M

ELEVEN GENERALS

Studies in American Command

DISCARD

By the same author

HAIL, CAESAR!

ROAD TO EMPIRE

EMPIRE AND THE SEA

THE EMPIRE AND THE GLORY

NAVY: A HISTORY

NAVY'S WAR

THE MARINES' WAR

ORDEAL BY FIRE

DISCARD

FLETCHER PRATT

ELEVEN GENERALS

Studies in American Command

WILLIAM SLOANE ASSOCIATES

Publishers   *New York*

"The Last of the Romans," copyright, 1938, by *The Infantry Journal;* "Sword of the Border," copyright, 1937, by *The Infantry Journal;* "Rumpsey-Dumpsey," copyright, 1934, by *The Cavalry Journal* under the title of "The Father of American Cavalry"; "Man on Horseback," copyright, 1940, by *The Infantry Journal;* "Little Phil," copyright, 1939, by *The Infantry Journal;* "The Rock of Chickamauga," copyright, 1938, by *The Coast Guard Artillery* under the title of "Old Pap"; "The Man Who Got There First," copyright, 1948, by *The Military Engineer;* "Sitting Bull II," copyright, 1939, by *The American Legion Magazine* under the title of "Then Came Summerall"; "Vandegrift of Guadalcanal," copyright, 1947, by *The Infantry Journal;* "Tactician of the West," copyright, 1947, 1948, by *The Infantry Journal.*

355.332
P914e

Copyright, 1949, by Fletcher Pratt

First Printing

Manufactured in the United States of America
Published simultaneously in Canada
by George J. McLeod, Ltd., Toronto

10/03

DEDICATION

The dedication of this book is
contained in the Preface

CONTENTS

PREFACE WRITTEN PRINCIPALLY FOR
PROFESSIONAL WRITERS

SOME YEARS AGO, WHEN THE THEN LIEUTENANT COLONEL
Forrest Harding embarked on a campaign to make the
Infantry Journal the No. 1 magazine of the profession
of arms that it later became, he asked a number of writers
from outside the service to contribute. His theory was that
soldiers get enough official gobbledygook in their manuals
and regulations, and when they are called upon to take money
out of their own pockets for a professional magazine they
expect to receive something that can be read with a certain
amount of pleasure, even if it does deal with technical subjects. The manner in which he proposed to accomplish this
for the *Infantry Journal* was to have more of his articles
written by professional writers and fewer by professional
soldiers.

I had written a certain amount of military biography
in a popular vein, so I was one of the writers to be approached.
Colonel Harding even suggested that it would be worth
while for me to look into the careers of one or two of those
American generals who had been overlooked or misinterpreted
by history.

The first result of this was the article on General Jacob
Brown which appears in this volume under the title "Sword

of the Border." Colonel Harding instantly accepted it and it was already on its way to the printer when there arrived in his office a very much longer and, I am sure, very much more thorough article on the same subject by a Captain Joseph I. Greene, then unknown to either Colonel Harding or myself. Of course, my gain was Captain Greene's loss, since the magazine already had an investment in the piece I had written. But the loss was not 100 per cent. It appears that the article directed some attention to Captain Greene, and when Colonel Harding retired from the *Journal* a little later (the editorship was then on a three-year tour-of-duty basis) the Captain was brought in as assistant to the new editor, Major John Burns.

That began a friendship of which I have always been particularly proud. Colonel Greene (as he became during World War II) succeeded to the editorship when Major Burns died as a result of the incredible accident of being hit on the head by a falling icicle. He has remained in that office ever since, following his retirement from active duty. In keeping him there, the Infantry Association, which owns and publishes the magazine, has made a singularly happy choice. Not only has the *Journal* become unquestionably the best service paper in the country or the world, one which can be read by any intelligent person whether he has worn khaki or not, but Colonel Greene has also carried the magazine and its attached press far out into other fields.

During the war Colonel Greene became quite the largest publisher in the country, turning out a great volume of cloth-bound books as well as an endless range of paper-backs, technical and nontechnical. They included those remarkable picture-and-text jobs on "How to Read Maps" and "How to Shoot the U.S. Army Rifle" which for the first time brought these subjects within the range of the ordinary reader and which have permanently affected textbook writing in general. It is probably known to very few ex-servicemen that Colonel

Greene, more than any other one person, was responsible for those volumes of good books, made up to fit the pocket of a uniform jacket and distributed without charge, which insured that no soldier or sailor was ever far from the kind of reading matter he wanted.

Nor is any ex-serviceman likely to learn it save from some such source as this. Colonel Greene is one of the world's outstanding experts in that form of modesty which consists in doing a tremendous job without saying two words to anyone about it. No one has ever seen him cross or tired or unreasonable; and when one adds to this an extraordinary kindness and breadth of view, it is not hard to perceive why one of the publishers who worked with him in the Council on Books in Wartime proclaimed publicly that as far as he was concerned Joe Greene could do no wrong.

It is because of that breadth and intelligence that he is introduced here, for this book, as a book, owes a good deal to him. He has given permission to reprint the seven articles which appeared in the *Infantry Journal;* the majority were prepared under his editorship and direction; and it was he who indicated that the series might be developed in the direction of a unity which would make it something more than a group of disparate articles about generals. The idea has been to make it something more; to present at least a partial picture of the American military tradition through the stories of some of the men who built that tradition.

Within that framework, the plan of dealing with the less-known or less-understood officers has been adhered to. Indeed, it is only by this route that one can get at the specifically military tradition, the ideas that soldiers have and civilians do not. The thoughts of George Washington about military policy and national defense, even his thoughts on tactics and strategy, have been matters of public debate. People outside the army, as well as those in it, are perfectly familiar with them. But even in the service it is by no means so generally realized that Nathanael Greene and Anthony Wayne contributed something to a specifically American art of war, an art of war so different from that practiced in Europe that the late Adolf Hitler's characterization of Americans as "military idiots" was one of his few technical judgments with which his generals fully agreed.

What is that American art of war, what is the summation of this book? I do not know that anything which has so many overtones and undertones can be stated in capsule form or that it would be worth writing a book about it if it could. But certain main lines can be indicated. The eleven men in this collection may not have been absolutely the most influential in producing the body of American thought on war, but they were certainly very influential, if for no other reason, because of their success—war being one of the most empirical forms of human activity.

It is noteworthy that all eleven were primarily battle commanders. If the conditions at any given time did not promise a battle, they went out to see if they could not stir one up—even Greene, who was so often beaten in his combats that he must have realized that there was something wrong with his technique of handling them or with his army. That is, these American generals were always on the aggressive, in striking defiance of Clausewitz, who calls the defensive the strongest form of war.

Secondly, there is a marked strain of amateurism. Greene, Wayne, Brown, and Johnson were amateurs pure and simple, who attained relatively high military rank on active duty without any military education and without passing through the lower grades in the field. Sheridan and Wilson were West Pointers, but reached their big commands with lightning rapidity and a minimum of combat experience. (In this connection, note that Grant and Sherman were long out of the service before the Civil War.) Of course as the country grows larger and war more technical, this amateurism tends to evaporate. One might expect it to disappear altogether; but is it not surprising to find that Bradley, the most recent of all, had never led troops until he took into action an army corps of over 50,000 men?

Along with this there is among the eleven a somewhat less pronounced but still visible inclination toward the book-taught soldier. Johnson and Vandegrift did no reading to speak of on the art of war, though in Vandegrift's case a considerable background of book learning was furnished by his able Chief of Staff, Gerald Thomas. It is doubtful whether Sheridan or Wilson had time to do much reading before they were in action; there is no record on Buford. But Bradley was a teacher who used books on military history as his familiar tools; Summerall was an avid reader who freely admitted getting one of his best tactical ideas out of a book; Wayne, Greene, and Brown all learned everything they knew about war from the printed word.

Finally, and very striking indeed, is the fact that all eleven of these successful American generals rested their hope of victory, their method of war, on one and the same thing— the fire power of attacking infantry. The eleven appeared in periods when weapons differed widely, they commanded men of different training under different geographic conditions. Two of them were trained as artillerymen, two belonged to the cavalry service (not counting Sheridan, a synthetic cavalryman), one was an engineer, but when the chips were down, they all thought alike on one point—that nobody is going to win a battle until somebody goes in there on foot and wins it with a hand gun.

There is in this connection an essential element of the American military tradition which cannot be told through any personal reference; the idea that wars are ultimately won through the aimed fire of individuals. This idea was perhaps first exposed to the public gaze at Bunker Hill, and it has persisted through World War II, as witness the chapter on Vandegrift. It had its most spectacular exhibition in the world field at the second battle of the Marne, when a German division attacked the 38th Infantry of the U.S. 3d Division. After the battle French officers who inspected the field came back to headquarters shaking their heads in incredulity; they had counted 3,000 German dead, "and every one," said one of the Frenchmen, "with just one little hole in the forehead."

After the battle a letter found on a German officer was even more emphatic: "God save us from these Americans. They kill us like animals with their rifles. They are the best marksmen in the world." Those riflemen of the 38th were U.S. regulars, professional soldiers, professional sharpshooters, if you wish to give them that name. But the aimed rifle fire in which General Pershing insisted on training his men (somewhat to the dismay of his European allies) is an underlying feature of American military thought—of our tradition. This is the tradition of Bunker Hill, and King's Mountain, and New Orleans, and Thomas' defense at Chickamauga, and Edson's Ridge, and Mortain. It always surprises European and even Oriental soldiers, who are not accustomed to dealing with marksmen who can kill you as soon as they can see you.

This part of the tradition comes down uninterrupted from the earliest frontier—in which connection we should not forget that the frontier was once a perimeter around Massachusetts Bay and Albany was a fort in the forest. Every American soldier of any importance has made the individual rifleman the foundation of his structure so thoroughly that, in considering the American art of war in this book, reference must be made rather to the method by which the rifleman is employed than to the fact that he is the center of the picture.

This explains the inclusions in the list of officers considered and some of the exclusions from it. George Washington was the dominating military figure of the Revolution, but his contribution belongs to the exoteric tradition and has been so elaborately considered by other students that there is no need to take it up here. Something might have been said of Benedict Arnold, but he belongs in a different kind of portrait gallery; of Philip Schuyler, but he never fought a battle; of Sharpshooter Morgan, "the Waggoner of the Alleghanies," but he never had an independent command. Greene and Wayne, the soldiers chosen from the Revolution, belong with the misunderstood rather than with the neglected generals. Hardly anybody understood Wayne (see the text). And Greene did not even understand himself; his letters show that he greatly admired his own skill in tactics but thought strategy an easy and obvious technology that any fool could acquire.

The reasons for omitting Andrew Jackson and Winfield Scott from the War of 1812 are similar to those in the case of Washington. (Incidentally, few commanders ever more fully understood or made better use of the rifle than Jackson.) The Mexican War was a cheap brawl, more politics than fighting; its chief contribution to our military history was probably that it convinced Jefferson Davis of his own military genius. There were two remarkable military achievements in that war, not without importance and influence—the march of Stephen Kearny to California and that of Doniphain's band all through the southwest. But neither one ended in a real battle and this is primarily a book about battles; the story of both these marches belongs where a Bernard De Voto has quite properly placed it in his classic *Year of Decision* —with that of the great westward migration.

From the Civil War the choices have been John Buford, Sheridan, James H. Wilson, Thomas. The justification for Buford and Wilson has been given in the text. With regard to Sheridan and Thomas, it is rather astonishing that they should have become obscure generals to the modern world. A biography of Thomas is in preparation as this is written; there has been no other since soon after his death and no consideration of his military career. On Sheridan there is only a book by Joseph Hergesheimer, of which it is adequate to say that, however sympathetic it may be as a portrait of personality, it would probably be hard to find another author less qualified to discuss "Little Phil" as a soldier.

There will probably be some moaning from the Dixie delegation over the fact that no Confederate generals are included. Well, who? Stonewall Jackson would be the obvious choice, and he certainly has been so influential on American military thought that his name is received with almost superstitious veneration among soldiers. But Colonel Henderson has covered that subject so thoroughly that anything anyone else could say would be repetitious. Of the other Confederate commanders, and of Lee especially, it can be said that one of the basic military reasons why they lost the war is that they never fought except when battle was forced upon them—a contradiction of that tradition of aggressiveness as the way to victory made by the eleven men mentioned here. There were occasional exceptions, to be sure, the most noteworthy being Forrest and John B. Hood. Some reference is made to Forrest, but Hood was so uniformly unsuccessful in everything he undertook that it is hard to see him as important except in an analysis of the reason behind defeat.

The Spanish War was so incompetently conducted that it has given the U.S. Army nothing but a negative tradition. The most important man connected with the military establishment was Secretary Alger, whom it would be nice to forget. The American phase of World War I was brief and under foreign command; hardly any of our generals had the opportunity to express ideas. Harbord, indeed, was one of the best men in the war, but his ideas were in logistics. Pershing had a large assortment of ideas and no hesitation about expressing them—like the maintenance of the American army as a unit, training for aimed rifle fire, and the proposal to follow St. Mihiel with an attack on Metz; but these were ideas of the council table, not of the battlefield. Summerall was chosen, partly to demonstrate that even under trench-line deadlock conditions there was still room for military originality, and partly because of all the American commanders in the war he has received the most attention from the Germans. They ought to know whose foot left the imprint on the seat of their pants, but, all the same and for an odd variety of reasons, Summerall was not particularly popular with the high-ranking officers of his own service. The article about him given here was published in the *American Legion Magazine* instead of the *Infantry Journal*.

On World War II we perhaps do not yet have quite enough perspective to decide who were the true master figures. It is already certain that Omar Bradley was one of them, and it seems equally certain that he is likely to join the ranks of the misunderstood, principally through the efforts of over-enthusiastic admirers to make claims for him that he does not make for himself, and to start quarrels in favor of one of the least contentious of military officers. Not that Bradley has any objection to verbal combat when there is a real issue at stake; he showed it in the famous 1946 speech before the American Legion Convention in which he attacked both the organization and its commander on the pork-barrel issue in veterans' hospitals. Bradley merely has no disposition for controversy over things past and especially things that have ended well. In view of this it seems fairly important to get the record straight before overzealous praise of the general draws down equally intemperate criticism. I think it can be maintained that he was the ablest soldier in any service during

World War II, as he was certainly the most successful; but to claim that he achieved what he did over the objections of his associates and by deceiving them, as Ralph Ingersoll has done, is to do an injustice to Bradley himself, one of the best men we ever had at accommodating his plans to those of others without losing anything essential.

As for Vandegrift, the fight for Guadalcanal is already very far away and long ago, somewhat dwarfed by the gigantic campaigns that later took place in the Pacific. The important thing about his story is that he stands with Buford and Johnson among the genuine American military inventors. His perimeter defense became a standard method of war; but in his case as in every other described in this volume, the heart of the matter is not in the method but in the spirit in which it was applied, not in the formula but in its use.

NATHANAEL GREENE
The Quaker Turenne

I

To most Americans the name Cornwallis represents a rather dejected figure handing over his sword to George Washington at Yorktown, while one of His Majesty's regimental bands plays, "The World Turned Upside Down." It surprises them as much to learn that the loser on this occasion was buried with honors in Westminster Abbey as it does the British to discover that Americans could imagine so trifling an occurrence was anything but a minor event in the career of one of the greatest of Britain's empire-builders and ablest of her soldiers.

The second Earl and first Marquess Cornwallis is ranked by English military critics only a shade below Marlborough and Wellington; he was almost uniformly successful as a military man and administrator; and it is quite reasonably felt that the conditions at Yorktown were beyond his control. No officer could have been expected to extricate himself from a position where he was faced by overwhelming numbers, his army lacking in supplies and pinned against the shore of a sea which, contrary to expectation and precedent, was held against him by a French fleet.

The only question not asked is how Cornwallis came to

be in Yorktown in the first place—a question which makes a good deal of difference. His florid lordship was supposed to be in command of the Carolinas; and, after the British armies had won a big siege and five battles, with the destruction of two American armies, he should have been. Cornwallis' commander-in-chief was inclined to regard the change of base to Virginia as something like a dereliction of duty—which only demonstrates that Sir Henry Clinton did not in the least understand the character of the opposition that had driven his lieutenant out of the southern campaign—as Cornwallis told him in an acrimonious pamphlet when both officers were back in England.

This is not surprising; Clinton had only to deal with George Washington, a great battle captain and a deadly strategist, but in the conventional mold, comprehensible. Cornwallis was fattened up for the kill by Nathanael Greene, to whom no rules whatever could be applied, and who, a hundred years after his death, was still a mystery, even to his admirers.

Even the ordinary sequence of cause and effect fails to apply. Greene was a practicing member of the Quaker Society until past the age of thirty, and he had almost no education but what he gave himself; he was a son of wealth, who was never required to work; he was jumped straight from private of militia to brigadier general of the regular army through a political job of the most shameless character; he lost every battle he ever fought—but he founded a new science of war and, next to Washington himself, did more to win the Revolution than any man in it. As though this were insufficient, he began life as a puritanical Rhode Islander and ended it as a slave-holding Georgia planter.

The only common element in this collection of paradoxes is that, all his life long, Nathanael Greene swam resolutely against the current. This character trait was in evidence as early as his fourteenth year, when Nathanael Greene, senior, a kindly father, but one whose "mind was overshadowed with prejudice against literary accomplishments," announced that the education of the younger Nathanael and his seven brothers was completed. An itinerant teacher had spent three winters in showing the boys how to read and to do simple arithmetic; from now on all necessary knowledge could be acquired from the Bible, Fox's *Book of Martyrs*, and the works of Robert Barclay, the Quaker theologian. The seven brothers accepted the decision without question; young Nathanael not only asked for, received, and made use of permission to study Latin and geometry under a private teacher, but also made some metal toys at his father's forge, and taking them up to the metropolis of Newport, sold them to buy a book.

"What book?" asked the proprietor of the shop when he made his request, and Nathanael Greene, who had not imagined that it would make so much difference, was too embarrassed to answer. By one of those fortuitous circumstances which lie near the root of every great career, there happened to be in the shop at the time a man who looked up sharply, took an immediate interest in the tall, shy boy and offered his advice.

The man was Ezra Stiles, future president of Yale, and the book he chose was John Locke on the human understanding. It was the first volume the boy had encountered that had anything to do with thinking, and for many years it was the only one he knew; and it is next to impossible to understand our soldier without realizing that he approached all problems with a mind formed by the father of empiricism.

II

For several years young Mr. Greene was not particularly oppressed by problems save the emotional one of being refused by the girl on whom his heart was set. He lived the normal life of a son of the local magnate, formed warm friendships with Hopkins and Ward, the perennially opposed candidates for the governorship of the colony, and in 1770, at the age of twenty-eight, was given the management of his father's mill properties at Coventry, being promptly elected to the assembly from that district. The conflict between the mother country and the colonies was now building up toward flash point, and the bill closing the port of Boston was passed through Parliament the spring after Greene married—another girl, not the one who caused his previous heartbreak. The bill provoked a new Continental Congress; as evidence of local unanimity, Rhode Island voted to send both the rivals, Hopkins and Ward, and at the same time to set afoot the organization of military companies.

Nathanael Greene became a private in one of these—the Kentish Guards. The act by no means met the approval of the governing fathers of his church. Three times previously they had warned him for talking in public about war and bloodshed, but they had been unwilling to proceed to extremities against the son of one of the richest and most respected Quakers in America. The enlistment was too much; they publicly expelled him; and Greene, without any comment that has been recorded, went to Boston to buy a musket and some military books, there being none of either in Rhode Island.

He not only obtained what he went for, but also secured the services of a deserter from the British army to drill the Kentish Guards. We would willingly know more about that deserter, whose name is nowhere mentioned; he drilled the Kentish Guards so well that they furnished no less than 32 officers to the Continental army, which must have been not far from 75 per cent of the membership of the company. But more interesting even than this obscure genius of a drill sergeant is the fact that the only military books Nathanael Greene could lay his hands on were a copy of Julius Ceasar's *Gallic War* and the memoirs of Marshal Turenne, to which he devoted himself with the same assiduity he had given to John Locke.

The news of Lexington and Concord reached Rhode Island on April 19, 1775. The Kentish Guards promptly mobilized and marched to the Massachusetts border, whence they were immediately recalled by an order from the colonial governor, an order which so little satisfied the Assembly that on April 22 they voted to suspend the governor and to raise an "army" which should consist of one brigade, three regiments strong—1,500 men all told. Nathanael Greene, the high private from the rear rank of the Kentish Guards, was named brigadier in command. He was thirty-two years old.

Now this appointment was politics of the purest kind. It is doubtful whether anyone in the Assembly knew about his purchase of Turenne's memoirs and Caesar's *Gallic War*, and it is certain they would not have cared if they had known. Nathanael Greene was simply a member of the wealthy Greene family, a personal friend of politicians in both parties, a man who had taken an interest in colonial defense. His nomination would offend nobody and might make some friends for the cause; the question of military qualifications for the post entered no mind save that of the new commander himself.

It entered his mind all right; there is the testimony not only of his own letters on the point, but also of General George Washington, a man not easily deceived. In June, after the Rhode Island army, somewhat below paper strength, had joined the forces before Boston, the commander remarked that "though raw, irregular and undisciplined, they are under much better government than any round about them," and watched with appreciation as Greene, fresh from an all-night study of Turenne, went out to the camp with his British deserter to put the men through some evolution he himself had just heard of for the first time.

In the meanwhile, the Continental Congress in Philadelphia had completed the setup of its armed forces by naming four major generals and eight brigadiers, with Greene on the latter list. This was politics once more; the Congress was deaf to Washington's recommendations and knew nothing whatever of Greene's merits as a drillmaster. They were interested only in pleasing the Rhode Island delegation, exceptionally powerful both for the political skill of its members and the fact that, with Boston in British hands, Rhode Island was the leading maritime colony, from which most of the support for the nascent Continental navy must come.

Fortune and his own carefully cultivated connections had now carried Greene nearly as far as they could, but they still had some slight service to render before he emerged as one of the master figures of the Revolution. For instance, it cannot be regarded as anything but a smile of fortune that he should be kept close under Washington's leadership during the long siege of Boston. Modern readers who devour a novel in an evening and a book of philosophy over the week end can have but little conception of the intensity with which the printed word was studied by a man of Greene's appetite for education, who had hardly seen as many as three hundred books in his life. All that summer, fall and winter found him studying Turenne and the *Gallic War* till he had committed practically every detail of both to memory, and the fact that he was in a static situation gave him time to learn from his books wihout making mistakes in the field.

It was doubtless from the Roman that Greene learned so much of the importance of such details as proper guard-mount and camp sanitation—he was the only officer in the

Continental army who gave much attention to either—but it could only have been from Turenne that he acquired a cognizance of the political relations of western Europe, which led him in October of 1775 to write to the Rhode Island delegation in Congress asking an immediate declaration of independence.

He placed the thing on two grounds—France was the natural rival and enemy of England, the only power in a position to attack her in Hanover, and so to engage the British in a major continental war, which would reduce the Royal army in America to that subsidiary status with which our native forces could deal; and France would "refuse to intermeddle until she is satisfied that there is no hope of accommodation." France was also the only power with naval strength enough to guarantee the shipment to America of desperately needed military stores and the supply of all the other articles of commerce upon which war ultimately depends. In short, France and France alone could break the blockade.

For an amateur strategist this is not at all bad (it is worth noting that the disciple of John Locke says nothing of rights or of Jeffersonian idealism, he is purely concerned with the empirical question of how to win a war), but the point that carried weight with the delegates in Philadelphia was less Greene's strategic ideas than the political fact that he had been one of the first in the field with the thought of independence. They made him a major general for it.

III

By time the army had moved to the New York area the Rhode Islander had formed intimate friendships with Washington, Henry Knox, and Alexander Hamilton, and was regarded by the chief as his best divisional commander, but he

Miles

RETREAT THROUGH N.J. → → → →

Ft.Ticonderoga Crown Point
Ft.Independence

NEW YORK

VT.
(CLAIMED BY NEW YORK)

N.H.

Ft.George Ft.Anne
Ft.Edward
Ft.Miller

Ft.Schuyler
Oriskany Mohawk R.
Ft.Hunter

Saratoga

M A S S.

Albany

Catskill

Hudson R.

Kingston

Poughkeepsie

C O N N.

Newburgh
Ft.Constitution
West Point Ft.Independence
Ft.Montgomery Peekskill
Ft.Clinton
Stony White Plains
Point Harlem Heights

PA.

Delaware R.

LONG ISLAND

Ft.Washington
New York

N. J.

New Brunswick

Princeton
Monmouth

A T L A N T I C

Valley Forge German-town
Brandy-wine Trenton

Philadelphia

O C E A N

Wilmington

The Hudson to Trenton

· 8 ·

was in bed with a fever at the time of the Battle of Long Island. He was still there when a council of war rejected his quite logical plan that New York should be burned to keep the British from using it as a base. The sick list released him in time to take part in that brief and confused Battle of Harlem Heights which did so much to restore the morale of the army. Washington promptly appointed him to the general command of New Jersey and specific supervision of Forts Washington and Lee, which barred the advance of the British up the Hudson. While waiting for the enemy to move, Greene prepared for a general retreat across the Jerseys by setting up a system of magazines.

It was on the advice of the Quaker general that Washington, himself dubious about the matter, decided to heed the resolution of Congress and attempt to hold the Hudson forts. The decision turned out very badly when Fort Washington was stormed in November, with the loss of 2,000 men and nearly half the artillery the Continental army owned, in addition to the position. Greene was naturally blamed for influencing Washington in the wrong direction, and it was suggested that his desire to stand well with his political connections in Congress had something to do with the matter. But this view is both narrow and unjust; he had no friends in Congress any more. Ex-Governor Hopkins was out and ex-Governor Ward was dead. As early as September, 1776, Greene's letters show him convinced that the Congress had become a useless debating society and its system of conducting the war was a mistake. He wanted a regular army, with enlistments for the duration, a corps of officers well enough paid to keep them from leaving the service in search of the enormous profits made by sea privateersmen, and real authority for the commander-in-chief.

Greene's reasons for wishing to keep the Hudson forts were purely military. The student of Turenne naturally thought well of fortified positions as furnishing pivots for maneuver, especially with troops whose battle discipline could not be altogether depended upon. Beyond this, and very prominently in Greene's mind, stood the strategic question. He had not the slightest inkling of the British government's basic plan for cutting the colonies in two by having Howe from New York and Burgoyne from Canada join hands along the line of the Hudson (for that matter, the British commanders had no inkling of it either), but he could see, and explained very clearly to Washington, that while the American forces held fortified bridgeheads on both banks, the British could neither move into New Jersey nor upstream without putting their communications in serious danger.

As to Fort Washington itself, Greene was not at all happy; he considered the trace of the works altogether too extensive for the number of men assigned to hold the place and wanted a better lot of men in there, not the offscourings who had run away before. In the actual event, Rawlings' Virginia Rifle regiment cost the storming party nearly 800 men before they ran short of ammunition, and it was the old inefficients who let the enemy in. The only fault that can be charged to Greene is that of failing to realize that there were no more or better men for the defense of the forts. During the seventeen months since the Rhode Island army marched to Boston, he had in fact become something like a professional soldier in interests and cast of thought.

It was as a professional and the most trusted lieutenant of his chief that he followed the fortunes of Washington's army down to December 2, 1780, when he took command of the forces in the South. There is not much detail of interest in his personal history during the intervening period. He commanded a wing at Trenton and saw victory for the first and almost the last time; tried to persuade Washington to follow up by an immediate attack on Princeton. When the commander-in-chief permitted his own acceptance of the idea to be overruled by a council of war, Greene made it his business to explain the matter in person to Congress. From the delegates he secured one of the key resolutions of the war, the one which completed the long process of placing the commander-in-chief really in command:

"That General Washington be informed that it never was the intention of Congress that he should be bound by a majority of voices in a council of war, contrary to his own judgment."

At the Brandywine, Greene commanded the reserve and did a creditable job of covering the retreat from that battle lost not without honor; at Germantown, he had a wing again and arrived late, but it was accurately felt that the failure of the operation was due less to his slowness (for he was not slow) than to General Sullivan's arriving early and attacking too sudden-soon. During the Valley Forge winter and in view of the success of his New Jersey magazine system, Washington persuaded him to take the post of quartermaster-general, which Greene accepted with the proviso that it should not prejudice his right to command troops. The experiment did not work out; while trying to make the office efficient, he fell on a violent quarrel with the self-seeking members of the Treasury Board of Congress and was ultimately forced to resign.

That last row furnished perhaps the one element in the Rhode Islander's equipment as a commander that he did not already possess on the day Fort Washington was lost. He was now convinced that the military ills which were the result of the congressional system would be incurable for so long as the war endured. If he were to achieve anything in the independent command of the South, to which he was assigned in 1780, it would have to be on the empirical basis of accepting that condition and making the best of it.

IV

When General Nathanael Greene saluted General Gates at Charlotte, N.C., all the surrounding conditions were of a nature to discourage. Congress, of which he remained a favorite, had authorized him to use all the regiments of Maryland, Virginia, the Carolinas, and Georgia, but this was no more than an expression of good will, since the British had taken Georgia before any regiments could be raised there, while the troops of the Carolinas and nearly all the Virginia line had been captured at the fall of Charleston. Gates had fought and lost a battle at Camden on 16 August; in it the Maryland troops and what remained of the Virginians had been practically wiped out. The returns received by the new commander showed 2,307 men on report, 1,482 present for duty, among whom the Continental regulars numbered 949, many of them newly enlisted.

A good part of these men were quite literally naked; Greene had to write to Governor Jefferson of Virginia that part of his diminutive army must be "sent away to some secure place in warm quarters, until they can be furnished with clothing." There were only three days' provisions in camp. Of the partisan leaders who had been so serviceable earlier in the war, Sumter's command had been nearly annihilated on the heels of the Camden battle; Marion's had much dwindled; Pickens was back in the hill country.

Cornwallis was the opposing commander; he had 8,000 regulars available, besides over 3,000 Tory irregulars. By that combination of firmness and reasonableness which was later to bring him interment in the Abbey, he had so subdued Georgia and South Carolina that the governor of the latter state was a refugee in Greene's camp, while the former had no government but the British. His lordship had already hit upon the military device for keeping down a revolted countryside which later became classic—a chain of strongly fortified posts, with patrols operating among them, while the locality was stripped of any resources that might sustain opposition.

It undoubtedly occurred to Greene that the Vicomte de Turenne had been confronted by a situation not dissimilar in a strategic sense during his Danube valley campaign in the closing stages of the Thirty Years' War, and again during the War of the Fronde in 1653, the fortified cities in each case playing the part that was here taken by Cornwallis' chain of posts. What had the great Marshal done? Divided his forces, each part striking toward some center the enemy could ill afford to lose; then led his opponents through an intricate series of maneuvers, always looking toward battle at some point near his own base and distant from theirs.

Something might be done along that line (Greene decided), especially since the American forces enjoyed one advantage Turenne had not possessed, in that the theater of war faded westward into the highlands of the Alleghanies, making it dangerous for the British to divide. The roads were bad in that region for one thing; but more important was the fact that these uplands were inhabited by backwoodsmen who knew how to ride and shoot. In October they had furnished an impressive demonstration of their skills, when Cornwallis sent his Major Ferguson into the back country with 1,100 men to keep the local people quiet while he operated near the coast. The effects of the battle of King's Mountain on the American military tradition have been bad in the long run; but Greene was not concerned with distant futures, he was only interested in the fact that the Ferguson command (a large one for the day and place, as witness the size of Greene's own army) had surrendered some 60 per cent of its effectives after all the rest had been shot by squirrel-killing rifle-men who quite literally sprang from nowhere without banners or organization.

The American commander did not think Cornwallis would forget that event; that is, the British would approach the hill country only in a body strong enough to dominate the local situation and their first care would be to break up any such concentrations as the one that had fought King's Mountain. *Per contra*, if the militia could, by careful timing, be brought to the support of the regulars when a battle was imminent, they could be employed as a genuine military instrument, though they always went home after a fight, and not infrequently during one.

In the opening move of the campaign, then, he sent Daniel Morgan of the famous Rifles far out to the right of the area of war to move light and fast, and gave him authority to summon whatever of the local levies he needed. Greene took command of the left of the strategic area with the remainder of the forces (about 1,100 men), planning to use his two field armies to keep the British from dispersing in pursuit of the partisan bands, who would hammer at their communications. If they detached against either himself or Morgan, the menaced commander would call out the local militia and fight. There was some danger that Cornwallis might concentrate against one of his forces; this Greene expected to discount through mobility, specifically by having boats built on the numerous wide rivers that cut up the country and planning to retreat across them if attacked.

This general plan appears above in a more organized form than it does in Greene's own papers. Actually, he developed it one element at a time and was so confident of his own ability in maneuver that he seldom bothered with laying down principles. The subjects that most intimately concerned him when he took command were those of logistics and recruiting. In the former he saw the fundamental reason for Gates' failure: that general's men were nearly always debilitated with hunger, and the fatal field of Camden had been lost just after they had received an ill-chosen purgative meal.

To solve the commissariat problem, Green selected Colonel William R. Davie, one of the most active of Continental officers, whose corps had reached the end of their enlistments in November, and who was now raising another group to serve with Morgan. Davie replied to the general's request by saying that although he knew something about troops, he understood nothing whatever about money or accounts; to which Greene answered that he might then accept the post of quartermaster-general in perfect tranquillity, since there was not a dollar in the military chest nor any prospect of there being one.

Davie accepted and went to see the North Carolina legislature, taking with him a letter from Greene, in which the commander remarked that "nothing but a good regular army can save this country from ruin," and made a remarkable demand on the delegates for the conscription of man power as well as of any stores that were threatened by the advance of enemy forces. He did not get his conscription law, and some collections of military material, particularly horses, continued to fall into British hands; but he obtained the essential authority to make requisitions, and it is worth anticipating to say that although the army was never opulently supplied, neither was it ever again in serious difficulties for provisions.

V

These were the preliminaries; now the campaign. Cornwallis lay at the hamlet of Winnsboro, with the important post of Ninety-Six on his left, that of Camden covering his right, and Fort Granby in his rear protecting his communications with Charleston. Before he turned over the command,

Gates had held one of the usual Continental councils of war, which voted to put the discouraged army into winter quarters in western North Carolina. It seemed clear to Greene that this would be fatal: Cornwallis had so large a mobile force afoot that he must be intending a winter campaign through the high, dry ground among the upper reaches of the rivers;

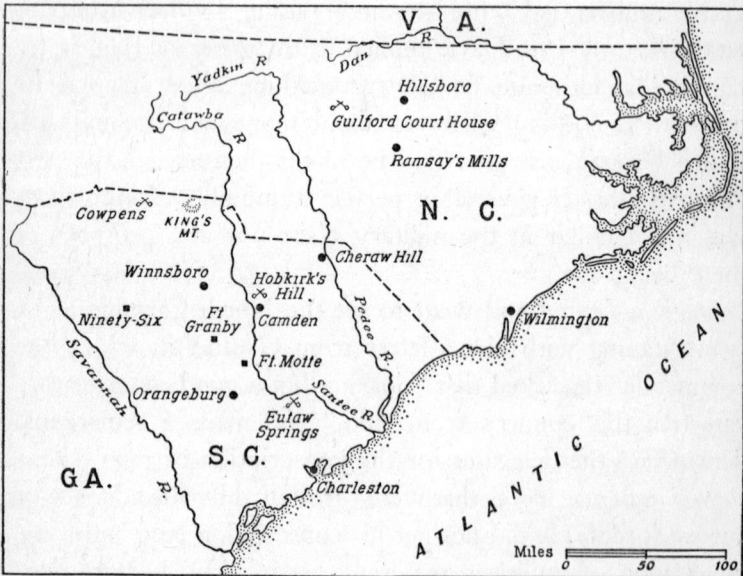

The Western Theatre

and for the Americans to await attack in quarters was to give the enemy every opportunity of approaching with concentrated forces, along well-established lines of supply and in such strength that the result of a clash would be disastrous. Greene therefore overruled the council of war and, as soon as his men had some clothes and food, moved the main body down to Cheraw Hill on the Pedee River, opposite the British right flank. Light Horse Harry Lee joined him there with a small but useful body of cavalry from Virginia.

Morgan had already moved out toward the other British flank in the region of King's Mountain, with 300 of his own Rifles and William Washington's regiment of dragoons, being joined there by 300 short-term volunteers and 4- or 500 Georgia and South Carolina militia. South of him Sumter's partisans were operating against British patrols and trains. Cornwallis, who was in fact purposing a campaign into North Carolina, did exactly what Greene expected and what most normal commanders would do—refused to be distracted from his own offensive move. One strong detachment was thrown out in the region of Camden to keep Greene from cutting into his right rear; another was sent against Morgan, to crush him or drive him off into the hill country. The main body prepared for its march.

Colonel Benjamin Tarleton, the restless and able cavalry leader, was given 1,100 men, all regulars, for the elimination of Morgan. He pushed forward so rapidly that on January 16, 1781, the British reconnaissance reported that the Americans had been forced to a stand at Cowpens, where they were waiting to receive attack at the foot of a little hill in open country. Their flanks were in air; there was an unfordable river behind them; Tarleton's numbers were slightly superior to their whole force, which the English commander knew to include a good proportion of the unsteady militia; and they seemed to be all infantry. The opportunity was ideal for a line attack, with cavalry circling the American flanks; Tarleton deployed and came on with a hurrah—to run into one of the deadliest tactical traps in military history.

For Morgan had been sure that his opponent would be unable to resist the temptation to finish the campaign with a single charge. Out in front of his lines at the base of the hill were 120 of the militia, selected for their skill with the rifle, in loose order, as skirmishers; behind them the main body of militia in line; behind these again, on the hill itself, Mor-

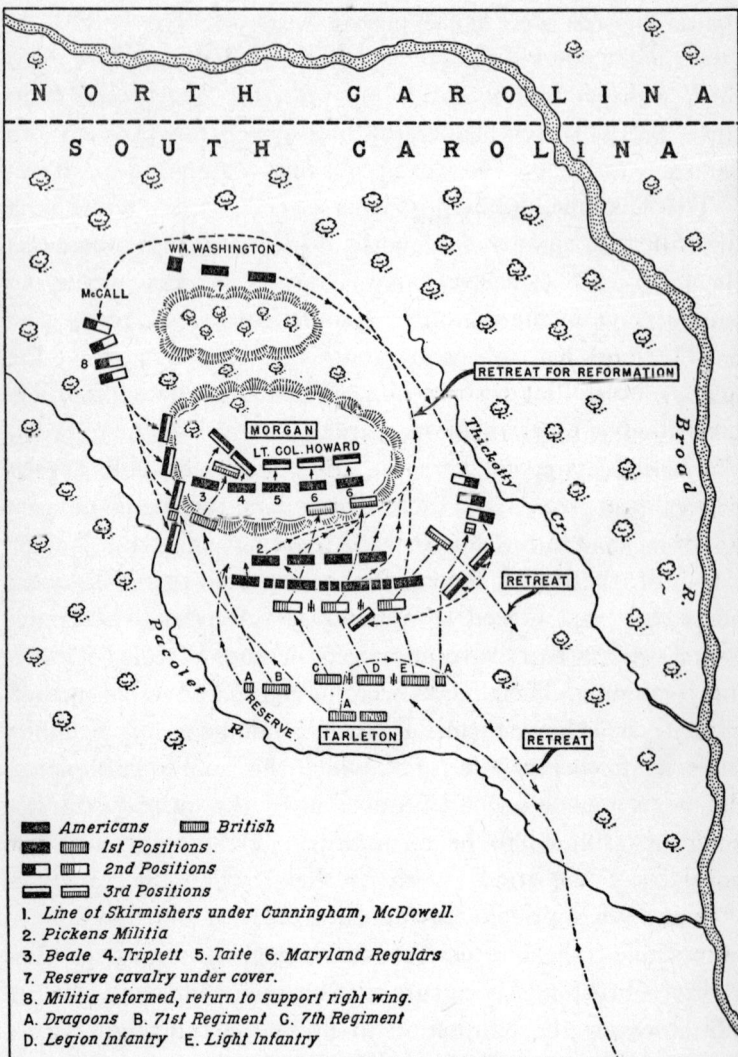

NORTH CAROLINA

SOUTH CAROLINA

WM. WASHINGTON

McCALL

8

RETREAT FOR REFORMATION

MORGAN
LT. COL. HOWARD

3   4   5   6

2

RETREAT

Thicketty Cr.

Broad R.

Pacolet R.

RESERVE

A   B   C   D   E   A

A

TARLETON

RETREAT

Americans   British
1st Positions.
2nd Positions
3rd Positions
1. *Line of Skirmishers under Cunningham, McDowell.*
2. *Pickens Militia*
3. *Beale* 4. *Triplett* 5. *Taite* 6. *Maryland Regulars*
7. *Reserve cavalry under cover.*
8. *Militia reformed, return to support right wing.*
A. *Dragoons* B. *71st Regiment* C. *7th Regiment*
D. *Legion Infantry* E. *Light Infantry*

Battle of Cowpens

gan's rew regulars; and out of sight behind the eminence, William Washington with his tiny force of cavalry. The militia in front were not expected to stand. "The Old Waggoner will crack his whip over Ben Tarleton tomorrow morning," Morgan told them. "Hold up your heads, give them three fires, and you are free"—adding that they should aim for the officers.

They did that; the riflemen in front and then the militia fired till their pieces were empty before taking flight around the hill (since they could not go up it), and they fired so accurately that there were gaps all along the British line and Tarleton had to put in his reserve before attacking the hill, swinging the horsemen of his right wing forward to take this third American line in flank. At this moment Morgan released William Washington and his own cavalry from concealment; they struck the British flanking cavalry themselves in flank and drove them from the field. At the center the lines locked, the British no longer so steady or with so many men, trying to climb the slope down which the Continental regulars fired by salvo into their faces. William Washington drove on to take them in one flank; and now Andrew Pickens, who had rallied the militia behind the hill, brought these men forward onto Tarleton's other wing and everything went to pieces. The British force was nearly exterminated—230 killed, 600 prisoners, and only those who still had horses could escape.

Cornwallis with his main body of some 4,000 was within thirty miles of the field. When the fugitives from the disaster reached him he immediately set the whole command in motion toward the northwest to cut Morgan off from North Carolina, imagining that the "Old Waggoner" would now press on toward Ninety-Six. But Greene's real strategic objective was not geographical and it had been achieved by forcing his opponent into detachments. Under his orders

Morgan was retreating straight eastward at the best speed he could make, and when Cornwallis reached the south fork of the Catawba it was to discover that the American commander had crossed two days before. The British commander decided he could catch Morgan between the rivers if he moved light and fast enough, burned all his own baggage trains, and pressed the pursuit.

The rivers were now swollen by winter rains. On the cross-country route Morgan could not move quite as rapidly as the trained and unencumbered British regulars, but at the main fork of the Catawba he crossed quite easily in the boats provided by Greene's foresight. Cornwallis was held up for a couple of days and was losing men all the time to snipers along the road, but he pushed on, hoping to catch Morgan at the Yadkin.

Greene himself had meanwhile ridden rapidly up with a small escort to join his lieutenant and direct the march, his main body following as rapidly as it could, his plan now being to concentrate at the Yadkin, call out the militia, and dispute the passage of the stream. When he heard that Cornwallis had burned his baggage, "Then he is ours!" cried the American general and sent messengers to summon every man who could march; for a battle with an enemy who had no great supply of ammunition and no ambulances to transport his wounded could not but work to the American advantage.

Some 800 of the militia did come out, but early and to the wrong place. They tried to hold the main branch of the Catawba, but Cornwallis broke through and dispersed them in a finely executed night attack. His service of information told him the Americans were still divided and that it was unlikely they could get across the Yadkin without retreating far into the mountains. But once more Greene's foresight paid off: when the British reached the Yadkin, Morgan was already on the other side.

The next of the rivers that flow southeast to the sea is the Dan, against which the British leader still hoped to trap the American forces, even yet not united. Rain, bad roads, and the lack of mounts had so delayed Greene's main body that already at the end of January the general had changed his concentration point from the left bank of the Yadkin to Guilford Court House, considerably farther inland, and had carefully surveyed the ground there, on which he meant to fight his battle. No effort was made to hold the Yadkin; to be effective it would have taken all Morgan's force, and Greene believed that an officer of Cornwallis' skill would find a way across in time to break up any force that attempted to conduct a delaying action.

But when the two bodies came together at Guilford, it was in an atmosphere of bitter disappointment. Greene found he had but 2,036 men, of whom but 1,426 were Continentals, and these mostly newly enlisted. The militia had not come forth in any great numbers from Virginia, where Benedict Arnold's raid was keeping them quiet, while the North Carolina men whom Cornwallis had broken through at the Catawba had dispersed. Against the 2,036 men, the enemy could still bring over 3,000, and a battle fought at such odds might easily end in a defeat that would destroy the cause of the Colonies in the South. For there was no army behind the body here present; it was the last focus of the Revolution below the Potomac, a fact which must always be kept in mind.

Greene retreated then, toward the Dan and Virginia, just barely winning a crossing of the stream ahead of Cornwallis' pursuit. By the map this new retreat looked bad; both Carolinas seemed to have been abandoned. But with the

British mobile forces far out to the north, Sumter was up again among the South Carolina hills, and Marion from the swamp country was operating against their posts near the coast. The little American army remained intact and in good spirits; had suffered few battle losses, while the vastly superior British force had been cut down by nearly 2,500 in Cowpens battle and by Greene's abrasive small war.

Moreover, Cornwallis' men had made a long, punishing march through used country and were very short on supply. The British commander turned aside from the pursuit to Hillsboro, N.C., to gather provisions and to raise loyalist support, reaching the place on February 20, 1781; and that date and place marked the high tide of English interest in the southern colonies.

For their whole structure was now internally shaken. As soon as Cornwallis reached Hillsboro, Greene again crossed the Dan, with Harry Lee scouting out before him. Late in February that leader fell in with a body of 300 Tories marching to join the British command and annihilated them at practically no cost to himself. The act practically ended Cornwallis' effort to make loyalist sentiment effective, and correspondingly encouraged the colonists, so that militia and a few volunteers began to join Greene on his return march. By time the American force again reached Guilford, it was 4,243 strong (of whom 1,490 regulars), and Greene considered this force sufficient to offer battle, which he did on March 15 by taking his stand in the previously selected position.

Cornwallis on his side was forced to attack, frightfully embarrassed as he was by lack of transport, running short of ammunition and having no base nearer than Wilmington, with his forces depleted to less than 3,000 men, and the certainty that if he sat still he might lose all. As he approached, the British commander took up a formation de-

signed to make the most of the military qualities, or lack of
them, among the American militia—his infantry in a deep single line, closed up, his cavalry under Tarleton in a tight col-

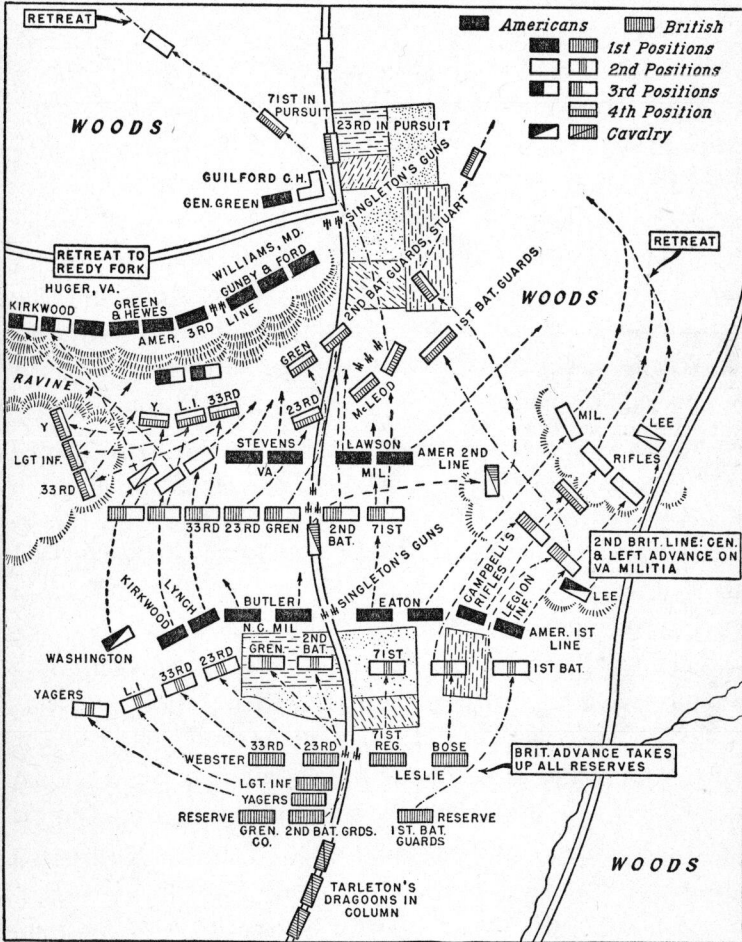

Guilford Court House

umn behind the foot, forming the only reserve there was.
The ground was much broken by trees; he did not think the
American rifle fire would cut down too many of his soldiers

before they were in on their opponents with the bayonet that green troops always so much fear, and he wanted to put as many bayonets in the front line as possible.

Greene drew up his own forces in obvious imitation of Morgan's trap at Cowpens—forward a line of North Carolina militia with some open ground at its front, trees behind and on both flanks; 300 yards in rear of them another line of short-service Virginia troops, all in trees, with William Washington's cavalry on one flank, Lee's on the other; 400 yards farther back, the Continentals, in open ground around the courthouse. The basic idea was valid, as Cowpens had proven; but Greene's lines were farther from each other than his lieutenant's had been, and the ground was less open, so that he lacked the close tactical control that had enabled Morgan to persuade his riflemen to withhold their fire till the enemy were only 50 yards in front of them.

These defects became evident as soon as the British line advanced, about one o'clock in the afternoon. Under cover of the trees and the smoke of their own artillery, they rushed across the open ground against the first American line so rapidly and so heartily that the North Carolinans ran away without firing a shot, and the country being wooded, there was no rallying point as there had been in Morgan's battle.

The short-service Virginians of the second line put up a firmer front, shot many of the British down, and were much aided by Lee and William Washington, whose men fired from the saddle. But Cornwallis' single line was so long that Greene's horsemen were unable to turn its flanks, the British broke through the Virginians and came washing up against the Continentals. There the fighting was hard; on the American right one regiment broke, but so did one of Cornwallis' on the opposite wing. Only the artillery of the attackers enabled them to hold on at all, and they might not have done that had Greene been willing to put in the three regiments he had in reserve for a counterattack, for the last British infantry was committed.

But Greene was not willing; that last small reserve was the last reserve of the Continental army. He formed it to cover a retreat and made one, leaving his enemies the field and the claim of victory that went with it—a victory truly Pyrrhic, for if Greene had lost 409 men, 300 of them from his small body of regulars, nearly a third of the whole British force was down, over half their regimental commanders had been killed, and Cornwallis was now cumbered with a vast number of wounded, in unfriendly country, without transport, and his ammunition very low. Two days after the combat he was driven to the inevitable decision; left most of his own hurt and all the American at Guilford, and began a retreat that was singularly like a flight to Wilmington and the support of the Royal Navy.

Greene pursued as far as Ramsay's Mills, trying to persuade the militia to come out and destroy the British force. The effort was useless; spring plowing time had come and the farmer-soldiers insisted on staying home for it. At Ramsay's Mills, therefore, the American commander reconsidered the strategic question. Cornwallis at Wilmington would be in no position to make a move upcountry at least until he had been strongly reinforced, and there was no passable road along the bottom lands by which he could join the British forces still operating in South Carolina. Why not carry the war back into that state?

VI

The over-all plan Greene worked out for this new operation was as original as anything he ever did. Lord Rawdon, whom Cornwallis had left in command in the southern state, had a total force not far from 8,000, but most of them were parceled out in posts, and the mobile unit consisted of only about 1,500 men, or not many more than the small band of American regulars. Rawdon was in the Camden region; Greene determined to close up on this mobile force and fix it in position, by battle if necessary, meanwhile detaching enough of his regulars to stiffen the partisan bodies of Marion, Sumter, and Pickens for attacks on the enemy forts. The three leaders were hard men to deal with, old Southern individualists, who considered obedience and servility as synonymous, and who were in the habit of putting plans to a vote of their men before undertaking anything, but they fell in with Greene's scheme, which promised both a chance to hurt the British and some very attractive plunder.

The elimination of Cornwallis had much encouraged the troops and they were in better condition as to commissariat: "they were regularly supplied with provisions for a day in advance, a gill of rum for the men and a quart for the officers forming part of the day's distribution." The main body marched cheerfully down toward Camden, where Greene made distant contact with his new opponent on April 14, shooting off Harry Lee to co-operate with Marion against Fort Watson, on the line of communication between Camden and Charleston along the left bank of the Santee.

It seems from Greene's letters that he entertained some hope of storming or besieging Camden, but a brief inspection of the place showed it was too strong for either, and he retired about two miles upstream to a strong position at Hobkirk's Hill, facing the fort. The intervening ground was heavily wooded; when a deserter carried word to Lord Rawdon that the American artillery had not come, that British general decided to try a surprise attack. It fell on the morning of April 25; he used a narrow front with two heavily supported wings. As soon as the lines closed in, Greene attempted a double envelopment around those wings, but the troops he used for it were new levies who could not drive the attack home, and he had so disgarnished his center that Rawdon broke it through. As usual Greene made his retreat in good order and without serious loss, writing to the French minister, "We fight, get beat, rise and fight

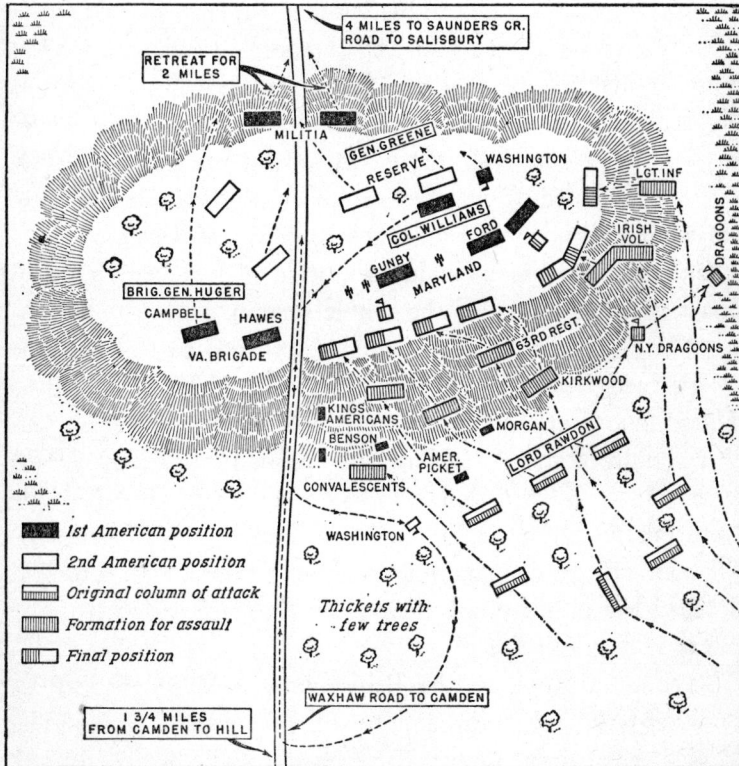

Map labels:
- 4 MILES TO SAUNDERS CR. ROAD TO SALISBURY
- RETREAT FOR 2 MILES
- MILITIA
- GEN. GREENE
- RESERVE
- WASHINGTON
- LGT. INF
- DRAGOONS
- COL. WILLIAMS
- FORD
- IRISH VOL.
- GUNBY
- MARYLAND
- BRIG. GEN. HUGER
- CAMPBELL
- HAWES
- VA. BRIGADE
- 63RD REGT.
- N.Y. DRAGOONS
- KIRKWOOD
- KINGS AMERICANS
- BENSON
- MORGAN
- AMER. PICKET
- LORD RAWDON
- CONVALESCENTS
- WASHINGTON
- Thickets with few trees
- WAXHAW ROAD TO CAMDEN
- 1 3/4 MILES FROM CAMDEN TO HILL

Legend:
- 1st American position
- 2nd American position
- Original column of attack
- Formation for assault
- Final position

Hobkirk's Hill

again." In fact, he was ready for another battle two days later.

Lord Rawdon was not. His losses had been by no means light, as British losses never were light when assaulting American riflemen in position; he now had a number of wounded to care for; the American force had neither been knocked out nor driven away, and while he was trying to pick up the pieces, word ran in that Lee and Marion had captured Fort Watson and his main line of communications. Rawdon made one more effort to drive Greene off so that he could see to his rear areas, marching out on May 8; but he found the Americans quite unwilling to go away; they were posted on a high hill surrounded by trenches and with so many guns that an attack was hopeless. Since his logistic difficulties were beginning to become serious and he could not send out patrols to cover his convoys while Greene remained so close before him, the British leader could only burn Camden and fall back toward Charleston.

Camden was the most important of all the North Carolina posts, the center of the whole system. Before its evacuation could begin Rawdon had been forced to call in some of his men from Fort Motte, on the opposite bank of the Santee from Fort Watson, whereupon Marion fell upon that place and took it, while Harry Lee pushed on to join Sumter in attacks on Fort Granby and Orangeburg, both of which were taken without difficulty. The total of British prisoners for a month of campaigning was now over 1,000, which is not bad for an army only half again that size which had lost the only battle it fought.

Beyond the seacoast the British now held only the forts at Ninety-Six and Augusta, controlling the routes to Georgia. Against the latter, Green dispatched the indefatigable Lee with a complement of artillery; Pickens, of the partisans, came up to join him. The place consisted of three strong forts, but they had been badly sited and were unable to support each other; Lee and Pickens captured them one by one, the last falling on May 22, after the Americans had built a wooden tower from which they could drop rifle fire into the stockade.

Ninety-Six was a more important proposition, controlling not only the main road into interior Georgia, but also the routes leading to the Indian country. It had a garrison of 550 men; Greene turned toward it with his main body, now 1,000 strong. He arrived before the place the same day Augusta fell, found it too well built and well held to be captured by a *coup de main,* and sat down to make a siege in form, with parallels and trenches.

That siege lasted just short of a month, the British making an extremely vigorous defense, with constant sorties which jarred Greene's men no little, while the besiegers tried the wooden tower again, fired most of the buildings with flaming arrows, and set sharpshooters to watch the fort's water supply, so that those within suffered frightfully from thirst. But British sea power now took a hand, bringing Lord Rawdon a powerful reinforcement that enabled him to march to the relief of his fort at the head of 2,500 men, all but a few of them regulars. Greene heard about the advance almost as soon as it began, and ordered Marion and Sumter to delay the British at the river lines as the militia had inhibited Cornwallis during his pursuit of Morgan's command. The partisan commanders took the orders as an insult and went off about their own business; Rawdon came marching on.

If he wanted Ninety-Six there was nothing for Greene to do but assault it, and assault the place he did, on June 18, from two directions, Lee leading one storming party and himself the other. Lee's group made a lodgment, but Greene's own was beaten off, and though a renewal of the attack might have broken in, Greene remained faithful to his principle of never committing his men to the limit, ordered a retreat, and raised the seige, with, for the first time, losses considerably heavier than those of the enemy and another fight lost.

But another campaign gained. When his lordship arrived at Ninety-Six with the army of relief he found there was no other place for him to go but back to Charleston. He could not leave enough men in the post to guarantee it against attack without leaving so many that they would be in constant difficulties about supply, since the line-of-communications posts were all gone. The loyaltists of the neighborhood were assembled and evacuated to Charleston under the protection of Rawdon's force; Ninety-Six was burned like Camden before it—and of all the South that was once so nearly conquered, the British now held only Charleston, Savannah, and Wilmington.

Greene followed the enemy as far as the High Hills of Santee, where he gave his hard-pressed men six weeks' rest. The British Colonel Stewart, who had replaced Lord Rawdon when the latter went home on leave, came forward to face the Americans from across the Santee River. The enemy were unwilling to abandon the upcountry altogether, since they drew much of their supply from it, and Stewart, like Rawdon and Cornwallis before him, hoped to break Greene in a battle and recover the lost ground. But he found he could gain no advantage in maneuver and was reduced to standing still while Greene moved around the circuit of the upper rivers to come down the right bank of the Santee.

At the beginning of September, 1781, the armies were in contact, Stewart falling slowly back to his base of supplies at Eutaw Springs. There on September 8 Greene prepared to attack him, each side having about 2,300 men, of whom only 1,254 of Greene's, but all of Stewart's, were regular soldiers. Stewart formed in a single, rather deep line, at the northern edge of some open ground in which his camp was situated. Greene advanced in two lines, his militia forward, the Continentals behind them, Lee's horse on the right flank, and a group of Sumter's partisans covering the left, while William Washington's cavalry were in the rear of the infantry lines to strike through the center down the road that lay there as soon as the British should have been driven back to open ground. The arrangement looks strikingly original till one recalls that it is almost exactly that adopted by Turenne for his famous battle at Sinsheim.

At Sinsheim the field was constricted; here it was the visibility, and because of that poor visibility, the British right

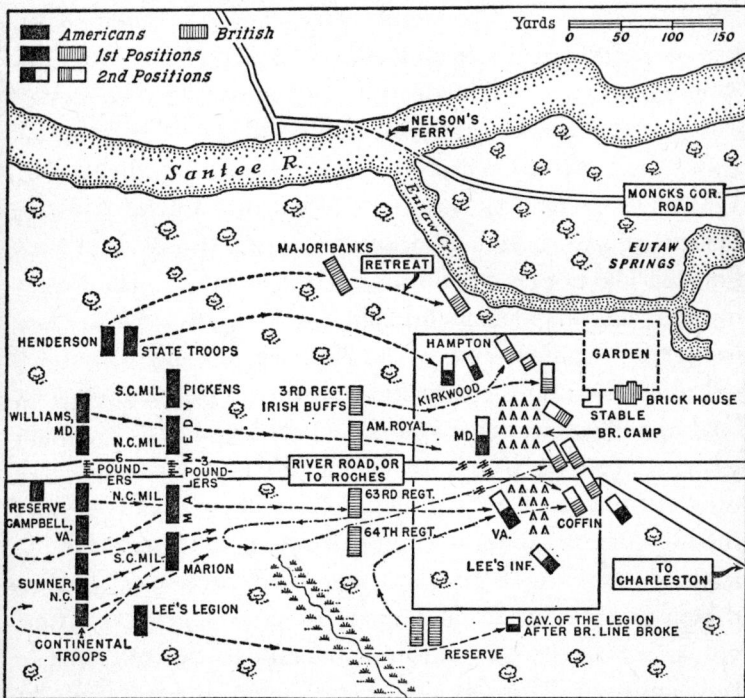

Eutaw Springs

overlapped the American left instead of the lines being parallel, as intended. The result was that, after Greene's militia had opened the ball at ten o'clock with a heavy musketry fight, in which they stood up surprisingly well, and had been replaced by the regulars, whom Greene ordered in with the bayonet, Sumter's men on the left were so menaced that Washington's cavalry had to be put in there.

The horsemen could not work up a swing among the trees, came head-on into unbroken infantry, and were driven back with the loss of nearly half their number, their leader wounded and captured.

But they fought hard enough to halt the British right, and on the other wing the bayonet attack, much aided by a rousing charge from Light Horse Harry Lee, broke down the British flank. The retrograde movement spread along the enemy line, and the Americans rushed in to capture Stewart's camp. Nathanael Greene had won a victory at last.

But there were two misfortunes that came with the victory. Washington's cavalry was gone; could not pursue; and the British camp was full of delicacies which the hungry Continentals had not tasted in years, including an abundant supply of rum. Regulars and militia alike fell out of ranks to celebrate the occasion, and while they were doing it, Stewart rallied his men on the formations of the unbroken right wing around a big stone house and walled garden behind the morning's camp. The troops remaining under Greene's control were too few to take the place; in the afternoon the re-formed British burst forth in a counterattack that drove back the leading American formations and was threatening to turn things into a rout when Greene ordered a general retreat.

He had lost his last and most hopeful battle—and won his last campaign. The action cost the Americans 503 men, but they retired with 450 British prisoners, and Stewart had lost 436 killed and wounded, for a total casualty list of nearly 40 per cent of his force, a figure that left him so weak he could do nothing but abandon his wounded and march back to the security of Charleston, never again to emerge on the landward side. The war in the South was over. In ten months, with a force that never counted as many as 1,500 regulars, Greene had captured all the British posts, taken 3,500 prisoners (more than double his own total!), and split their armies in half, shutting one remnant in Charleston and the other in Wilmington.

For Cornwallis in Wilmington could still reach the Rawdon-Stewart force only by another march into the uplands, and "this," he wrote, "might enable General Greene to hem me in among the great rivers and by cutting off our subsistence render our arms useless. My situation here is very distressing." In other words, he knew better than to try with inferior forces the campaign he had just lost when his numbers were superior. There was, he decided, only one real way to escape from his distressing situation—march into Virginia and add the armies there to his strength. Under the circumstances and in the state of his knowledge it was a logical decision to get away from Greene. There was nothing in the book or his knowledge to inform him that George Washington would throw an army down from New York in one of the fastest marches of history or that Chesapeake Bay would be full of French battleships.

VII

Analysis makes it easy to see how Greene won his campaign; the question is how he contrived to lose all his battles. The matter has received a certain amount of critical attention, and the conclusion usually reached is that the reason for the defeats is that Greene simply did not have a stomach for battle; that if he had possessed the fighting leadership of Wayne or Stark, he might have utterly broken the forces opposed to him at Guilford or Eutaw Springs.

This is a misreading of Greene's character as a leader and a misunderstanding of the battles he fought. They were carried to the last bullet and bayonet; in all our military history no series of combats saw battles fought so desperately or losses so high on both sides, till the U.S. Marines began to assault the Pacific islands, where the rule was no quarter.

Few commanders fought so hard as Greene. He led the assault on Ninety-Six in person; at Trenton he showed an even greater capacity for battle than Washington himself; and that exacting leader had no criticism of the way Greene led his division in the furious fighting at Monmouth.

There is an explanation of the defeats which does not involve such contradictions as maintaining that one of the most thorough battle captains in the Continental army had no appetite for battle. Greene was simply the pupil of Turenne and of John Locke, of the delicate tactician and the pure empiricist. His personal preference was doubtless for fighting at any time and continuing to fight as long as anyone could stand on his feet, but in his Lockeian role he had learned to set preference below the evidence of surrounding conditions.

What the evidence said at Guilford and Eutaw Springs was that while putting in the last man might produce an immediate spectacular result, it would not solve the larger strategic problem. The very fact that the two battles were fought against different forces proves this. A really solid defeat for Greene in either action, or even a ringing victory that left his little army crippled, would have set the remaining British force free to spread out across the country, recover the lost posts and set up new ones, hold the centers of communication, and in the long run break down both the colonists' capacity to resist and their will to do so. While Greene's army retained its power of maneuver, the British were forced to concentrate, could not distribute their forces on police duty, and must allow the partisans more or less a free hand. The system of a chain of posts, so successful in dealing with rebellions elsewhere in the world, failed in the southern colonies because there was an army in the field to support the raiders, even though a very small army compared to the forces facing it. The situation is closely analogous to that described by Mahan in his classic work on sea power—a raiding war can be a great success when there is a fighting force to back it up.

In working this out, in carefully husbanding his power of maneuver, Greene was to a degree following Turenne, but he was also producing something new in war—making real strategic use of irregular troops. Nor was it the only new thing he introduced. With his background and training he would certainly have preferred to live out of magazines by regular logistic convoys, as the custom then was in all armies. When he took over the command in New Jersey, Greene's first care was to arrange such a system for Washington's army. But in the Carolinas this was impossible; magazines would have been as much hostages to fortune as were the posts set up by the British, and would have hamstrung Greene's power of free maneuver as the posts hampered theirs.

The Rhode Islander was more or less forced, not by financial difficulties alone, to live off the country. In the long run this proved to be the key factor of the campaign, but it hardly would have been had not the American commander been willing to accept and to make use of whatever he had, without inquiring why it was not better.

In only one respect does Greene seem to have allowed preconception to cloud the mirror of his empiricism. One of the reasons why he lost his battles was clearly that they were planned on too intricate a basis, one that could only be executed by trained troops, moving precisely. Eutaw Springs was an obvious borrowing from Turenne, as we have seen; Hobkirk's Hill less obviously, but still a borrowing, since it demanded that a thin line of infantry stand firm under fire till free-moving bodies struck in on the enemy flanks. Obsessed with the idea of a regular army, Greene could never quite understand why the men called regular did not behave like trained troops when the shooting started.

But in every other respect, in the handling of every other detail, Nathanael Greene made himself master of the circumstances he found, and left to the American army a tradition it has never quite lost, of considering each problem in the light of its surrounding conditions rather than in that of received opinion.

ANTHONY WAYNE
The Last of the Romans

I

IN AN AGE WHICH SET GREATER STORE BY CLASSICAL COM-
parisons than does ours, college orators found a favorite
subject in drawing a parallel between the reception of the
news from the Teutobergerwald by the Emperor Augustus
and the not dissimilar moment when George Washington
heard of St. Clair's crushing defeat by the Indians. It made
an arresting antithesis—the emotional Roman ordering off
heads, running wildly through his palace, shouting "Varus,
Varus, give me back my legions!"—the Virginian carrying
on with unalloyed courtesy the dinner party in which he was
engaged and only when the guests had gone bursting forth
with, "Oh, God! Oh, God! He's worse than a murderer! I
warned him! To suffer that army to be hacked to pieces!"
Then the sudden pause, the self-mastery: "This must never
go beyond this room. St. Clair shall have justice."

To modern ears the story lacks point, for the underlying
circumstances seem so utterly unlike. But this is because we
suffer from chronic historical myopia. To the first president
of the United States and his contemporaries a comparison
with the first Emperor of Rome was not absurd. The young
republic, like the young empire, had lately closed a desperate

war with an exhaustion of the national military spirit. Both were in economic confusion; each was faced, across a great river, by an irreconcilable and active barbarism, whose previously disjointed tribes had lately coalesced under good military leadership. In each case these barbarians inhabited an unsurveyed forest; both republic and empire had made settlements across the frontier river and had seen them wiped out. Now each had lost, in a single catastrophe, the best army it could muster. What difference the analogy held was unfavorable to the Americans; for the confederation of tribes that held the Ohio, unlike that which held the Rhine, was receiving munitions, advice in diplomacy, and the support of military posts and civilized officers from the first power of the world. Moreover, the army that had perished at the headwaters of the Wabash was the only American army; after St. Clair's defeat there were not 300 men left under the flag. Nor was it heartening to realize that the long-range result of the Roman defeat in the forest had been the submergence of their civilization.

The United States was, then, in 1791, faced with a crisis as grave as any that ever confronted a government; and it was rescued from it by a man who had been praised for qualities he would have regarded as faults. His own generation often ridiculed Anthony Wayne as "Tony Lumpkin," a name intended to carry an implication of stupid, bulldog courage. The present one knows him only as "Mad Anthony" and seldom sees him except in a picture of fifth-reader days, wounded but carried on the shoulders of his men during a charge—a brave thing to do, perhaps, but not very intelligent.

It is with something like surprise that one finds his lesser known portraits exhibiting a man of delicate features, with dark-brown eyes deep set under long lashes. Personal memories confirm the evidence of the painter's brush; speaking of his extraordinary vivacity, quick wit, intellectualism, and deep reading, they tell how he was the only man in the Continental army who could bandy persiflage with the French officers—and also (alas!) how he was the greatest Ben Blowhard the Army of the United States ever knew.

Modern psychology would describe the last habit as a defense mechanism. Wayne's position at the beginning of the Revolution was not a happy one. He was the youngest and most ignorant colonel in the Pennsylvania Line, a civilian officer who owed his appointment to social gifts and financial position. From the beginning he was thrown into contact with three incompetent and envious professionals—Charles Lee, Arthur St. Clair, and James Wilkinson.

From the beginning also it was his fate to be given impossible missions. His first contact with the enemy came at Three Rivers (Quebec), where the Pennsylvania Brigade had been marched in support of the faltering Canadian expedition. It was the spring of 1776. Scouts had reported a weak British vanguard pushing forward beyond contact with its main body. The Pennsylvanians were footsore and in rags, badly done-up after a long march, ill supplied; had never been under fire. The British were regulars in beautiful shape, but the chance was too good to be missed. A peremptory attack was ordered, with Wayne leading.

Well, the scout reports were wrong. The young colonel found himself at the head of two regiments of militia attacking the main British army. The action he took might be set down as pure combative instinct, were we not aware that Wayne was already well known in Pennsylvania for his persistent reading of ancient military history. There is more than a memory of the tactics of Marathon in the way he ployed his little command into column and tried to push through the British center with cold metal, regardless of flanks. Of course he was beaten back, with his brigade badly mauled; but in the process he acquired a piece of knowledge not without importance—he learned that green troops can be held steady as long as they are moving forward, but tend to go to pieces in a retreating fire fight.

Another lesson in the art of war as practiced in the Continental army soon followed. Wayne was made commandant at Ticonderoga, the key of the northern lakes and the spot where the British invasion was obviously coming through. Conditions there were simply horrible—mutinous troops whose service had expired, no clothes, no food, no ammunition—but not much worse than elsewhere during the Revolution. They were of importance to Wayne's story chiefly in that they seem to have convinced him that the whole militia system was wrong and would have to be rooted out.

It is more significant in general history that his surveyor's eye (he had been a surveyor before becoming wealthy as a tanner) detected the fact that Ticonderoga was dominated by Mount Defiance, across the river. He reported in this sense; General Gates came up with St. Clair, looked at Defiance, and said it could not be climbed. Wayne climbed the peak himself; St. Clair remarked that even so, a cannon fired from there could not hit the fort. Wayne fired one of his fort guns at the mountain. The ball landed better than halfway up; the two professional soldiers sniffed, said no action need be taken, and went home. Only a few months later the British dragged a couple of guns straight up Mount Defiance and bombarded the most important fortress in America into submission without even a decent resistance. From that moment on, Anthony Wayne never trusted a professional soldier save in routine matters where judgment did not enter.

II

By the time Ticonderoga fell, however, "Dandy" Wayne had entered on a new phase of his career, as a division commander in Washington's main army. His first engagement was the Brandywine, where he held the center. Early in the day he divined the British movement opposite him as a feint and asked permission to attack, believing such a move would dislocate whatever plan the enemy had. There seems to have been some wretched staff work: by the time the permissive order came through, Wayne's supports had been withdrawn and once more his Pennsylvanians took a pounding.

It was apparently with some idea of allowing the command to win itself a victory that Washington confided to them the operation of surprising the British camp at Paoli, near Wayne's own home, a week later. Wayne did his own scouting, discovering the Redcoats camped in a valley, badly outposted, and quite oblivious of the presence of enemies. Their numbers were too much for his single brigade; he asked and was promised the support of Smallwood's, and on the evening of September 9, 1777, withdrew a little distance to wait overnight for the reinforcement. He had already retired when a country boy was brought to headquarters who said he had been in the enemy camp and learned the British were planning a countersurprise on Wayne for the next day. The general, groggy with sleep, remarked that when Smallwood arrived in the morning, they would set an ambush to make the Lobster-backs' ears tingle, then returned to his rest.

The trouble was that the British came before Smallwood, caught the Pennsylvanians just crawling out of their blankets, and rumpled them up. That finished Wayne as far as the professionals were concerned; they tagged him "Tony Lumpkin" and began an organized effort to get him dismissed as an impetuous, boastful, and stupid officer. The picture did not agree with Washington's own; he had noted that, since Wayne was in command of them, the Pennsylvanians bore themselves more pridefully than any other troops in the army, and their commander was the only one of his subordinates who thought in terms of battle rather than position. He clung to the brigadier and even gave him charge of the leading column in the attack on Germantown two weeks later.

That was another American defeat, but by no fault of Wayne's. He went charging into the town like a whirlwind, pierced the British center, and would have won the battle out of hand, had not Stephen's brigade, with its commander silly drunk, come up to fire into his rear.

There was no other officer in the Continental army who could carry through an attack like that, and at Monmouth in the following spring Wayne was placed under Charles Lee to be the spearhead of the movement. The British were retreating through New Jersey in a long column; the general battle plan was for Lee to strike their big rearguard, halt it and contain it, while Washington himself swung a deep flank move around to cut it off.

Wayne started with the day, one of the hottest days of which we have historical record, June 28, 1778, fell on the hindmost element of the march, punched it hard with a bayonet charge, and brought the whole British rearguard down on himself. Heavily outnumbered, the Pennsylvanians drew back to a little rise of ground and waited for the rest of Lee's men to fall in on their flanks.

They did not come. Lee, with some remark that "Americans could not be expected to stand up against British grenadiers," had given orders for retreat which left the Pennsylvania general (whom he did not like) to stand the full force of the enemy counterstroke. Washington, midway in his turning maneuver, received the dismaying tidings that the whole British army, not rearguard alone, was united and beating at Wayne, rode to Lee's front, found the corps going back in rout and the general who should have been leading the advance conducting a disorderly retreat. He "swore like an angel from heaven," called Lee a damned poltroon, and instantly ordered a new line formed on Wayne, who had made a desperate retreating fight till he reached an orchard at the edge of the road between two hills.

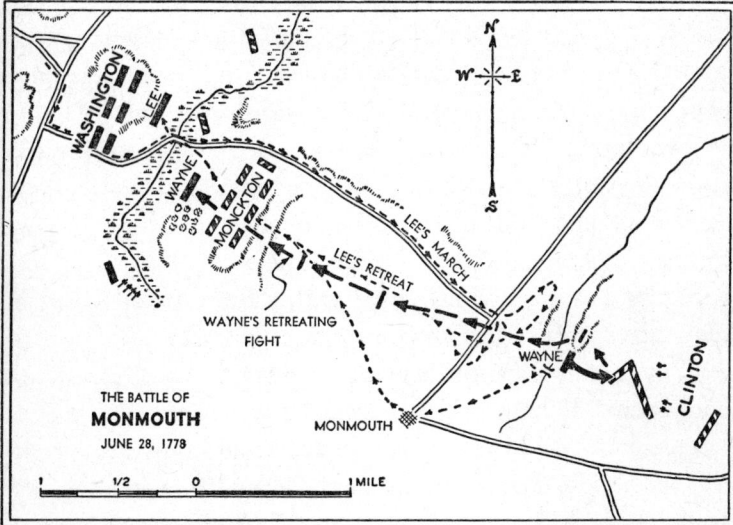

THE BATTLE OF
MONMOUTH
JUNE 28, 1778

The British tried the left, did not like their reception; tried the right, liked that no better; then, with their grenadiers in the lead, came rushing along the low ground to drive through Wayne. Charles Lee had his answer there; for the tired Pennsylvanians, who had fought all day under heat that cost them nearly as many casualties as bullets, held their fire till the British closed, then broke the grenadier column, killed its colonel (Monckton), and then finished the job with a rousing bayonet rally, Wayne himself leading right into the thick of it.

His reward was a court-martial on the Paoli business. It found him blameless. But in the reorganization that took place shortly afterward, his enemies gained the upper hand in the state, and he was retired. We do not see him again until a twelvemonth later, and then through the eyes of an officer sent by Washington to inquire whether Squire Wayne will take command of the new corps of light infantry. "A man remarkable for his skillful manners and skill in carving," the emissary found him, "in a fine broadcloth suit, highly polished boots, ruffled waistband and bosom, with a tricornered beaver hat set to one side . . . " and explained about the new command. The war has shown signs of dying by inanition; the light infantry corps, to be composed of companies of 41 men each, picked for their activity from the regular regiments, is to roam the country, marching fast and hitting quick in an effort to ginger things up.

Squire Wayne was delighted with the prospect; joined his diminutive corps (less than a modern battalion in numbers) on July 1, and instantly began to complain about his soldiers' equipment. "I have a prejudice," he writes to Washington, "in favor of an Ellegant Uniform and would rather risque my life at the Head of the same men Clothed & Appointed as I could wish with a Single Charge of Ammunition than to take them as they appear with sixty rounds of Cartridges." The commander-in-chief replies that as a matter of principle Wayne is perfectly right; the difficulty is to find the material, a business that shall receive his earnest attention—and will General Wayne consider Stony Point as the objective of his operations?

Stony Point is one of the Gibraltar-like peaks glaring across the Hudson at the southern gate of the highlands. In 1779 it was a position of great strategic and economic importance, for it was the western ferry terminus of the great traffic artery from New England to New York and the southern states—the only highroad of union while the King's men held New York City. The British had taken it that spring; it was now strongly fortified and strongly garrisoned, and had warship support. Yet it was so essential, that Washington felt it would be worth all it might cost to win it by storm.

The correspondence has been preserved, giving us for the first time in Wayne's career the full picture of how an operation of his was arranged in all its detail. To our astonishment, the roles assigned by history to the two men are reversed. It is the cautious commander-in-chief who is all on fire, urging the place be stormed out of hand, while the impetuous, rash, careless subordinate does not think a storm possible, but believes he may do the matter by surprise and careful pre-arrangement. Wayne is busy with minutest details; orders the men to wear white cockades or slips of paper in their hats for night recognition; sets the hour for midnight because surprises generally come at dawn and the British will be keeping shrewd watch at that hour; orders his officers to inspect every musket to be sure it is unloaded and has the bayonet fixed; rehearses the movement against a hill back in the Catskills to insure timing. He rejects Washington's suggestion that the column attempt the side of the fortress that lies along the river beach, on the ground that he has consulted tide and moon tables, and found that at the hour when the water is lowest the light is brightest.

The fort lies on a peninsula, with a marsh and brook separating it from the mainland. At the north end, the easiest slope, a small party is to advance with noise and parade, let themselves be seen, take over, and open fire. At the center, where the marsh is worst, French Fleury will lead half the light infantry; at the south end, Wayne himself will come in, across a marsh not so bad, but piled with rocks and heavy abatis. So—we are ready, and on the night of July 16 will start. "The fort's our own" is the watchword.

Do start; in column of platoons. By one of those accidents that always attend concentric attacks, the northernmost movement, the feint, strikes first, for the marsh lies under the tide and the other two are twenty minutes getting through it when they should have spent but three or four. By the time Wayne's own column arrives at the abatis the feint is marked as a feint. A few intelligent British soldiers have brought themselves and their muskets to the south end of the line and, though the night is black as pitch, blaze away in the dark to-

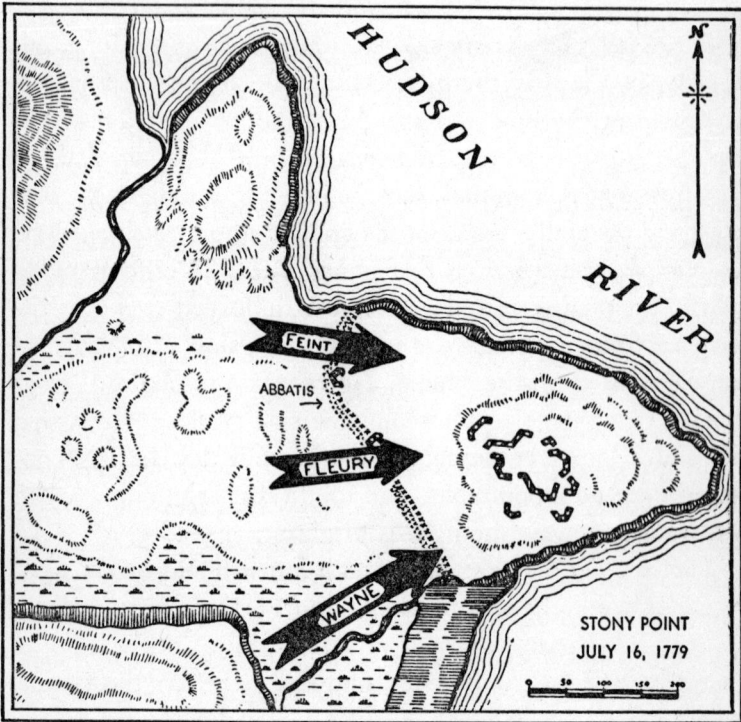

STONY POINT
JULY 16, 1779

ward the sound of the axmen chopping abatis. Men are hit in the storming column, which has no way of replying, cannot even move, only wait. Wayne himself is hit, a gashing wound along the head, and flails on the ground, half-conscious, unable to rise. They try to stanch his wound; through a veil of blood he notes how the column weaves and murmurs in those first uneasy movements which are the beginnings of disintegration. He summons all his strength. "Carry me into the fort," he cries, "and let me die there!" and then goes off into another faint as they pick him up.

That was how and why Anthony Wayne was carried up the slope of Stony Point; and that shout of a man who truly thought himself dying supplied the Tyrtaean touch. The soldiers gave a shout; poured over, around, and through the abatis, went rushing up the hill, and at the crest of the rampart met Fleury just as the British began to shout, "Mercy, Mercy, dear, dear Americans!"

Five hundred of them and fifteen cannon were taken in the post; and the feat of arms roused the Colonies from near apathy with so strong a shock that Congress voted to the general who had lately been under a cloud one of the first Medals of Honor given any man. The public voted him the name of "Mad Anthony" and pronounced it in a way to indicate that there was a certain divinity in that kind of madness.

But Stony Point, if it marked for the Continental army the beginning of a new era of operations not only well planned but well carried through, also marked for the successful commander the end of active service in the north. The Arnold treason began to coil out of its hole; Wayne had to clean up the mess, which took him the rest of the year. The next found him back with the Pennsylvania Line and that body of troops in a mutiny. It was not his fault nor did he settle it; but it was 1781 before he took the field again, now under Lafayette in Virginia.

The campaign was that of Yorktown, and Wayne's only action came when Cornwallis was making a retreat across the James River near Green Spring. The Pennsylvanian had the vanguard, eight hundred men; thought he might get in on the British rear in time to smash it against the unfordable stream. The approach was through a morass both wide and treacherous, down a single corduroy road, which ended in a wide space of savannas and groves just north of the river. The Americans pushed into this space, but too late; discovered that the British were aware of their presence and, instead of crossing the James, had turned back with some five thousand men. Wayne was in much the same situation as a man in a cage with a tiger who can get out only through a single door just big enough to be negotiated at a crawl.

His cure for the trouble was to hit the tiger in the eye. But he now knew more about tactics than he had at Three Rivers; deployed his slender force across the open spaces so that every man was visible and came on in line. The British could not but take this bold advance as the presage of something much more formidable. They imagined Wayne had been unexpectedly supported by Lafayette's whole force, took defensive positions, "beat off" the first rush, and spent so much time waiting for its renewal that Mad Anthony slipped away down the road of danger.

After Yorktown, the Pennsylvania general was sent south with a semi-independent command against the Indians on the wings of Nathanael Greene's campaign. He had one small fight, of which the details remain obscure, but in general achieved his object so well that when the war closed the Georgia Legislature voted him eight hundred acres of land.

He tried to farm this estate, but the successful northern businessman proved an indifferent planter. The place had been lost through foreclosure proceedings when a letter came from the Secretary of War of the then newly organized nation. The United States Army had been practically destroyed in the Ohio wood; President Washington wished him to take command, reorganize, beat back the Indians, and save the Northwest Territory.

III

The basic situation was that there were a good many tribes in the ground beyond the Ohio, with overlapping and ill-defined rights, since the idea of territorial sovereignty was one foreign to the Indian mind. Purchase treaties for trans-Ohio lands had been negotiated with some of these tribes. The successive American governments took these agreements as binding on all the Indians, but the more stiff-necked tribes refused to recognize them as binding on any. This attitude received warm support from the English, who had never evacuated the forts and trading posts throughout the northwest, and who continued to regard the country as a field reserved for their commerical exploitation. Scalps passed as current coin in The Honourable The Hudson's Bay Company's posts.

The background is important, not merely to the origin of the war, but also to a comprehension of the specific problem facing Anthony Wayne. It was not the common problem of dealing with a dispersed enemy in wild country. A good case could be made out for the view that the braves could muster a better-trained regular army than the United States. They had weapons as good as the Americans; they were experienced in a system of tactics admirably adapted to the country in which the war was to be fought; British support took care of the logistic question which trips so many savage armies; and for the time, at least, they had adequate leadership in chiefs Thayendanega, Little Turtle, and Blue Jacket, three of the ablest men the forest Indians ever produced.

At least this seems to have been the view that Wayne himself took. When he came up to the badly frightened trading hamlet at Pittsburgh in April of 1792, he set himself not merely to organize a new American army, but also to train it along special lines that would give it permanent field superiority over the enemy. Under the conditions of the conflict he could hardly improve on the Indians in the school of the soldier or in minor tactics, and he adopted their method as far as it went. The strategy of the struggle was not a matter of training. The question of making certain of victory in advance therefore boiled down to one of discovering an impregnable system of major tactics. Disgusted with the professional military science of his day, Mad Anthony went straight back to the first principles of those grand masters of frontier warfare, the Romans.

It was thus not merely a taste for the classic phrase that led him to name the new army "The Legion" and to organize on the basis of 5,120 men (though it never reached this figure) with a troop of irregular mounted auxiliaries of similar size; or to arrange that the bulk of the Legion should be heavy infantry, with small bodies of light footmen and elite cavalry. This is precisely the size and organization of the legions Marius used against the Cimbri. Similarly, we find Wayne training his legion to operate in small squads of 40 men each, maneuvering not in the long lines that dominated every European battlefield of the century, but in checkerboard formation (maniples!) with skirmishers round front and flanks. He gives the most stringent orders that each night half the infantry shall stand to arms in hollow square while the other half constructs a stockade, then installs redoubts 300 yards out from each angle. Nor was this Roman camping arrangement confined to orders; it was daily practiced in the wooded hills around Pittsburgh.

Wayne's subordinates had not thought the thing through as he had. Most of them were frontiersmen of the most violently individualistic type, and they imagined the veteran was suffering from softening of the brain. As far as they were concerned, a man who was brave and knew how to shoot was a soldier; discipline, Roman tactics, and camp-building were so much *opéra bouffe*. The camp was filled with violent wranglings, and the marplot Wilkinson, who had turned up as one of the subordinate commanders, sent to President Washington a circumstantial and mendacious account of how the general had killed not less than three men by his cruelties.

It went into the no-attention file, and the drills continued while peaceful efforts were made to arrive at a settlement with the tribes. But the complaints had the result of making enlistments slow, and it was with less than half his full legionary organization that Wayne drifted down the Ohio and camped at Hobsons Choice, near Cincinnati, in May of 1793. He based on the latter town, drawing supplies both by the river and by Kentucky, and began at once to make a hard cleared road up into the Indian country. By September he had pushed beyond Fort Jefferson, a distance of over seventy miles, not the least feat he accomplished. Arthur St. Clair resented it bitterly. Still Governor of the Northwest Territory, he complained that he was conducting delicate peace negotiations with the tribes but Wayne was breaking down everything by a show of force—an odd complaint from a man who had shown force himself till it was struck from his hand.

Like the other appeals against Wayne, this one went into the presidential scrap heap. The General spent the fall building his force in for the winter at Fort Greenville—a stockade fort as near as could be in all its arrangements like the fort Quintus Cicero set up among the Nervii, as Julius Caesar tells us. For light-traveling men the spot is but three days' journey from "The Glaize" and the headwaters of the streams flowing to Lake Erie, a fine strategic situation.

That fall, the peace negotiations broke down, as Wayne knew they must unless the United States conceded that its citizens would not settle beyond the Ohio. The announcement came in typical Indian fashion, with a surprise attack in force against Wayne's provision convoy on the road up from Cincinnati, twenty-one wagons under a strong guard, which beat off the attack, though not till fifteen men were killed. Two days later the commander emphasized the point of watchfulness by shooting two sentries who had slept on post, then sent forward Colonel Francis Hamtramck to the spot of St. Clair's defeat, twenty-two miles farther out, where a strong advance post was set up and named Fort Recovery.

Like all the barbarians of history, the Indians lacked both skill and stamina for sieges. Wayne was unmolested till spring broke in a cloud of hot little combats along the line of communications. Doubtless he would have liked to take the offensive early in the year, but the Kentucky irregulars he was counting on did not join at Fort Greenville till the end of June, and he stoutly refused to march without the help of these squirrel-killing riders. When he did move, it was with 2,000 of the Legion and 1,500 volunteers, among them a certain Lieutenant Clark, one day to journey to the Oregon, a man with a marvelous gift for observing detail and setting it down. To him we owe most of our knowledge of the campaign, and his testimony is all the more valuable because he did not like the commander.

The march started July 28, 1794. The order for it placed the legionary infantry in the lead, then the baggage, then the mounted Kentuckians, with light infantry and the legionary horse far out on the flanks, where they "Sustain'd considerable fatigue & injury from the thickness of the Woods and Brush thro which they passed" but furnished effective security, as the same arrangement had for Julius Caesar's men in the land of the Belgae.

Each night they set up camp in the Roman fashion Wayne had taught them. When the site was good the camp became a permanent post in a line of blockhouses up into the country, left in charge of a lieutenant with a hundred sound men

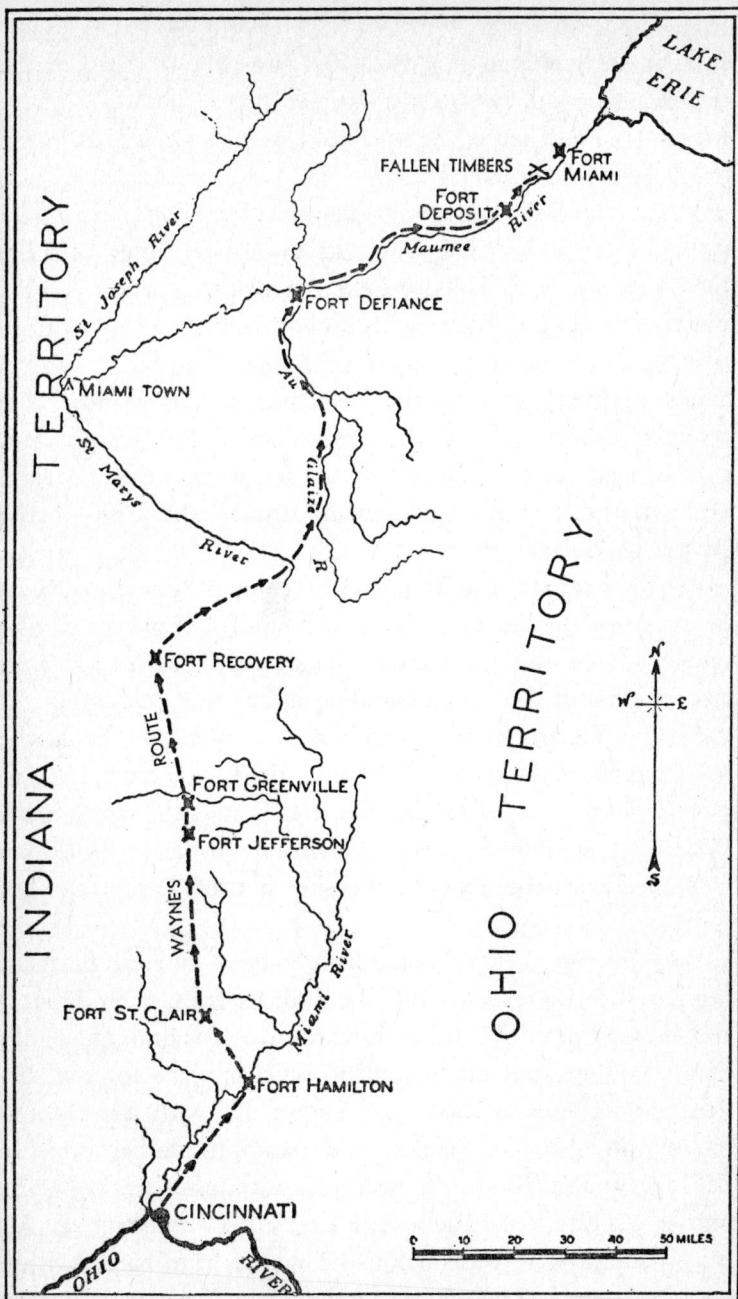

Wayne in the West

and the accumulated casuals of the date. The strategy of the march was good, pointing up to the valley of the Maumee, which was, in a sense, the savages' base of supplies, for these were Indians who tilled the ground. At the western end of this river line lay their great village and capital, Miami, and the most fertile of their fields; its eastern terminus, at Lake Erie near modern Toledo, held the British outpost, where there were still more cornfields together with the link to England and the Indians' source of military supplies. Wayne aimed midway between the two, and we know now that this concealment of his ultimate objective was wholly successful, many of the Indians falling back west to cover Miami, while the rest went downstream toward the base of the British post.

On the banks of the Maumee the column "immerged Suddenly into an open, extensive and bountiful Plaine or Prairie which offered ellegant Scenery handsomely interspersed with Small Copse of Trees & abounding in every Species of Great variety of Herbage which enspired new animation" in all the soldiers, who fell to work destroying the Indian crops. At this point, where the Au Glaize River falls into the Maumee, a great fort was built, Fort Defiance; and here Wilkinson quarreled with the general, accusing him of "irritating" the Indians.

Now, at last, Wayne made his choice of objectives, turning east downstream to cut the Indians from their base at the British fort. The tribes hovered thick round the flanks of the column, but could find no time or place for the surprise attack they wished. On August 17, with the column moving down the left bank of the stream, the Indian pressure became intense, for the British post was just ahead. Wayne halted, built another stockade, Fort Deposit, and in it left his heavy baggage. It was obvious he would have battle within a day or two, but he sat still in the enemy's presence instead of attacking, a move based on his knowledge of Indian psychology. They cherished a theory that a wound was always fatal to a man with a full belly; therefore they refused to eat

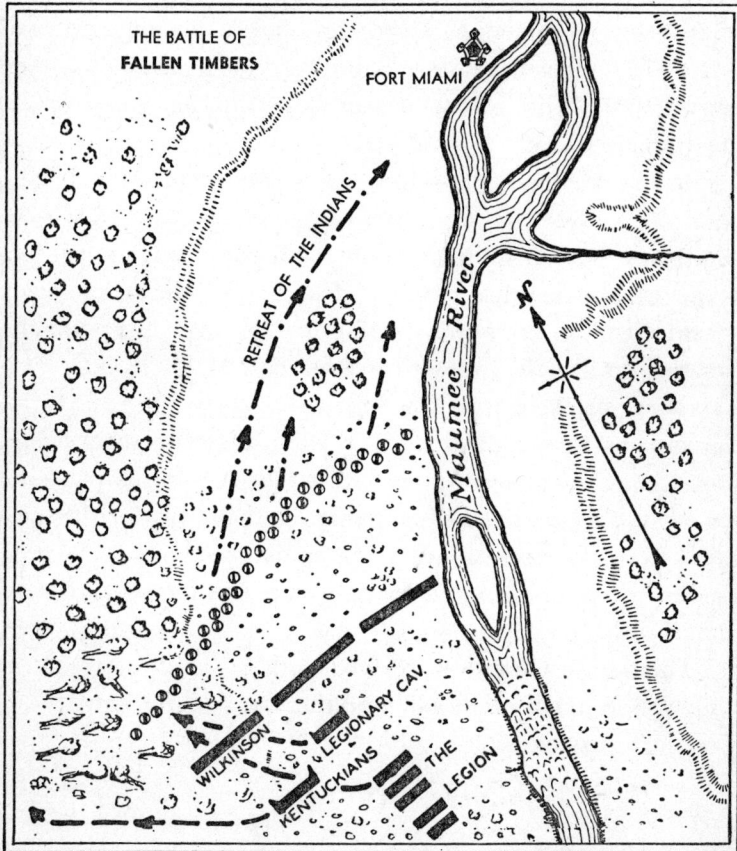

THE BATTLE OF
FALLEN TIMBERS

FORT MIAMI

RETREAT OF THE INDIANS

Maumee River

N

WILKINSON

LEGIONARY CAV.

KENTUCKIANS

THE LEGION

on the day of a fight. Wayne kept them hungry for three days by constant feints forward, before he took up the march again in earnest on the 20th.

In his path was a place of broken rocks where some great storm had brought down trees in large numbers, with second growth pushing through the mass in a perfect jungle. Here the troops deployed into battle order, infantry ahead, cavalry behind, with the right wing on the river; and as they began to enter this place of the fallen timbers, the left wing, Wilkinson's, was violently attacked. Mad Anthony had a bad leg, product of an old wound, but got to horse with tears of agony streaming down his cheeks, looked over the situation, saw his elastic formation was holding well in front, and dispatched the Kentuckians in a circuit to get deep around the Indians' flank.

For a couple of hours a heavy fire fight went on in front, with the Indians getting much the worst of it. Wayne noticed they were beginning to give, but there was no sign or sound of the Kentuckians; and fearing the choice moment would pass, he flung the small force of legionary cavalry forward on his left, followed by the foot. Major Robert Mc-Campbell, of the horse, was killed, but they burst through; the Indians broke all along the line. Many of them were rounded up in the open plain that reached from the place of the timbers to the British fort, which to the horror of the savages closed its gates against them as the steady ranks of the Legion, company on company, came trotting out of the underbrush.

"The troops were now revived with ½ a gill of whiskey which they much required," and the war for the Northwest Territory was over.

IV

It did not seem so at the time, particularly to Anthony Wayne, who considered his battle a very unsatisfactory affair. But the preponderant results in war are moral, and he had destroyed the Indians' confidence both in themselves and their faith in British support by his watchful, irresistible advance, as much as by the battle. The struggle was not revived until the organizing genius of Tecumseh, the religious revivalism of the Shawnee Prophet, and overt British aid brought it to life again fifteen years later; and then it was revived in far different terms. In 1812 it was no longer a question of whether the United States should possess the great West, but of how long it would take them to achieve possession.

For Fallen Timbers was a decisive battle, one of the most decisive in our history; and it reached a permanent decision because Mad Anthony Wayne planned it to the last saber cut more than two years before he began. The really striking and surprising thing about Wayne's career is that on the only other occasion when we know what he did before a battle, at Stony Point, we find the same minute pre-preparation. Even the wild act of the wounded general being carried in a charge turns out on examination to be a calculated effect, as sound as it was theatrical.

Is it, then, going too far to suspect that the same intensive preparation went into the rest of those whirlwind charges— at Germantown, Monmouth, Green Springs? I think not; even at Paoli we find him taking pains. All we need to do is deny the classic myth of Tony Lumpkin's rashness, which was carefully fostered by the three evil geniuses of the early army—Arthur St. Clair, Charles Lee, and James Wilkinson. We have the best of testimony on which to deny that myth: the testimony of General George Washington, who made Wayne's men the spearhead of every attack and called him from retirement to a position which required, if anything, the utmost caution.

When that denial is once made, we have left an extremely curious case—a great soldier who learned everything he knew out of a book. A Latin book; for the whole cast of his mind was Roman. His preoccupation with appearance, his insistence upon long drill in preparation for Indian warfare, his segregation of the Legion from the Kentucky volunteers, all bespeak an effort to instill into the American army that pride of race and service which was the distinguishing characteristic of the Roman legionary. Examine his tactics—almost excessively simple, but stamped with the Roman imprint, the imprint of an idea that heavy infantry in close action can master the world, and that a commander's duty is practically over when he has placed such infantry in contact with the enemy under conditions as favorable as he can arrange.

It would have been interesting to see what results Wayne's Roman-model army would have produced in later Indian troubles and in the War of 1812. It would have been interesting to compare the results of his neoclassicism with those of the revolutionary tactical system through which Napoleon Bonaparte was even then trying to escape. Both were plagued by the strait jacket of eighteenth-century war. But such comparisons must be forever futile theory; for the only man who understood what Mad Anthony was trying to do was Mad Anthony himself, and he died less than twenty months after his great victory, leaving behind one of the least-comprehended names in our military history, and a record of service with hardly an equal.

JACOB BROWN
Sword of the Border

FATE TRIED TO CONCEAL HIM UNDER ONE OF THE MOST common of names; Time, by pitching him into the most unmilitary period in the history of our peaceful republic; his parents, by bringing him up as a Quaker; the commanding general of the U.S. Army, by reporting him as the most stupid and insubordinate officer under his command; and the government by giving him neither men nor horses nor guns. Yet he saved our northern frontier twice; he won one of the most desperate battles in American history, and with raw militia at his back he broke the veterans who stood unwavering before Napoleon. Not Sheridan nor Longstreet nor Mad Anthony Wayne more furiously rode the whirlwind. Gentlemen, I give you General Jacob Brown, the best battle captain in the history of the nation.

A pleasant-faced man with rather sharp features and curling hair looks at us out of his portraits; there is a keen eye, an erect carriage, and a skeptical line to the mouth. He was born into a family Quaker for many generations, in Bucks County, Pennsylvania, a month after Lexington, son of a prosperous farmer who fished in the troubled waters of commercial speculation in the years following the Revolution and lost all his money. His education, says a man who knew him young "was accurate and useful as far as it went, without

aspiring to elegant literature or mere speculative science."
He supplemented it by reading everything he could lay his
hands on, and when the family fortunes shipwrecked at the
time of his eighteenth birthday, young Jacob Brown easily
fulfilled the requirements for becoming a country school-
teacher, a trade which he followed for three years.

At that period the Ordinance of 1787 had recently gone
through and the West was opening to ambition. Brown
went to Cincinnati and had enough mathematical equipment
to get a post as a surveyor. It is interesting to note that he
followed Washington in this profession; and that biographies
of such otherwise diverse captains as Frederick the Great,
Napoleon, and Julius Caesar speak of the "surveyor's eye"
—the sense of distance and direction possessed by these men.
Perhaps there is here some clue to the secret of leadership in
battle.

Yet Jacob Brown was still far from battles and the thought
of battles when he came east again after two years of failure to make his fortune in Ohio, and secured the position of
head of the New York Friends' School. The life does not
seem to have afforded enough scope for his intellectual activity, which was considerable; he left the post to take one
as Alexander Hamilton's secretary. The table conversation
at that house must have frequently turned on the Revolution
and its military history; at all events we are told that it was
at this period that Brown began to read Quintus Curtius and
the strange military-philosophical works of the Maréchal de
Saxe. His commercial fortunes also improved about this time,
and in 1799 he bought "several thousand acres" of land near
Watertown, N.Y., and formed there a small settlement which
he called Brownville.

As the squire of the district and county-court judge, he
was elected colonel of the local militia in 1808, apparently
less because he was thought able to command a regiment in

war than because his big estate and comfortable house made a good spot to hold the quarterly drinking bouts which passed under the name "militia exercises." He was politically active at the period, holding several pocket boroughs in the northern part of the state and his appointment as brigadier general in the state service by Governor Tompkins in 1811 was in the nature of a reward for services rendered at the polls, and not because he had shown military ability—for which, indeed, there had been no opportunity.

The appointment made him ex officio military commander of the northern district of the state, and when news of the declaration of war was followed by that of a proposed British descent on Ogdensburg, it was Brown's duty to keep them off. His men (militia) and munitions were all at Sackett's Harbor, some distance away, with the roads so deep in October mire as to be positively impassable. The British had naval command of the lake and a fleet cruising on it, but Brown boldly loaded his force into bateaux and pulled along the shore. He remarked that he could always make land when topsails came over the horizon, and if the British stopped to attack his little force he would deal them such a buffet as would make them forget Ogdensburg. The topsails did not come until he reached his destination. There Brown received the landing party with an amateurish but energetic fire, and after a few languid efforts the British went away.

That closed Brown's service till the following spring, when a rather peculiar strategic situation brought him out again. The American military and naval base on Ontario was Sackett's Harbor at the eastern end, faced across the lake by the British base of Kingston. Winter building had given the United States command of the water, but instead of striking at the enemy base, Chauncey commanding the fleet, and Dearborn the army, decided to trot off to the western end of their little inland sea for an attack on the Niagara

frontier and Toronto, then called York. Lieutenant Colonel Backus, of the "Albany dragōons" was in charge of a
small detachment and a hospital at Sackett's. He should have
been in general charge, but Brown was a landed proprietor of
considerable substance, and Dearborn, a toady if there ever
was one, asked the latter to take charge of the post if any
emergency arose.

Fortunate blunder! For the British learned of the American preoccupation at the wrong end of the line and Sir George
Prevost, governor of Lower Canada, came down on Sackett's
Harbor with all the force he could muster. He had a fleet, not
large by any absolute standard, but of overwhelming power
in relation to the defense; for a landing party he had some
600 Lobster-back regulars and 300 marines and sailors. The
British sails were visible in the offing on the evening of May
27, but the airs fell light and baffling, and they could not
close. All that night and the succeeding day messengers were
out rousing the countryside. When the morning of the 29th
came up, sunshiny and hot, Brown was at Sackett's and in
command. He had 400 regulars, invalids, of whom half were
sufficiently convalescent to fight; a regiment of Albany cavalry, 250 strong, who fell in line dismounted, and 500 militia,
whose experience was limited to the quarterly keg-tapping
aforementioned.

The only place where a landing could be made was on a
spit west of the town, where a broad beach led some distance toward the line of barracks that formed the outer
boundary. Along these buildings Brown deployed the regulars under Backus, with a couple of guns. He posted the
militia at the landing point behind a gravel bank. Cowpens
was the obvious model, where Morgan, of the famous Rifles,
had placed his militia in the front line, sure they would run,
hopeful they would not do so till they had delivered a couple of telling volleys.

Colonel Baynes, of the British 100th Regiment, led the landing party and advance; his report speaks of a "heavy and galling fire, which made it impossible for us to wait for the artillery to be landed and come up," so that he had to charge, out of hand and with infantry only, against the gravel bank. In fact, the "heavy and galling fire" was a single and ragged volley; as soon as the militiamen found their guns empty they became obsessed with the fear the British would be among them before they could reload, and vanished into the woods on their left.

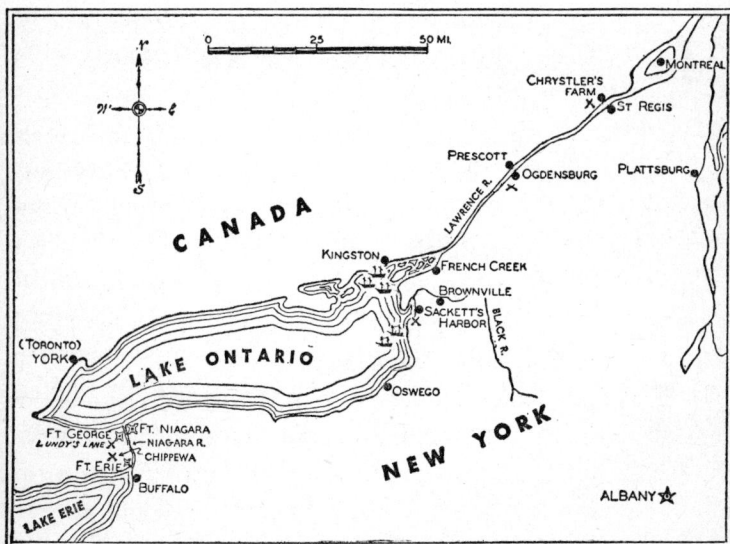

The Canadian Frontier

The attackers cheered and came on; the fleet warped in and began to cannonade the flank of the battle line of regulars. The naval lieutenant in charge of the building yard, foreseeing that they could not hold out long, set fire to everything, so that Backus' tiny group fought with the town and dockyard blazing in their rear and double their strength of enemies closing on their front. They fought well; but the British got a lodgment at one of the barracks and prepared to sweep out the line; Backus was mortally wounded, Brown nowhere to be seen.

As a matter of fact, he was off in the woods, addressing the militia in somewhat un-Quakerly words. "Victory!" he was shouting, waving his sword, "Victory! Will you let the (perjorative) regulars claim your credit?" and rode on among them, gathering a little group and then a big one, like Sheridan at Cedar Creek, half a century later. Just as Sir George Prevost reached out to grasp his own victory, the militia suddenly came storming out of the forest into his flank, with fixed bayonets and Brown at their head. They did not fire a shot; simply yelled in answer to their leader and flung themselves through a scattering volley into the British regulars from whom they had run not half an hour before. Colonel Baynes ordered a precipitate retreat, covered by the ships. He had lost 259 men, nearly a third of the force, and Prevost, when criticized for not countermanding the retirement order, pointed out with some energy that he was in an excellent position to lose everything if he stayed.

The armies were diminutive, but the results prodigious; certainly the victory saved Sackett's Harbor and probably the whole northern frontier. In the then existing state of affairs, it is difficult to see how the United States could have recovered from the loss of their one good base on the lakes. For Sackett's Harbor was the point through which went all the supplies for Oliver Perry, who had not yet fought the battle of Lake Erie, and for Harrison, who had not yet driven the British from Detroit. Secretary of War Armstrong, greatly impressed by Brown's rare talent for making militia fight, rewarded him with a snap promotion to brigadier general of the United States Army and the command of one of the four brigades being organized for the "conquest of Canada" that fall.

The officer in general charge and the ranking leader of the army of invasion was General James Wilkinson, traitor, spy, liar, and hopeless incompetent, completely antithetic to the militia general of the north. He had not been in camp with him a month before he was demanding Brown's removal because the latter refused to serve under a personal friend of the commander's, General Boyd, and because he was ignorant as well as insubordinate. "He knows not enough of military duty to post the guards in a camp," wrote Wilkinson, "and he compelled his batteries to form in a hollow for the advantage of elevating the pieces to fire at the opposing heights."

The last item is too odd to be imaginary; one can only wonder what in the world Brown was thinking of—but the point is that Wilkinson's criticism can be admitted as perfectly just without denying Brown's usefulness as an officer. Winfield Scott, certainly with no animus against the fighting Quaker, said much the same thing in more friendly fashion—"Not a technical soldier; that is, he knew little of organization, tactics, police, etc."—but thought him of great value, for he was "full of zeal and vigor."

He had something else as well. In those lugubrious fall months while the high generals wrangled over this plan and that, their men dying like flies under pouring rains and "lake fever" (whatever that was), Brown's brigade had fewer men on sick report than any other, and was the only one that kept its strength. Why? We have one flash of insight into his methods. Alone among the brigade commanders he made his man build proper huts with fireplaces, drainage, and clean latrines. They worshiped him. Wilkinson complained he was coddling the privates for political purposes. Wilkinson would.

In November the expedition finally got untracked and wandered vaguely down the St. Lawrence, with its commanding general spending his days in bed aboard a bateau, weeping that he had a flux when called on to make decisions and sustaining himself with rum. The British fired at them from the bluffs. At first the opposition was not serious, but it showed an annoying tendency to coalesce. On the 7th, Macomb, with the small reserve, was landed on the north bank to drive them off. He could not handle the situation he found, so on the next morning Brown's brigade also was put ashore, and by night had bruised a path through the gathering clouds of Canadian militia.

Wilkinson next turned his attention to Captain Mulcaster, of the British navy, who was following the expedition up with about 800 men. Since it seemed that some reputation might be gained by driving him off, Wilkinson put another brigade and a half ashore under his favorite Boyd, to turn back against Mulcaster, while Brown was instructed to keep straight on away from the battle. On the 11th came the clash at Chrystie's Farm—it represents perhaps the lowest point the American regular army ever reached. In a blinding sleet storm Boyd fed his triply superior force into the fight in small parties, saw them riddled one by one, and himself led the disgraceful rout that ensued. Mulcaster might have cleaned up the whole force, but for the brilliant covering charge of Walbach's small cavalry regiment, and the skill and steadiness with which Brown, who had marched without orders toward the guns, covered the retreat.

The expedition, however, was ended, and that winter there was a house-cleaning among the higher officers. Wilkinson, Boyd, Wade Hampton, Dearborn, all the old period pieces from the Revolution, were shoved into retirement, and to their horror Jacob Brown was appointed major general of the United States and commander at Sackett's Harbor. Secretary Armstrong seems to have had a clear sense of Brown's limitations as well as his merits, for he gave him for brigadiers two of the strictest professional soldiers in the service—Ripley and Winfield Scott. It was a happy combination.

The campaign of 1814 started badly when Brown permitted the timorous Commodore Chauncey, with whom he had been instructed to confer, to convince him that nothing could be accomplished against Kingston. Accordingly he moved his troops to the Niagara frontier. A talk with Scott and Armstrong showed him the strategic error of trying to lop off a branch when he could strike for the trunk of the tree. "I am the most unhappy man in the world," he wrote, and hurried back to have the matter out with the naval commander.

But the latter was one of those officers whom nothing can persuade to fight unless odds-on. He flatly refused to give naval support for a move on Kingston or any other point until midsummer had brought his new battleship from the building ways. So Brown had to return to Niagara and make the best of things there. Meanwhile, Scott, left in charge of the little army, had drilled the troops well; but the strategic situation his commander found at the Niagara was bad.

The Americans held only the ashes of burned Buffalo and the Lake Erie inlet of the Niagara. Facing that place, on the Canadian side, was a strong, only half-complete work, Fort Erie, in British hands; at the Ontario outlet of the river were similarly paired fortifications, Niagara on the American side, George on the Canadian, both excellently planned, well provided with guns,and both in British hands. This gave the British three corners of a quadrangle, split down the center by a river, which was passable only at the fortified points. Their commander, General Riall, had something over 4,000 men, all regulars and veterans. His mobile force, however, numbered not more than 2,800 men; the others were parceled out in garrison.

Brown's men, though nominally regulars, were actually the greenest of recruits, with no drill but what Scott had given them during the three spring months. This force comprised three brigades:

SCOTT'S

Organization	Commander	Recruited in	Number
9th Inf	Maj. Leavenworth	Massachusetts	642
11th Inf	Maj. McNeil	Vermont	577
22nd Inf	Maj. Brady	Pennsylvania	287
25th Inf	Maj. Jesup	Connecticut	619
Staff			4
			2,129

RIPLEY'S

Organization	Commander	Recruited in	Number
21st Inf	Maj. Miller	Massachusetts	917
23rd Inf	Maj. McFarland	New York	496
Staff			2
			1,415
Artillery	Maj. Hindman		327

PORTER'S

Pennsylvania Militia		600
		4,471

The size of the 21st Regiment is accounted for by the fact that it included some detachments from the 19th. The total number of effectives was certainly not over 3,500 and probably much less, when the campaign began in July.

The war in Europe was drawing to a close and heavy reinforcements were already on the sea for Riall; his plan was simply to wait until he got them and then crush the Americans. On our side Chauncey's new warship was nearly completed. It would give him command of the water and he had promised Brown a naval blockade and bombardment of Fort George for the early part of the month if the army were at hand to co-operate. Brown therefore planned a quick stroke at Fort Erie, a sweep down the Canadian side of the river, and a siege of Fort George to chime with the arrival of the fleet. Fort Niagara would fall of its own weight once its companion piece was gone.

The move began on the first day of the month, Scott landing below Fort Erie, while Ripley crossed above. The two pinched out the area between them, taking 170 prisoners, and sustaining no casualties. Riall, who had not thought the Americans so bold, was taken by surprise. He gathered what troops he had, not over 1,500 men, and came forward to hold the line of the Chippewa River, which flows into the Niagara some sixteen miles below Fort Erie.

Brown threw forward Porter's militia and a handful of Indian allies as scouts, with the design of feeling along the Chippewa for a spot where a crossing might be forced. They encountered Riall's skirmishers, Indians and Canadian militia in about the same number, and there was a little desultory firing. Scott was back at a smaller stream, Street's Creek, holding a parade. He had with him the three small guns of Towson's battery. Ripley was in camp behind Scott, and Brown up on reconnaissance. The date was July 4.

Riall's experience of this war had been that Americans always ran when attacked by British regulars. He ployed his 1,500 into column, whipped them across the Chippewa hard by its mouth, and punched through the scattered scouts of Porter's brigade with a cloud of militia and Indians round his front. Porter's men went back in disorder. Brown, galloping past Scott to bring up Ripley, shouted, "You are going to have a battle!"

Scott remarked that he did not think there were three hundred British within miles, but scarcely had he got his men across Street's Creek and into a crescent formation when

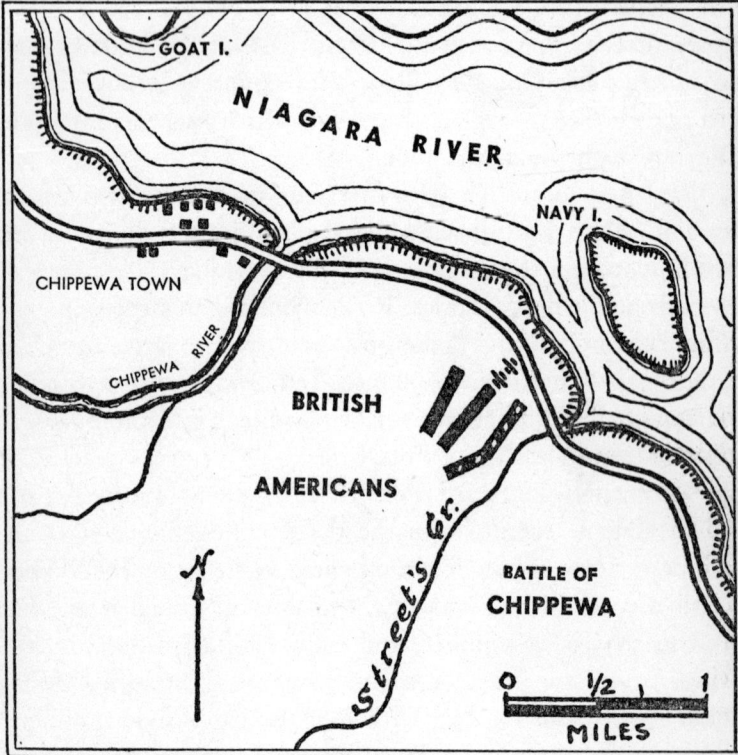

GOAT I.

NIAGARA RIVER

NAVY I.

CHIPPEWA TOWN

CHIPPEWA RIVER

BRITISH

AMERICANS

N

Street's cr.

BATTLE OF
CHIPPEWA

0   1/2   1
MILES

Riall topped the last rise and came down toward him with two 24-pounders and a big howitzer banging away. The Englishman got the surprise of his life. Not only did these Americans fail to run, they received him with volleys hotter than he gave. His column hesitated, came to a halt, and hung fixed in the semicircle of fire. Towson's little battery dueled fiercely with the British guns, mastered them, blew up an ammunition wagon in the English rear, and turned on their column of assault just as Scott, catching a hint of wavering in the line opposed to him, rode out in front with his sword swinging for a countercharge.

Brown came rushing across the creek with Ripley's men to put them on the American left for a sweep, but before they reached position it was all over; Riall had lost 515 men, a third of his force, and was behind the Chippewa trying to rally what he had left. The American casualties, including Porter's, were only 297.

Brown followed his opponent in crisply, touched the shore of Lake Ontario, and there received the dismaying news that Chauncey's new two-decker was not ready and would not be before September. The navy could give him no help of any kind. Meanwhile the British had been heavily reinforced by a corps of Peninsular veterans under Major General Gordon Drummond, an officer who had made a considerable reputation in Spain.

The precise extent of the British additions and their plan of campaign was unknown to Brown. He fell back to the Chippewa River, Scott's brigade holding there for observation with the rest behind. On July 25 Drummond and Riall were ready; the latter came forward and established himself in a strong position along Lundy's Lane, at right angles to the flow of the Niagara, with 1,200 men and six pieces of artillery. Three miles behind him was Drummond in person with the reserve of his forces, another 1,200 men and two guns. Up near Fort George were another 1,700 men under a British colonel, Scott, all ready to cross to Fort Niagara. Their plan was simple and should have been effective; Riall to hold hard in his prepared position, Scott to cross and turn the Americans out of their position at Buffalo or trap them in Fort Erie,

Drummond to throw his reserve in with whichever force met the more opposition.

Winfield Scott and his brigade were 1,400 strong, with those same three little guns of Towson's; Ripley was behind near Fort Erie with 1,200 men, and Porter near the same spot with about 600 militia, maybe less. The American position was truly desperate: they had not enough men and artillery to put up a defense and there were no good defensive positions; heavily outnumbered at every point, they had no place to which they could retire nearer than Albany.

The best device Brown could think of was to keep the British so occupied that they could not finish their turning maneuver. As soon as he had plumbed the situation he ordered Scott to hit Riall with all his strength. At the same time he ordered Ripley's brigade forward and followed with Porter. He was staking everything on one blow.

Scott formed the 9th on his left wing, with Towson's three guns next, facing Riall's battery; then the 11th, the 22nd, and the 25th, the latter's right against the river. The setting sun threw long shadows across the field as they took their positions in the hollow below Lundy's Lane. There was a brief cannonade; Riall, a trifle disturbed by the unshaken bearing of those regiments he had so good cause to remember, had just ordered a retreat when Drummond in person arrived with his division, giving the British a two-to-one superiority in numbers.

Scott came right on. In the center the fighting was fierce, but the three regiments could accomplish nothing against slope, numbers, and cannon; but on the right Scott himself burst through the British line at the head of Jesup's men, hurled back their flank, wounded Riall and captured him, and completely broke up one of the British regiments before artillery from the flank and Drummond's heavier weight drove him out again.

Towson's guns had now been silenced, but Scott ordered another charge and then another; three charges we count on the right and center before nine o'clock. Scott himself took a wound that finished him for the rest of the war; Majors McNeil and Brady were down; the 9th, 11th, and 22nd had lost nearly all their officers and organization, but Major

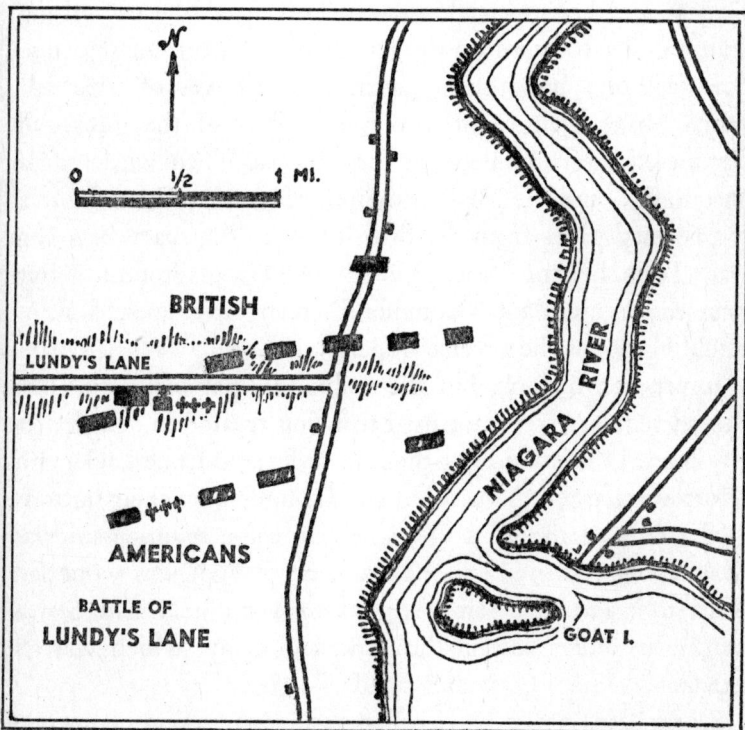

BATTLE OF
LUNDY'S LANE

Leavenworth formed what was left of them into one single mass and was planning a last-ditch defense in the hollow against the now advancing British when Brown came up on the run with Ripley and Porter. He seized the situation at a glance; nothing would go right until he got rid of that British battery which was tearing his center to pieces. Meanwhile

Drummond had called the British Colonel Scott and there were now over 3,000 men along Lundy's Lane, less than 2,000 below it.

"Can you take those guns?" Brown asked Major Miller.

"I'll try, sir," in the words that have become a regimental motto, and went up the hill into the dark with the 21st. Brown gave him all the help possible, himself leading the 23rd as an advance echelon on Miller's right, Porter and the militia going forward on the left in loose skirmishing formation around a big stone church. Under cover of their advance Miller went right into the muzzles of the guns and bayoneted the cannoneers at their pieces. Then with militia on one side, and the 23rd on the other, he formed a new line, not twenty paces from the British while "the space between was all one sheet of flame." The raw Americans stood it better than the Peninsulars; Drummond's men gave up and went tumbling down the reverse slope.

It was ten o'clock, but the stubborn fight went on. The British regulars were not used to being treated in so cavalier a fashion. Drummond got them in order and came back with a furious charge—"You could see the figures on their buttons in the light of the guns"—was beaten, came again, again was beaten, but returned still a third time. Brown was wounded now, too, and in a faint; so was Leavenworth. There was hardly an officer left in the American army, which was all one mixed line, militia and regulars together.

As the last English wave rolled back, Drummond's confused ranks began firing into one another and collapsed. The battle was won and the whole British army was taken had there been a regiment of cavalry or the tiniest reserve. But there was not, and Ripley, left in command, counted his own desperate state and ordered a retreat to Fort Erie.

The wagoners sent back for the captured British cannon found that a British wagon corps had had the same idea, and earlier; and when Brown recovered consciousness and heard of it he called Ripley a coward and sent for General Gaines to take command till he should be on his feet again.

The charge was not just, as Ripley had proved before and would again, but this was a tiny wrangle; the important thing was that Drummond's hopeful movement was stopped as though he had been poleaxed. He had lost 878 men in the battle (Brown lost 853) and, insisting to his dying day that he had fought not less than 5,000 Americans, won commendation from the Cabinet for his "gallant stand against superior forces." "I never saw such determined charges," said the man who had faced Junot and Murat.

He was immediately and heavily reinforced; strategically his turning maneuver was as good as ever, but Lundy's Lane had embedded itself in his mind. He did not dare try anything until he had got rid of the little American force. Therefore he came down to lay siege to Fort Erie, where Gaines could muster but 2,125 men, including some militia that came up. On August 15 the English tried a midnight surprise; it ended in a frightful disaster (Ripley seems to have predicted it to the day and almost the minute), with 900 British casualties against only 84 American. A boat-landing off Buffalo ran into a company of squirrel-killing Kentucky riflemen who emptied two of the boats so rapidly that the rest pulled away in a hurry.

At the beginning of September the swing was toward the American side, the more so since Brown was recovered. He held a council of war, wishful to attack the British lines. The regular officers, particularly Ripley, objected that the lines were well planned, adequately supplied with artillery, and defended by some of the best troops in the British army, including the Scots Highlanders. Assault was madness. Brown began to fidget, finally snapped that the council was closed and sent off for some more militia. He got about 1,000, which gave him a total of 3,000 against Drummond's 4,500. This seemed to the fighting Quaker about the proper proportions for battle.

Colonel Wood, of the engineers, under cover of the racket made by the siege artillery, cut a path through the brush to a point within 150 yards of the battery on the extreme British right. On the morning of September 17 Brown took this path with his militia and the little remnant of the 23rd, which was to serve as stiffening and example for the rest. Major Miller had orders to throw a column at the British center as soon as the militia began to shoot.

The attack went off like clockwork. The Scots stood their ground, but the untrained, rowdy militia—the same men who failed every other general of the war—followed Brown in on them and, in a wave of fury, took losses that would have staggered most regulars (over a third!), killed the Scots where they stood, captured the battery, and spiked its guns. Miller's column punched through the second battery and spiked that too; there was a little fighting around the third, but Brown pulled out before getting too deeply involved.

That finished Major General Gordon Drummond. He was a good officer and a bold man, but the sortie had cost him 700 more casualties, bringing his battle losses to more than 3,000 for the campaign. And there seemed no limit to his opponent's stomach for combat, nor to his ability to inflict further damage. Then, too, the British artillery was spoiled or spiked. Nor had Brown neglected to burn their barracks during the sortie and the autumn rains had set in; his own men were housed in comfortable huts. Finally, it is probable that Drummond knew Brown was being reinforced at no distant date, for it was difficult to keep any big news quiet along the border. By sum total the British position had become untenable; a week after Brown's sortie Drummond beat a retreat to his fortress.

The following week General Izard came tramping into Buffalo with 7,000 regulars, including a strong brigade of that cavalry for the lack of which on the night of Lundy's Lane Brown had wept. It is a matter of speculation as to what might have happened after another spring, of course, but in view of what Brown accomplished with inferior forces, no cavalry, and little artillery, the likelihood is that with superiority in all three arms he would have made things extremely warm for his opponents.

He was prevented by the end of the war, which also ended active service for him, though he remained in the army, becoming its head in 1821. In 1828, still chief, he died of the aftereffects of his Lundy's Lane wound, leaving behind a record of service second to none, but a reputation shadowed by that of the more colorful and politically minded Andrew Jackson. Yet it is not mere wonder-hunting to say that Brown did more than Jackson; for New Orleans was fought after the war was over, while Sackett's Harbor and Lundy's Lane were won at its height. The loss of either might have entailed the loss of the whole Northwest, and certainly would have afforded a solid basis for claim to a foothold south of the lakes that the British put forward with such persistence at the conference at Ghent.

When it comes to analyzing the reasons for Brown's achievement, as startling as it was brilliant, one is a little at a loss. It is the easy and the common habit among military writers to attribute everything to Scott and to set Brown down as a sterling fighter with but a single military idea— that of getting in contact with the enemy and hitting him as hard as possible. But this picture will not quite do; Brown won at Sackett's Harbor before he had Scott, and in the Fort Erie sortie after Scott was gone.

Chippewa was largely Scott's victory; the discipline he put into the raw recruits did much to win Lundy's Lane; but it is surely taking nothing from the credit due him and his men to say that they behaved on both fields as they never did before and never did again. And nobody but Brown ever thought of leading militia in a charge against veteran Scots, or would have got away with it had he done so.

There was, in short, some ineluctable secret of leadership, something in Brown's presence and manner, that made green country boys fight like the devil, and it would be worth a good deal to know that secret. But it would be silly to account for Brown's success on this basis alone. Scott complained of the general's ignorance of tactics, yet Brown's major tactics were, on the whole, better than Scott's. At Chippewa Scott's plan of a crescent resting on the river with the right wing supported by artillery was good; yet Brown had a better one—to hold hard in the center, bring Ripley in on the left and knock Riall's whole column into the Niagara. At Lundy's Lane Scott conceived the classical plan of breaking down a flank, the flank where the enemy thought himself the strongest; but it was Brown who saw that the big British battery in the center would queer any flanking sweep while it stood, and that its fall would entail the wreck of the whole line—he saw it in an instant, in the darkness of the night, in the midst of the battle. Again, at Sackett's Harbor it would have been easier and more normal for Brown to bring his rallied militia in on the line where the regulars were holding—but no, he had to lead those troops, already once broken, in a cold-metal charge against Prevost's sensitive wing. The essence of Brown's concept may be expressed by saying that while Scott played, and played well, to beat the enemy, Brown meant nothing less than his destruction at every stroke.

This suggests, then, that major tactics is something innate and not to be learned; all these ideas came out of Brown's own head, without benefit of military education. One would expect the same native genius to make him a good strategist also; but oddly enough this turns out to be his weak point.

Then there is another suggestion in Brown's career, perhaps even more important. The fact that the general's political influence in his home district was an influence of affection makes it clear that he treated the tenants of his estate much as he later treated the soldiers who fought so well for him—that is, with an attention to their physical well-being even rarer then than it is now. It was not only Scott's drill that made the men of Lundy's Lane follow their Quaker up the hill; it was those comfortable huts and the fight the general had made to provide good food and good clothes.

Yet neither these nor any other details can be tortured into a Jacob Brown formula. His secret was the secret of all great leaders, and what man can discover that?

RICHARD M. JOHNSON
Rumpsey-Dumpsey

I

"NO CAVALRY," WRITES BRACKETT, THE HISTORIAN OF the U.S. mounted arm, "was ever better than that which belonged to Wayne's army in 1794, and, I fear, no cavalry was ever much poorer than that which belonged to us in 1813–1814."

The latter half of the remark is certainly true as it applies to the hastily raised and ill-trained squadrons of "regulars," and it is even an understatement of the military qualities of the militia dragoons, who at Bladensburg acquired the well-deserved reputation of being the fastest-running cavalry in the world. But in overlooking one remarkable regiment formed and led by a remarkable man, Brackett runs too lightly past one of the key military inventions of American history.

He is not alone in this neglect. Our forces by land were so far from covering themselves with glory in the War of 1812 that military historians have tended to use the whole episode as a basis for general criticisms of the Brackett type rather than looking into it to see what is really there. Actually it was in that conflict that the techniques were learned which later proved decisive in the winning of the West, and which have left indelible marks on the profession of arms in America.

No doubt the West would have been won in any case by mere population pressure. This does not alter the fact that the method employed was fundamentally military conquest, in a form which allowed the settlers to achieve nearly maximum efficiency in both the military and civil branches of their calling, and which had something to do with the political pattern that developed throughout the upper Mississippi basin. Gaul was conquered for Rome by a race of foot soldiers, who worked out of fixed posts under tight military discipline, even when they doubled as settlers, and whose success destroyed the republic that sent them forth. The American West was gained by men who could assemble so rapidly on horseback that military authoritarianism was unnecessary to the success of their enterprise.

It is possible to be deterministic about this point also. But the fact remains that the recipe for fighting an Indian war—the one that was continued practically unaltered to the end—was discovered and applied by a man whose distinguishing ideological possession was a liberal individualism, and who made this cast of mind a part of his military technique. Moreover, the application of his method resulted in the most spectacular success achieved against Indians after the turn of the eighteenth century, and it was achieved against the most formidable opposition the tribes had succeeded in producing. However historians might neglect the matter later, the men on the spot knew that something had been discovered.

The man who discovered it was Richard M. Johnson—Colonel Richard M. Johnson, one of that first energetic generation born outside English citizenship and west of the Alleghanies. His father (also called "Colonel," of course, since he was in Kentucky) had followed Daniel Boone across the mountains while the Revolution was still being fought—one of those pioneers in the grand manner, a self-made man who was a good workman and turned himself into a local magnifico.

His children "were taught to endure hardship and privation as a guide to self-discipline," says a note. There was also a good deal of early American whoopee around the house, and it is somewhat surprising to learn that young Richard took up the study of Latin under his own power at the age of twelve. At fifteen, in 1796, he had the language by heart and left home for Transylvania University, the only one west of the mountains. There were two courses, law and medicine; he took the former. By twenty-one he was an attorney with a flourishing practice, chiefly concerned with land titles, for ownerships in early Kentucky were hopelessly intricate and, as in most pioneer communities, litigation and politics were the only winter amusements available.

Court cases were largely decided on flowery Ciceronian eloquence in that jurisdiction, and Johnson's classical education gave him an advantage possessed by few. He was a success; received the normal reward of being elected to the state legislature; then, in 1806, while still short of his twenty-fifth birthday, to Congress. He went as a member of the Jeffersonian Republican party, naturally; there were no Federalists beyond the mountains.

Campaign biographies of Johnson were written later, but they are in the highfaluting tone normal to that species of literature, and it is only when he reaches Washington that we begin to learn what manner of man he was. He was a liberal —not in the quasi-political sense in which that term is used today, but in the full dictionary meaning, a man who believed that every issue should be decided on the basis of ethics and abstract justice, without reference to party policy. One of the very first items before Congress when he took his seat was the matter of Alexander Hamilton's widow, who had been left practically penniless, though the estate had a considerable claim against the government. Party policy was against allowing the claim, but the junior representative from

Kentucky led the fight for it and cried "Shame" so effectively that he pushed it through.

Like most of the western and southern members, he also went beyond the party line with relation to English aggressions. The men of the old Northwest came from a country where if somebody hit you, you hit him back, and damn the consequences. They knew the English were hitting at them, and they were not in the least interested in the profits being made by New England merchants willing to submit to Orders in Council and impressments that took no men out of shipowners' offices.

Specifically, the British were stirring up a major Indian war which was designed to keep the young republic too busy along its frontier to worry about anything that happened on the Atlantic. It is a little hard to realize today how serious that threat looked—and was. The endemic defect of the Indians as a military power was their inability to combine or to continue. Their tactics were nicely adapted to the country in which they operated, but they were essentially the tactics of the squad; and once the Iroquois were out of the way, no group of Indians could hold together long enough to conduct a campaign. Their leadership was subject to repeated palace revolutions, and they lacked leaders capable of thinking in large terms—at least down to the first decade of the nineteenth century.

At this point the race threw up two of the greatest men it ever produced, in Tecumseh and his twin brother, Tenskwatawa, "the Shawnee Prophet." The latter was a mystic and religious leader, the exact nature of whose doctrine is still so uncertain that an examination of it would be worth while as an item in the comparative history of religion. What we do know about it is that there was a considerable resemblance to the religious militancy that Mohammed had preached to a disunited people under circumstances not altogether dissimilar. Like Mohammedanism, the revelation of the Prophet proved extraordinarily attractive to the congregation.

Tecumseh was the Khalid ibn Walid of the movement, a leader of enormous ability, both as a military captain and as an organizer of the enthusiasms set free by his brother's heady preachings. The two persuaded Indians all the way from the Great Lakes to the Gulf to depose the old tribal leaders and join the central authority that radiated from the "City of God," near the headwaters of the Wabash. A central location of the Indian capital would probably have secured better communications and a more cohesive organization among the tribes, for most of Kentucky was held against them, but Tecumseh seems to have felt the necessity of keeping his headquarters near the base of military supplies, the British holdings in Canada.

II

In the Eleventh Congress the balance of power passed into the hands of the young men of Johnson's own generation— Henry Clay, John C. Calhoun, Peter B. Porter, and Langdon Cheeves, "the War Hawks," as they were immediately called. By the Twelfth Congress they had gained a clear majority as pressures piled up on the ocean and in the West. Within two weeks of the new session they passed a resolution calling on the executive for "more active measures," a bill tripling the army, and then a declaration of war.

The last was a formality; the war had already begun, as Johnson reminded someone on the opposite side of the house. Even for Tecumseh, it had proved too much of a task to restrain the religion-and-sword enthusiasm of the young warriors till he could co-ordinate his movement into a simultaneous rising all along the line. There was a series of raids into the Indiana settlements, and William Henry Harrison, governor of the territory, counterattacked in force, broke the back of the Indian empire, and killed its Prophet in the prelude to valor at Tippecanoe.

The death of the Prophet removed the mainspring of the long-range danger, but as soon as the weight of England was thrown openly into the struggle the military situation in the Northwest became precarious. British forces pinned down the only available American mass of maneuver, and Tecumseh immediately demonstrated his mastery of the strategic use of irregular troops by simultaneous attacks on Fort Dearborn, Illinois (which was taken and its garrison wiped out), Fort Wayne, Indiana, Fort Defiance, Ohio, and posts far down into Alabama.

It was at this juncture that, under some vague permissive authority from the President, there appeared a card in the Kentucky papers:

"Richard M. Johnson, Esquire, will accept of the companies which first tender their service to the number required; and will attend at Georgetown until next Monday Evening for that purpose. It is expected that each man will furnish himself with 20 days' provisions, ammunition and arms (musquets)."

This was raising an army in the old gentlemanly tradition that had come down through the Revolution from the English shires; the difference lay in what Johnson did with his companies. More men came out than he could use, and all those he chose were individuals who had brought horses as well as musquets; an act which could possibly be considered as an obeisance to that other part of the gentlemanly tradition which holds that a man who goes to war mounted is socially superior. It happens that Johnson himself did not think of it this way. He was too much of a liberal in the first place, and in the second, he placed on record his reasons for the make-up of his regiment.

He expected to be fighting in forested country, mainly against enemies who did not know how to form the tight

Campaign in the Northwest

Frederician line or to fire by volleys, and who became panicky when they had no easy line of retreat. Under these circumstances what was needed was "a force that could penetrate the ranks and throw into confusion" whatever it encountered. Johnson believed that his rapidly moving riflemen, firing from the saddle, could accomplish this even against regular troops among the woods. There was also the not inconsiderable point that, since they were mounted riflemen, they would always be working in loose formation, pretty much out of tactical control in battle; and in their other function, as scouts and flankers, would operate as individuals. That is, these men already possessed the skills necessary for employment on Johnson's lines; special training and close discipline were unnecessary.

A month after organizing, Johnson reported with between 300 and 500 men (the records are very inaccurate) to Harrison, who had taken command in the Northwest by virtue of the authority implied in his governorship and a militia commission from the state of Kentucky. There was no one else who could command; all the regular forces north of the Ohio had been surrendered to the British at Detroit. The American line of defense now followed the Wabash and Maumee Rivers, with a fairly strong post at Fort Harrison on the former stream and another at Sandusky on Lake Erie. The wide gap between these terminals was covered by the little stockade at Fort Defiance and the somewhat more considerable work at Fort Wayne. Harrison had concentrated behind the center of this line at St. Mary's, Ohio, with nearly 5,000 men under his command, Kentucky militia for the most part. They were the stuff of which good soldiers can be made, but the process had not even been begun, and the men were so lacking in training that Harrison's range of operations was limited.

It was still more limited in the geographical field by logistics. The little army was desperately short of supplies and had almost no transport; the season was that of the autumn rains, which is to say that forward movement was virtually impossible. Yet forward movement of some kind was necessary, for Tecumseh had assembled a considerable Indian army and was holding Fort Wayne under close blockade. If the place were taken, the line of the two rivers would be broken, as the defense line of the Southern Confederacy was later broken at Fort Donelson; all Indiana and most of Ohio would follow the rest of the Northwest Territory into the hands of the English-Indian alliance.

"Old Tippecanoe" was not exactly the most brilliant general the U.S. forces had, but he did possess the ability to take straightforward action. He dispatched Johnson and his completely amateur soldiers to the relief of Fort Wayne as soon as they arrived, the mounted riflemen carrying their ammunition and whatever dry provisions they needed on their horses' backs. The result completely justified Johnson's method. Whatever logistic superiority the Indians had over infantry, they had none at all over these riders, who experienced no difficulty in finding food during their three-hundred-mile march.

Tecumseh had enough warning of their coming to throw out war parties which tried three seperate attacks on the camp of the force, and near Fort Wayne itself the favorite device of a big ambush was attempted. The camp attacks were beaten off with ease; the ambush counterambushed and the Indians driven in sharply under considerable loss. Tecumseh was wise enough not to risk another defeat that might have ruined the always delicate morale of his men. He raised the siege, Fort Wayne was saved, and Johnson went back to Congress for the winter to find himself something like a national hero.

III

For his had been the only positive and successful action on land in the war. All the rest was defeats, including the big black one at the River Raisin, when a whole brigade was wiped out, the capitulation of Detroit, and the disgraceful campaign on the Niagara frontier. The mounted riflemen dispersed to their homes that winter, having enlisted for the campaign only, in the jolly fashion of those days. But Johnson was now a personage and during his experience with them he had done some thinking on the strategic problems of Indian war. He distilled the result into a long resolution, laid before Congress during the winter; it comes fairly close to being a manual for conquest in all the region east of the Rockies.

Johnson points out that the difficulties of fighting Indians spring from their fluidity. They disperse before any force strong enough to crush them and reassemble on its line of communications. The problem is one of forcing them to concentrate before striking.

Indian fluidity has one drawback which offers a point of attack. In winter they are forced to concentrate to live from stored supplies, and at such times they can be dealt with by troops sufficiently independent of their own trains to be capable of long marches through snow—that is, mounted riflemen. These men, as Johnson had demonstrated, could be taken directly from the civil life of the frontier into action without training. He proposed that before the spring of 1813 broke, a powerful army consisting of mounted men exclusively should be sent into the Indian country to attack the villages and force the braves to fight pitched battles in the snow or starve.

The plan went to Secretary of War Armstrong, who was by no means as much of a fool as many people thought him, then and later. Armstrong passed it along to General Harrison with approval, but Harrison, after the manner of military conservatives of all places and ages, reported it was "impractical" without giving any reason other than that he, as commander, thought it impractical. The matter rested, and is of importance only in showing that Johnson was approaching his problem in a fine, free-thinking spirit of amateurism, conceiving the mounted arm not so much as an accompaniment to infantry, but as an independently operating body, able to care for itself against any opposition it was likely to encounter.

Harrison did assent to, and even asked for, another and larger regiment of mounted riflemen. Early in the year the young Congressman-Colonel went home to raise it. It was the first of May before he was ready to take the field again, this time 1,000 strong. The delay was partly due to the fact that Johnson's command was only a wing of a large group of Kentucky militia, 3,500 all told, which was going up to reinforce Harrison under the personal leadership of Governor Shelby.

But this was not the real determining factor, since Johnson was intended to operate as the head of the semi-independent striking force, and in the actual event he went on without waiting for Shelby and the infantry. The real reason for the delay was that this amateur captain of cavalry was now far less of an amateur than he had been in the previous year, and was no longer willing to take men as they came and let them fight as they pleased. He introduced discipline among men who had never known anything like it; and, with a degree of care quite astounding in those casual days when even the regular army gave little attention to such matters, provided for the logistic services by hiring gunsmiths, blacksmiths, and doctors, out of his own pocket.

"Every captain [of thirty] is charged to have the arms put in prime condition" was one of his first general orders. He held personal flash inspections and actually broke a couple of junior officers who had violated the first rule of Indian warfare by not requiring their men to have every weapon ready for instant action. Most important of all, he trained his men in a common tactical doctrine, apparently of his own invention, an extension of the normal Kentucky frontier method of war into operations of larger and organized units. The central feature was that any group making contact dismounted at once, took cover, and constituted itself a holding force which engaged the enemy in a fire fight; while any unit not in contact remained in the saddle and kept moving toward the sound of the guns, dismounting when contact was attained.

When the Kentucky mounted rifles joined Harrison in May, the situation as seen from the American side of the line appeared more desperate than in the previous year. There had been new posts built along the two rivers, but the main infantry command was down to 1,000 men, and with these Harrison had just undergone a siege in Fort Meigs on the Maumee, between Fort Defiance and the lake base at Sandusky. Tecumseh's Indians were raiding all through the line, deep into Ohio.

Actually a major change had taken place in the British-Indian operation. The able General Isaac Brock, who had given Tecumseh the fullest co-operation, was gone—killed in a battle on the Niagara frontier—and the command had fallen into the hands of General Henry Proctor, of whom the Indian leader expressed his opinion by telling him, "Go home and put on petticoats." The accusation was one of stupidity as well as cowardice. Having failed in his siege of Fort Meigs, Proctor withdrew the British troops to Malden on the Canadian shore and let the Indians alone try a stand-up assault on Fort Stephenson, near Sandusky, in which they were, of course, heavily defeated.

Nevertheless, there was a reason for Proctor's retreat—the old question of supply, which could move effectively only by water on a lake whose naval control was still under contest. He may also have considered the Indians quite adequate to the task of clearing out the American posts, which were so weak that Forts Wayne and Harrison held but 70 and 50 men respectively. Harrison certainly took the view they were unsafe; when Johnson arrived with his thousand, the order was that they should go into garrison at once.

There was a headquarters argument, one of those arguments that decide the course of wars, with Johnson spouting in his best Ciceronian style to the effect that garrison duty would break the spirit of his restless, uncontrollable Kentuckians. He carried his point, the order was changed, the riflemen went out on a long patrol toward Fort Wayne; and the day that patrol began the northwestern war was won.

For the mounted rifles had been experienced woodsmen to begin with and they were by now thoroughly trained in a system of war to which unsupported Indians, even under a man of genius, could find no valid reply. The marches made on the series of sweeps that began with the journey to Fort Wayne are astounding by any standard. By 9 July the Kentuckians had covered 730 miles in 40 days, and in one stretch they made 63 miles through forest country in thirteen hours against some opposition, without losing a man or a mount. The itinerary took them all round the defensive crescent, on a long raid up to Lake Michigan, and another to the Lake Huron country, where they surprised the British post at the scene of the earlier American defeat on the River Raisin. During this series of patrols they ruined the Indian villages and in effect destroyed Tecumseh's base, both physically and morally.

The procedure was not merely one of answering raids

by counterraids. Johnson's patrols produced numerous fighting contacts, of a character so minor that no one ever thought of giving them names or calling them battles, though their aggregate was of considerable importance. The sequence of these little combats was always the same. On contact the riflemen dismounted and engaged the Indians in one of those bushwhacking frontier fights with a great deal of yelling and banging and not many people getting hurt. In the middle of this the redmen would wake up to the fact that they were being surrounded by mounted men. Among trained troops it is an act of special constancy to fight facing in two directions; with barbarians it simply does not happen. Result: panic, Johnson's men shooting down a few more Indians as they scattered, and the patrol moving on.

By mid-July the offensive had passed definitely into American hands and Tecumseh's war parties were running away at the approach of a handful of these troopers. Johnson gave them a brief period of rest, and in mid-September was dispatched on a two-hundred-mile march to Kaskaskia, during which he took an encampment which proved to be the main distributing headquarters for British arms and money. He was still on this patrol when, on September 16, the news of Perry's great naval victory ran in.

Proctor at Malden was now subject to being cut off by a landing in his rear, and though Tecumseh wished to defend the place, there is no doubt that the British commander's decision to retreat eastward was correct. Harrison did land at Malden on 27 September, with 2,500 infantry, taking up the pursuit at once. For a time it seemed as though the British might get away; Tecumseh covered their retreat so skillfully that the Americans could not gain a mile. But two days later Johnson fell in on the main body, coming through Detroit, and as usual, they could do nothing with the mounted rifles. Johnson began to pick up British stragglers, captured some of their trains on October 3, and moved so threateningly toward the flanks of the retreating column that Proctor came to a stand at the River Thames.

The position he chose was across the neck of a narrowing funnel of land between the river and an impassable cypress swamp, the latter covering his right. At the center a smaller swamp divided the position; leftward of it the British regulars were drawn up in three lines, covering the highroad down which they had been retreating. Tecumseh and his Indians were placed to the right of this small swamp, with a British regiment in support; a very considerable number of Indians were thrown forward as skirmishers along the edge of the big swamp.

Johnson, young and ardent, asked Harrison's permission to attack without waiting for the infantry; received it, and flung rather more than half his force against the regulars, the rest, with himself leading them, onto Tecumseh. On the American right the ground was too much cut up by trees for infantry to stop horsemen by volley fire; the Kentuckians carried everything right away, breaking through all three lines, killing or capturing all but 200 men, who escaped with Proctor himself.

On the other wing Indian leadership and the Indian tactical arrangement of a defense in depth proved better than British, and almost too good for the mounted rifles. They suffered from the flanking fire of the skirmishers at the edge of the big swamp and could not ride home against the position beyond. Johnson himself was hit four times, all light wounds. He brought the attack to a halt, dismounted his men, sent for infantry, and pressed on. For twenty minutes there was a hot little fight, in the midst of which a tall brave with a chief's feathers fired a ball which smashed Johnson's left shoulder, and was balancing a tomahawk for a throw when the young cavalry leader pistoled him. As though this were a signal the infantry came streaming through the trees under Shelby himself, and the Indians broke.

IV

That break was the end of all serious wars in the old Northwest Territory. The Kentuckians always maintained that the tall chief shot by Johnson was Tecumseh himself, and cut razor strops from the skin of his legs as trophies. (They could be sufficiently grim on the frontier in those days.) Later, when Johnson was running for the Vice-Presidency on Van Buren's ticket, there was a doggerel tune about it:

> *Rumpsey-dumpsey, rumpsey-dumpsey,*
> *Colonel Johnson killed Tecumseh.*

Obviously, the opposing Whigs had to deny that the colonel had killed Tecumseh or any other chieftan, so there was a controversy. The point is hardly important today, save to note that somebody certainly killed Tecumseh in that battle.

What is important is that Richard M. Johnson had found the one best answer to a question which had vexed colonists since King Philip's War. Actually, he had discovered something more—the answer to a problem of warfare in general, not merely that of the frontier; but that answer was lost to sight and had to be rediscovered by other men in other circumstances.

This was partly due to the sequence of events, but still more to Johnson himself. He remained a citizen-soldier in that tradition which believed that a military man was a landowner who gave some of his time to the general defense in hours of national danger. As no national dangers came up during most of his career, he went off into politics and did nothing to press forward what was really a major military invention.

At the time of the Mexican War, when the subject might

have come up again, the Colonel was already in some dis-
repute—had been living publicly with a mulatto mistress, was
drinking a good deal and somewhat incoherent in his speech.
The result was that such analysis as took place concentrated
itself around Johnson's achievement as an Indian-fighter and
quite overlooked the fact that in the pursuit to the Thames
and the battle there, the mounted rifles had proved singularly effective against regular troops—just as Johnson said they
would. His school had to be refounded by men who received
his ideas in the form of tradition and through the route of the
Indian wars.

JOHN BUFORD

Man on Horseback

I

T IS IN THE LAST DEGREE IMPROBABLE THAT ANY OF THE
officers in Eylau cemetery, peering out into the snow
scurries of 1807, as glittering Murat thundered past at
the head of 14,000 horsemen, realized they were taking part
in the closing event in a series than began with the destruction of the last of the legions at Adrianople, more than fourteen centuries before. They were more concerned about the
cold and the Russian infantry; and they were not men given to
long-range speculation of any kind. They watched, then;
and saw for the last time cavalry armed with cold steel
wreck infantry defending itself with hot lead.

Not that there was any cessation on the part of the cavalrymen. They tried the thing again at Wagram, at Leipzig, and
notably at Waterloo, but some accident—the slope of the
ground, Scharnhorst's batteries, or the sunken road of Ohain
—seemed always to give the man on foot the advantage during the rest of the Napoleonic struggles. Local accident
seemed again to have intervened against the man on horseback on the battlefields of Latin America, the Crimea, and
North Italy, but these were local wars. It was only when the
commanders of the American Civil War failed to use their

big masses of cavalry as such squadrons had been used by Zieten and Murat that the case seemed to call for explanation; and the explanation found was that of a terrain unsuited for cavalry operation, and a people who did not understand it save for the brilliant exceptions of Forrest and Stuart.

It has taken three-quarters of another century to demonstrate that at least three officers on the Northern side understood the uses of cavalry very well; that the true brilliance rested with the men who beat both Stuart and Forrest; and that the Union cavalry technique in its final form was not a mismanaged form of the war that had gone, but a startling anticipation of the war to come. Not merely of the war to come in 1914; for the more attentively one studies the Civil War, the clearer it appears that the Union cavalry movements of 1864 are the perfect pattern for the infantry operations of future war—whether that infantry obtains its mobility with a set of tracks or a pair of wings.

In a sense this anticipation was an accident, but only in the very broad sense that after the surge of the French Empire rolled back from La Haye Sainte, chance should order the next major war to be visited on a nation whose only cavalry traditions had been derived from Indian skirmishes; and that it should be opposed by armies whose cavalry was drawn from a landed class that considered mounted action the only chivalric method of making war, the mounted charge the crown of every horseman's existence.

From the start of the war the Confederate cavalry was good in the traditional fashion; from the start it achieved a decisive superiority over the Union horse, which was composed of a few squadrons of regulars trained in the scatter tactics of the Indian wars, and a considerable number of plow horses. Cavalry contacts in 1861 and the early part of 1862 were so uniformly Confederate victories that when

General John Pope came east, "Who ever saw a dead cavalryman?" was already a catchword in the Army of the
Potomac.

II

All things considered, Pope was probably the weakest
general Lee faced, but there is one thing to be said in his
favor. He insisted that combat intelligence was the only
kind on which a commander should base his own operations,
and that cavalry alone had the mobility to get such information and bring it home while it was still warm. McClellan
had relied on spies; they filled his nights with dreadful bug-
bears about a Confederate army 250,000 strong. At the same
time, as the result of several distressing encounters between
his own troopers and Jeb Stuart's command, he had given
orders that his cavalry should not get out of sight of its supporting foot, which was about like putting it in rocking
chairs.

Pope did not regard the early work of Stoneman and
Pleasanton as exhilarating examples of cavalry technique,
and when he organized the Army of Virginia his first care
was to find a new chief for his mounted arm. The man was
one he had known during frontier days—John Buford, then
a mere brevet major in the Inspector General's department,
while men in West Point classes junior to his already had
their stars. A big, blond, slow-moving man with a curly
beard, who had been in the West since his graduation in '48,
had played quartermaster during a celebrated thousand-mile
march to Utah, and had more currently seen one or two of
those distressing encounters with the Rebel squadrons.

A man from the Inspector General's Department is in a
peculiarly good position to make observation in minor tactics.
Except for his subsequent actions we have no clue as to the
precise nature of Buford's observations (the only papers he

GLENDALE COLLEGE LIBRARY

left were reports distinguished for their brevity). But those actions speak with the tongues of men and of angels, and the thing they say is that John Buford found the existing minor tactical doctrine of the United States cavalry entirely wrong.

It is probable that he explained his views to Pope; he explained something to the general, who jumped his new chief of cavalry through the grades to brigadier and put him in charge of the horse of Banks' II Corps. In theory this made Buford only equal to the cavalry brigadiers of the other two corps, but he had five regiments, and those the largest, while Bayard of the III Corps was given four weak regiments and Beardsley of the I Corps was kept in army reserve with three regiments. Buford had 3,000 of the 5,000 horsemen with the army, and within ten days of his appointment was at the front, testing his ideas in battle.

It seems that he thought the horse had no more place on the battlefield than the elephant; rejected utterly that European idea of heavy cavalry delivering a violent shock which was so wholeheartedly adopted south of the Mason-Dixon Line. There were several press artists at the front, good observers. They have given us drawings of cavalry under other officers charging in three or four lines or by checkerboard companies, tightly knotted. On only two occasions are charges under Buford pictured; in both, his horsemen are riding forward in a loose, irregular line, for all the world like an assault wave of World War I infantry. More remarkable still, only one man in the line has his saber out in either drawing; all the rest grip pistols, and the captions show that these "charges" are pursuits of an enemy already on the reflux.

Nor did Buford (apparently) make any bones about admitting that the Union could never meet the Confederate cavalry on equal terms—as cavalry, in the saddle. His departmental experience assured him that the defect was mainly one promoted by nature, which had given the Southerners so much the better mounts. He accepted it and turned it into a virtue, and there is a striking passage in the records of August 13, 1862, which shows how he did it. Kilpatrick, with a force of Union cavalry, encountered some Rebel troopers on that date. His report tells how he routed the first detachment he met in a rousing surprise charge, held his own against a second, and was only driven from the field when a third fell on his flank. What lies behind this mass of Rebel riders he can only surmise from their number and presence in such a place.

On the same day Buford's brigade was in action. "A strong line of dismounted skirmishers was thrown out," he reports, "who soon drove away the enemy pickets," and goes on to tell how his men took cover, using the support of their artillery. Confederate cavalry swoops down on them and goes back again, with a good many saddles empty. Buford does not retire till two brigades of enemy infantry have come into action, have been identified, and are feeling for his wings, when he gets to horse and rides away, with insignificant loss.

The source of this new tactic is evidently the Indian Wars, in which the saber had already become vestigial during the early fifties, and where a massed cavalry charge only afforded a good target for Indians who lay on their bellies all over the landscape. The interesting thing—we can see it now—is that contemporaries were right in maintaining that Buford's was not a cavalry technique. It is precisely the method of a fast motorized column of infantry, with the difference that the transport runs on oats instead of gasoline.

III

The first clashes of the campaign took place at Cedar Mountain, where General Banks' corps was badly broken in an ill-advised attack on the nearly triply superior force of Stonewall Jackson, and at Madison Court House, out on the right flank toward the mountain corridors, where Buford fought Stuart. Bayard was covering Banks' front while Buford was away on his mission for Army HQ to the west; and Bayard failed to break through the Rebel screen. Both he

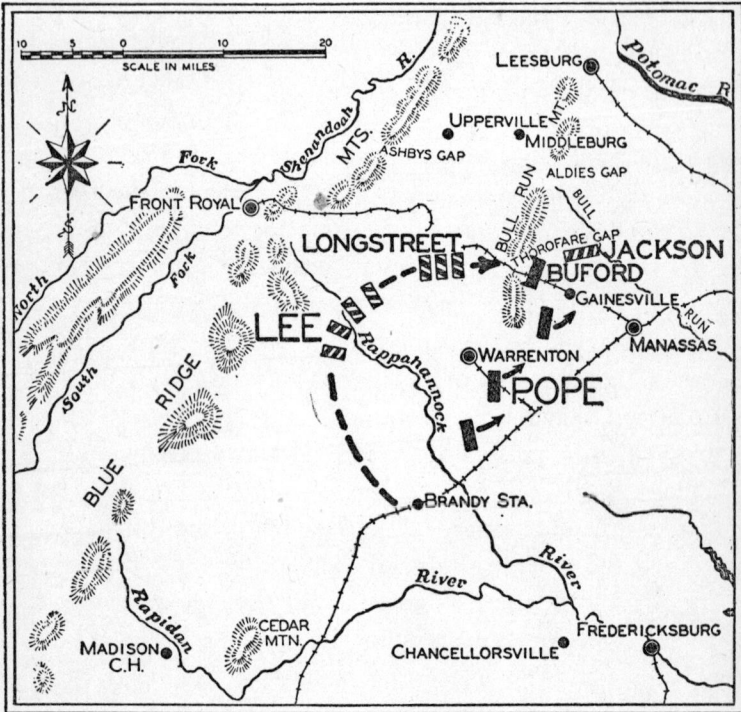

Second Manassas

and Banks wrongly estimated the enemy were in no great force, and Pope's orders being ambiguous, there was an attack and disaster.

Stuart attacked Buford from the saddle; Buford defended from the ground. He was heavily inferior in numbers, his men not quite used to the new tactic; but he managed to pull out with the command still in shape to march and fight, and what was more important, a good bag of prisoners, including Stuart's adjutant who had in his pocket a letter from Lee clearly outlining the ground plan of the campaign. The letter told Pope what to do and he did it—namely, retired to the angle where the north fork of the Rappahannock meets the Manassas Hills and prepared to hold the line till reinforcements reached him through Washington. Buford covered his right flank, in broken ground.

It was out of this arrangement that Lee drew his wonderful plan for Second Manassas, sending Stuart on a long raid around the Union left to draw their attention thither, then Jackson on an equally long circuit, behind the hills and through Thorofare Gap around the other flank onto Pope's rear. One critic has remarked that the execution of such a plan required a Stonewall Jackson. It required more than that; it required that the Union cavalry should be what it had always been—prone to energetic and futile charges against the first enemy element it encountered, or to equally strategic flight. But the Union cavalry on the sensitive flank was not what it had been; it was Buford with his "motorized column." He clung to Jackson's skirts like a burr; when he encountered the enemy, spread skirmishers, brought up his guns, and shot it out till the full Confederate strength was developed. Before Jackson had gone two days Buford knew his full strength and purpose; and history has had nothing to add to the reports in which they were described in every detail.

Pope correctly planned to turn and throw his full force on Jackson. The move failed through the fumblings of inefficient corps commanders and the fact that the General simply could not write a clear, definite order. Lee followed Jackson through Thorofare Gap. Now as Pope wheeled back to deal with Jackson, the Union right had become its left, and Buford on that flank was at Thorofare Gap when Longstreet came through it at the head of Lee's column.

The tragedy of the campaign was that the Union cavalry leader did everything right and the Union high command everything wrong. The Gap, though not a true pass, had fairly good ground for a defense. A whole day before Longstreet began climbing the slope Buford had correctly identified seventeen regiments of the Confederate infantry, Stuart's horse, and the Rebel reserve artillery, had reported their presence, and asked for support. Pope had only to put in one of the corps which were wandering muzzily about Gainsville; he would have the Confederate wings cut apart and could deal with both at his leisure.

What he actually did was altogether to lose sight of Buford in a fog of war, even withdrawing the single division of Ricketts' which was giving the cavalry brigade distant support. Longstreet rushed on; Buford dismounted his men and made a defense truly heroic, holding 27,000 men of the main Rebel army with his little 3,000 for six whole hours, till the Confederates were around both his flanks and partly in his rear, till they brought up their big guns—sending off appeal after appeal. Pope was beyond paying attention, Longstreet broke through, and Second Manassas followed as inevitably as four follows two plus two.

After the defeat the duty of covering fell on Buford's brigade; both Bayard's and Beardsley's commands were too worn out with mere riding to be of service. In action at Lewis Ford, Buford took a wound believed for a long time to be mortal, which effectively eliminated him from the campaigns of Antietam and Fredericksburg, though he held a nominal staff position during both.

It is noteworthy that after Second Manassas, Stuart reorganized the Confederate cavalry into sharpshooter and saber companies and increased the attached artillery. This was not "proper" cavalry technique either, but at least it furnished a partial reply to the intolerable nuisance of Buford's new method.

IV

Chancellorsville found Buford back in the saddle, now in command of one of the three divisions of the new Cavalry Corps; but bad weather, Hooker's impatience, and General Stoneman's case of piles spoiled whatever chances the horse had in that campaign. Brandy Station came next; Pleasanton commanded the corps there, an old-style cavalryman who preferred mounted action and the saber, but the new technique was spreading, and the battle turned into a wild melee of charges mounted and dismounted, skirmishers on horseback. Pleasanton accomplished nothing positive and his command was badly mauled; but Stuart was cut up too, and found it quite impossible to clear the Union horsemen from his path for an advance by Lee outside the Blue Ridge, so that the great invasion of Pennsylvania went wide, up the valley of the Shenandoah.

All along the mountain gaps there was fighting through that June—at Aldie's, Upperville, Middleburg, Ashby's. Buford did most of it in person, and Buford's new system all. "There were no regular line formations," says one who was there, "but the Indian mode of fighting was adopted on both sides, by taking advantage of every stone, fence, bush or hollow." The index of tactical victory swung to and fro; strategically the gain was all to the Union, for Stuart could get no certain news of Hooker's movements, and the very incidence of the fighting ticked off the steps in Lee's progress. By turning his horse into a flying wing of infantry, Buford had forced his opponent to do likewise, and the great invasion moved half blind.

Stuart fretted; Lee, under the impression the Union main force was south of the Potomac and could be held there, shot him off in a spectacular raid between Hooker and Washington, and marched on. But the day was passed when the Northern high command could be disordered by such empty menaces. Hooker, and Meade, who succeeded him about this time, simply fanned out Gregg and Kilpatrick with two small cavalry divisions on Stuart's trail, and kept right after Lee, with Buford hanging to him as he had hung to Jackson before Second Manassas. Stuart was not caught, but neither did Lee learn Meade's whereabouts till the last day of June, when his scouts brought in a German farmer with a Washington newspaper in his pocket, which told of the Army of the Potomac already in Pennsylvania and feeling toward the Confederate communications. The Rebels could get food from the country, but not bullets; they had to turn back.

Meade had expected Lee to come down on him, and was all ready, with a line of entrenchments along Pipe Creek, but his plan was an engineer's plan, physically perfect, but faulty in psychology. His troops were already north of the Pipe Creek line; retreating before battle is probably the world's best way of discouraging your men, and the Pipe Creek position imposed no compulsions on Lee, who had only to drop a containing force and throw the rest of his army toward Philadelphia in order to force a fight on his own terms.

But John Buford had been assigned to scout through Gettysburg on June 30, and, in the chain of causation that led through the next three days to the hour when Pickett's high tide ebbed, was to play the first and perhaps the greatest role. Late that afternoon he had ridden through the town, driving a Rebel detachment before him to the west. The road there runs across a chain of ridges; he took possession of two and flung his pickets far on the heels of the retreating Gray-

backs, both west and north, nearly ten miles beyond headquarters. Before his men bedded down they had been disposed as skirmishers, the horses had been sent to the rear and
the artillery posted for a regular infantry battle; couriers were
burning up the roads with dispatches to Pleasanton, Reynolds
of the I Corps, and Howard of the XI.

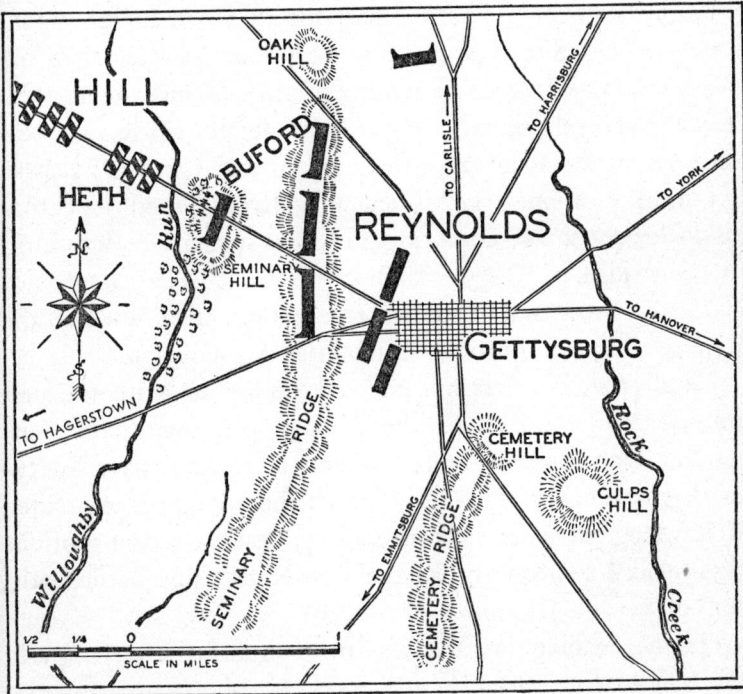

Buford at Gettysburg

The Confederates had been encountering some absurd local
militia, armed with nothing more lethal than shotguns. As
Heth with the first division of Hill's Confederate corps
came along the road from the west in the flat dawn light of
July 1, he thought the first elements of Buford's deep defense were more of the same, and did not bother to deploy or

report anything unusual. There was a little wood on the first ridge Buford held; as Heth's men came in sight three cannon shots came from it and then a storm of rifle fire that surprised and disconcerted the Confederate advance. The Rebels deployed and formed for an attack; and as they were forming Reynolds was rushing in with I Corps as fast as his men could march.

At half past nine Buford beat off that first attack. Heth waited for artillery. At ten Reynolds rode forward ahead of his men and climbed with Buford into a steeple, where the cavalry general pointed out the Confederates advancing west and north, and away from the huge mass of Cemetery Ridge, an ideal position. "Tell General Howard," said Reynolds as he came down, accepting Buford's suggestion, "to form on that ridge."

It was the crucial order of the battle, and now came the crucial moment. Buford's dismounted horsemen had just retreated from the first hill and were mingling with the first regiments of the I Corps; the black-capped men of the Wisconsin Iron Brigade and dismounted cavalry went in together in a countercharge. "There's those damn black-hatted fellows again! That ain't no milishy, that's the Army of the Potomac!" someone heard the Rebels cry, just before they broke.

Heth's leading brigade was through for the day, nearly all killed or captured. It was noon and afternoon before he could get his front rearranged, his other brigades into line. Meanwhile the I Corps had reached the field complete and Howard's stubborn Germans of the XI Corps were just beginning to file in behind. But Ewell had now appeared on the north road, with a third of Lee's army behind him, and if they got through, it would be onto the rear of the I Corps. Buford had had part of one brigade out that north road since early morning; in the lull between Heth's drives he got the rest of his men into the saddle, took them to the north, and dismounted them again, for an encore of the performance he had just given.

Doubleday, who had succeeded to the command of the I Corps when Reynolds was killed in the morning, complains that this line of Buford's was too far out, leaving his right flank in air. Perhaps so; but Buford showed himself a capital tactician on other occasions, and this time he made his first defense so far to the north that Ewell and Hill were unable to establish communications with each other and coordinate their attacks. Moreover Ewell, like Heth before him, had to deploy at an unreasonable distance from the line where he was to do his main fighting, in midafternoon, with Howard all in line against him. In his advanced position Buford was eventually overwhelmed by main force, but when he was finally driven in, Hancock was already at hand, the XII and part of the III Corps were closing in and it was too late for Lee to win his battle that day—or any other.

During the evening Buford's division was taken out of the line and sent back to guard the trains. It was completely shattered, but it had gained two hours—the two hours most needed—for Reynolds, and two hours again for Howard, each time by standing off a Confederate corps. It was more than any other cavalry leader in the Union army could or would have done. One can imagine an able ordinary cavalryman—say Kilpatrick or Pleasanton—at the head of Buford's men in the morning, and the result. A brilliant charge on Heth's head of column, a brief showy victory, the division broken by the steady surge of Confederate regiments behind, and Ewell or Hill or both on Cemetery Ridge by noon. If the picture seems overdrawn, it is only necessary to remember that this is exactly what happened when Kilpatrick did come on the field in the evening, with the difference that Cemetery was already gripped tight.

It was Buford's last service, except for minor bickerings during the retreat from Gettysburg. In December, '63, pneumonia and his old wound brought him to bed, and there in Washington he died what the Vikings called "a straw death." But by that time he had raised a torch to be caught by a stronger hand; the order had already gone forth that brought Philip H. Sheridan from the west.

PHILIP H. SHERIDAN

Little Phil

I

THE DECISIVE HOURS OF THE CIVIL WAR ARE GENERALLY considered to be those of the afternoon of July 3, 1863, when Pickett's column moved through the long grass, while 1,500 miles away flags of truce hung limp in the heat along the ramparts of Vicksburg. This is accurate if the war be thought of in the light of European precedent, and only untrue when we remember that for the Union mere victory was equal to defeat. It should not be forgotten that a soldier's work is incomplete until he has decisively influenced the political situation, and the double victory of 1863 did not achieve that result. A year after Gettysburg and Vicksburg—a year that had seen the Chattanooga battles and the better half of the titanic Atlanta campaign piled on the summit of these triumphs—the Democrats were seeking control in the North by denouncing the war as a failure. It seemed to many intelligent men, among them Thurlow Weed, Salmon P. Chase, and Lincoln himself, not unlikely that the Democrats would convince the country they were right and make a peace that left two nations.

The "decisive" battles of the Civil War thus decided nothing but that the Confederates could not win in the field. They might gain their essential point by default. The task that faced the North at the beginning of 1864 was infinitely more difficult than anything it had yet accomplished. It was required not only to achieve military victory (though this was an indispensable preliminary) but to achieve it in a manner that involved the extinction of Southern morale and the prevention of that guerrilla conflict which most European observers considered likely to follow the operations of the field armies.

In this sense both Vicksburg and Gettysburg were indecisive. They damaged, but did not slay the Confederate spirit. If Pemberton had been less a ninny, the one would not have been lost; if Lee had not made one of his rare errors, if Stuart had not been absent and Longstreet sulky, the other might have been won. The Southerners reasonably felt that a comparatively minor change in the conditions of either conflict would have reversed the results. They went on fighting in the expectation that the law of averages would provide changes in another combat. The battles that broke their hearts as well as their heads did not come till later; and these were named Chickamauga, Yellow Tavern, Cedar Creek, Five Forks.

The first was Thomas' battle and affected the western theater of war alone. But the other three have four elements in common. Each took place in that eastern piedmont on which the attention of the people on both sides of the strife was riveted, and thus yielded the maximum moral effect; each was the crowning act of a campaign; in each, cavalry, the special and favorite arm of the South, was deeply engaged; and in all, the Union commander was Philip Henry Sheridan.

With Sheridan there triumphed in these battles not only the Union army. There triumphed also an entirely new, purely American doctrine of war, of the use of the mounted arm—an idea that had been struggling dumbly for expression since Richard M. Johnson's Kentucky riflemen made razor strops of the skin from Tecumseh's legs after the Battle of the Thames. It was a doctrine that could not possibly have been framed south of the Potomac, in spite of the fact that the Confederacy entered the war with an aristocracy habituated to the saddle and with considerably more than its proportionate share of the cavalry officers of the old army.

In fact, it was a doctrine that could hardly have been born in the mind of a cavalryman at all. For cavalry officers, North and South, were so imbued with the history and tradition of their arm as to be incapable of perceiving that the advance of mechanical science had deprived this history and tradition of all meaning. They continued to think in terms of the days when the infantryman's gun was ineffective beyond a hundred yards and could be fired at most twice, while the cavalryman was crossing that distance. They thought of Murat and regarded the charge of the gallant six hundred as an example of courage and not of stupidity.

The Northern cavalry service had clearly failed as a Napoleonic arm when the Mine Run campaign closed out 1863, with its demonstration that the most serious part of the war was still to be fought. The reaction of an ordinary commander to this failure was that cavalry, having become an arm useless for heavy fighting, should be turned into a kind of military police force, charged with convoying trains and doing picket duty for the rest of the army. This had been Hooker's reaction after Chancellorsville, and Meade inherited it from him. It took something more than an ordinary commander to throw all received ideas out the window and start afresh from the concept that a cavalryman was only an infantryman with four detachable legs.

This was Sheridan. He pronounced a bill of divorcement between the cavalryman and his horse, a thing unheard of since true cavalry was born and the Goths came riding across the steppes.

The basic doctrine was not altogther novel, and perhaps not even independently original with Sheridan. John Buford, for one, had held the idea and might have pushed it further had he not been debarred by death from becoming more than a subordinate commander whose originality was limited to the tactical field. It was Sheridan's special merit that his precise and orderly brain evolved a harmonious and logical structure from the various elements he found already existing. It was his special accomplishment that through his treatment of cavalry, not as a separate arm with peculiar disabilities, but as a kind of fast-moving foot soldier, he achieved the only pure offensive to be found in the Civil War.

For Lee, a master of the tactical attack, always developed his successes out of the strategical defense, against enemies moving in, with lengthened communications, across ground he intimately knew. In both the battles he fought during advances he was beaten. Grant and Sherman, who might have possessed parts of the same brain under two different skulls, exactly reversed Lee by acting on the strategic attack but tactical defense. They aimed to place armies in positions where the enemy must hit out at them. Both failed (Cold Harbor, Kenesaw Mountain) when they violated this principle. Thomas was strictly a counterpuncher, waiting for an enemy advance, which he parried with one hand while knocking out his opponent with the other. Only Stonewall Jackson approached Sheridan; and there is more than a verbal coincidence in the fact that Stonewall's men were known as "the foot cavalry" while Sheridan's were cavalry who fought on foot.

At the time of the great winter conference of 1863–64 on military affairs, with Lincoln and the army leaders present, nobody was thinking of getting a man of genius or a new doctrine of cavalry. It occurred to nobody that defeat of its mounted arm might have ruinous effect on the morale of the Confederacy; though for political and military reasons everyone seems to have agreed that they could not afford to have Stuart riding circles around the Army of the Potomac any more. In other words, the views of the conference were negative. The decisive campaign of the war was approaching, and it was important to get something more than a minimum yield from the human and mechanical power the Union cavalry possessed.

The best way to do this was a change in command. For Pleasanton, then commanding the cavalry corps, had been given a thorough trial and he was simply not good enough. But who would be better? The three divisional commanders in the corps were Buford, Gregg, and Kilpatrick. Kilpatrick was a hard fighter but a still harder rider. The men knew him as "Kill-cavalry"; he normally arrived at the scene of action with horses blown and panting, men dropping from the saddle with weariness. Gregg was just the sort of mercurial leader Grant most distrusted—perhaps the best of them all when swinging to victory, perhaps the worst when things went wrong. Custer and Wesley Merritt were too junior. Grant asked for old General Franklin, whose talents he held in incomprehensible respect, but the others frowned him down and there was a silence till General Halleck cut the knot with the suggestion, "How would Sheridan do?"

"The very man!" cried Grant, and that night a telegram was dispatched for Sheridan.

II

Who was this Sheridan? Practically unknown in the East, he had flashed only once across the front pages of war history—when he stood in the captured rifle pits at the foot of Missionary Ridge, and lifting his whisky flask toward the

Rebels on the towering summit, shouted "Here's how!" before he drank the toast. As the last drops trickled down his gullet a shot from a big gun up there threw dirt all over him. "I call that damned ungenerous!" cried Sheridan. "I'll take those guns for that!" and flinging the empty flask up the slope he started after it—the beginning of that incredible charge up a mountain like a mansard roof.

Army circles knew slightly more about him. They knew him for the hero of the fighting at Perryville, where he had held his division all day against overwhelming Rebel attacks, and in the evening put on a counterstroke that tore Bragg's line to pieces. He had done well at Chickamauga where, though his division had been one of those carried from the field, he rallied it in time to come back and cover Thomas' retreat. At the dreadful battle of Stone River he had done surpassingly well; had slowed and then halted the Confederate attack of the first day and formed the anchor of Thomas' line. In the dramatic midnight council of war he stood with Thomas against retreat, and even asked permission to lead the counter that eventually won.

Most of the rest was gossip that drifted up by word of mouth through junior officers, for Sheridan was the youngest division commander in the armies of the West, belonging to a later generation than most of the high command. That gossip would tell, for instance, how he came to West Point, a tough little Mick of a store clerk from Ohio, poor as Job's turkey, with a chip always on his shoulder; how he wrangled during drill with Cadet Sergeant Terrill, and after trying to jab that student officer with a bayonet, had challenged him to a fist fight behind the buildings, coming out of the encounter with a black eye and a year's suspension; how he had been graduated in 1853, an undistinguished thirty-fourth among fifty-two, and was ordered to Fort Duncan, Texas, as lieutenant of infantry.

There again he fell on stormy weather, which can perhaps be traced to the fact that all his life long Sheridan was a picturesque and vivid swearer, while the colonel in command was equally noted as a God-fearing man of the Puritan type. There was as much disagreement as there can be between a very junior lieutenant and a very senior colonel, with petty persecutions on one side, petty sabotage on the other. Sheridan finally escaped via a requested transfer to the 4th Infantry, then on duty against the Yakima Indians in the Pacific Northwest.

The country was ill explored, the Indians almost inveterately hostile, and young Lieutenant Sheridan was very much on his own in leading detachments out to deal with them. But in that hard service he found himself. He displayed a perfect passion for topography; never went out on an expedition without taking surveying instruments along and mapping every inch of the country he covered. Two other details of this period have survived, interesting in view of his later career. Lieutenant Sheridan formed the habit of requisitioning all the mules he could lay hands on and mounting his infantrymen on them for movements up to the scene of action; and in dealing with the Indians he displayed a wonderful gift of blarney, could always talk them out of hostile intention if he could get them to powwow before the shooting started.

Much of this, however, was not to be dredged from memories and records till the young lieutenant was famous. The service papers lying before Lincoln, Halleck, and Grant at that winter conference would have stated only that Lieutenant Sheridan was ordered east at the outbreak of the war, arrived late because of the distance, and was assigned to the Herculean order of auditing the accounts left in confusion by the ornamental Frémont. A year after the war began he had only attained promotion to a captaincy, and was quartermaster of southwestern Missouri, that is, effectively buried. Grant and Sherman were generals, the former already a famous general; Thomas had an independent command, and McClellan more military authority than any American since George Washington.

But at this juncture Sheridan caught his tide. Quartermaster business brought him frequently to the headquarters of the western armies, where he was met and liked by Gordon Granger, then a brigadier of several months' standing. Granger's old regiment, the Second Michigan Cavalry, had gotten into bad shape since he moved upstairs. He wanted an officer to straighten the command out, and the name of the young quartermaster, who was running his department like a clock, naturally suggested itself.

Granger put the matter up to Halleck, then commanding the West. That formalist, who had already been impressed by the neat way Sheridan ran his freight schedules and his fastidious paper work, gave the promotion his blessing. This was how Sheridan, whose nearest approach to mounted action had been muleback operations in the 4th Infantry, came to be pitched into the Corinth campaign at the head of a regiment of horse. He was to be a lieutenant general before he received his colonel's commission.

Fortune rode with him on his first mission, a detached one to hold Boonville, Missouri, with eleven companies of his own regiment and the 2nd Iowa, about 750 men all told. Most might not consider it fortune, however—Confederate Chalmers came down to shoot up the place on July 1, 1862, with 4,000 men. Sheridan had chosen a position where his flanks were covered by a pair of swamps, and the attack was canalized into a narrow front where his dismounted riflemen waited, but the disparity in numbers was so great that by noon things began to look grim.

Sheridan summoned a trustworthy officer, Captain Alger;

gave him ninety men, armed with Colt "revolving carbines"; told him to go by a circuit and fall on the enemy's rear, shooting for all they were worth from the saddle, making a racket whether they hit anything or not. Now, says Alger, who has told the story, he understood why his colonel had spent half the previous night poring over maps of the region. In the heat of the conflict, among the ceaseless attacks, Sheridan gave him road directions as clear and precise as though he were telling a man how to find the post office. Alger rode off with his ninety; made his circuit, and charged the Rebel rear with guns banging. At the same time Sheridan threw forward his own dismounted men in a countercharge against the Confederates, who were mostly still in the saddle.

There is one thing about mounted cavalry. If it once gets started going either forward or back, it is very difficult to stop. Chalmers' men had already started going back when Alger struck. Sheridan's charge kept them going with doubled speed, and in half an hour the four thousand had left the seven hundred fifty in possession of the field and the enemy wounded.

It was an outstanding feat of arms in a campaign that had very little outstanding about it. The young commander was given a young brigadier's rank and was sent by Grant to Buell a month later, when Grant's invasion of Kentucky caused the Army of the Cumberland to ask for help. Sheridan was taken from his two regiments of horse to arrange the defense of Louisville, which he did so well that he was placed in charge of one of the new divisions of infantry in the campaign that led to Perryville. While ex-Cadet Sergeant Terrill was being killed at the head of his brigade in one part of the line that day, Sheridan in another was the heart of the Union defense, the best man on the field, winning his step on the ladder that had now brought him to Chief of Cavalry in the Army of the Potomac.

III

There is a certain amount of mystery in how Grant came to assent so enthusiastically to the nomination, for the most important cavalry command in the nation, of a young man whose ten years of active service had included only four months with cavalry, and those at the head of a single regiment. The commander-in-chief did not know Sheridan well. He had seen him in action as a general officer only during the week or two of the Chattanooga fighting, and the most favorable reports on Sheridan came from men Grant was rather inclined to distrust—Buell, Rosecrans, Halleck.

The choice is perhaps explained by a remark of Grant's long later: "No man ever had such a faculty of finding things out as Sheridan. He was always the best informed man in his command as to the enemy." This is full of illumination, not only on Sheridan, but also on Grant's own theory of the employment of horsemen in a world where they had been banished from the battlefield. He evidently thought of the arm as screen and counterscreen, whose function was to conceal the movements of one's own forces and to acquire information about those of the enemy. Sheridan's preternatural activity, physical and mental, his deep interest in and knowledge of topography, his ability at questioning prisoners ("That there man, he'll talk the eyes right out of your head," said one of them)—these things impressed Grant as the proper equipment of a cavalry leader.

Yet both Grant and Halleck had misgivings when the man arrived in Washington on April 4, too late for any change to be made before the opening of the campaign. Grant particularly, as he confessed later, "formed a very unfavorable impression." Seen in a drawing room Sheridan was a "most extraordinary figure. His chest was large and full, his legs short and small, and his arms so phenomenally long that his hands reached down below the level of his knees." Above this was a small head, bearing little bright eyes like those of a bird and a face that registered doubt both about his own ability and the wisdom of accepting the new appointment.

Sheridan was, in fact, inclined to view the cavalry command as a demotion. He was due to take over a corps in the western armies and liked service there, among the free-and-easy veterans who turned out on parade to bleat at an officer when they considered his behavior sheeplike, or offered him chewing tobacco as a special delicacy when they liked him. The Army of the Potomac, he understood, was more strait-laced in discipline. He doubted his ability to give satisfaction under the conditions. Grant eyed him ruminatively, puffing cigar smoke, and was ultimately delivered of the remark that the new Chief of Cavalry would have pretty much of a free hand on one condition—that he keep Jeb Stuart out of mischief. Sheridan's face cleared at once, and two days later he was riding down to inspect his new command.

There were 10,000 effectives in three divisions, commanded by Gregg, Torbert (a new man come up through the ranks to replace Kilpatrick, who had gone west to join Sherman), and Wilson. This last was another of Grant's surprise appointments—the youngest man so far to bear stars on his shoulders, an engineer of the West Point class of 1860, who had been a kind of secretary and personal inspector-general to Grant in the west, but who had never led troops. The men looked strong, healthy, smart—Sheridan has recorded his pleased surprise at their appearance—but the horses were the merest flea-bait. It did not take the inquisitive new commander long to discover the reason for a state of affairs that would be pardonable only at the close of a long and hard campaign.

The cavalry were doing picket duty for the entire army, round a circuit of sixty miles, besides having the standing assignment of furnishing heavy escorts for every provision train and every column of infantry that moved on the roads in back areas. Sheridan went to Meade with a demand that his corps be concentrated as a fast battle wing of the main army and relieved of drafts for the service of security.

Meade's concept of cavalry was that which had grown up in the Army of the Potomac. It was not thought out at all; it was imposed on the army from outside, by the pressure of Mosby's lightning jabs and Stuart's long rides around the rear; and it was essentially defensive. The commander was horrified by Sheridan's demand. "What will become of my trains, my flanks, my moving columns?" he asked.

Sheridan: "If you let me use the cavalry as I wish, you need not worry about trains or flanks. As for the infantry, it ought to be able to take care of itself on the roads."

Meade demurred, filled with the engineer's distrust of new ideas that could not be expressed in figures, and Sheridan had to develop his theme. The infantry, he said, were about to attack the enemy's infantry; why, then, should our cavalry stand on the defensive against the Confederates'? If our mounted men be concentrated, the enemy will dare just one more of those long raids—his last. For a concentrated cavalry corps will then face him from a prepared position across his line of retreat, or alternatively, deliver 10,000 men at any desired spot on the enemy rear at any time desired.

"It is the business of cavalry to fight cavalry," Sheridan went on, "and if there is no cavalry there to fight, to attack the enemy's infantry in their most vulnerable point." Warming with his own logic he demanded thrice the normal equipment of artillery for his horse, as much artillery as infantry would have. Cavalry used as he meant to use it would be seizing positions behind the enemy, points vital to that enemy, which he would fight like the devil to regain. Cavalry mobility was a means to the end of arriving at an effective point for an infantry battle—

At this point Sheridan had parted company not only with

Meade but with Grant also. The latter's theory of cavalry was different from that of either Meade or Sheridan, but he possessed a brain so habituated to following the essential through mazes of side issues as to resemble a mechanical instrument. The registering dial of that machine reported to him that Sheridan was proposing to submit the Rebel cavalry to the novel experience of being attacked. This chimed with his own idea of cavalry as a service of information and anti-information. He decided the argument about concentration in Sheridan's favor, but as for the extra artillery—no, not at present. The decision accurately reflected Grant's questioning middle-ground attitude at the time.

IV

The inquiries and arguments took two weeks. Sheridan was granted two weeks more in which to assemble his men and to rest their horses before reveille on May 3 blew the opening of the Hammering Campaign. Two of Sheridan's divisions led the two columns of infantry across the Rapidan that morning. Division Torbert, by Meade's orders, was held back to guard the rear—a perfectly proper employment for the nimblest troops of the army by Meade's ideas. Though Sheridan could hardly have agreed, he forbore any protest at the time.

On the 5th the Battle of the Wilderness broke among the tangled thickets south of the stream. Only two of the three big Confederate corps reached the field that day. On Lee's left, Ewell, with ground and good tactics in his favor, held Warren and Sedgwick around Wilderness Tavern amid appalling losses on both sides. On the Confederate right, A. P. Hill did not get his men up quite so soon, and when he did arrive, found Hancock's II Corps, with the best battle captain in the Union army, facing him. The fighting went ill for the Confederates; Hill lost ground, men, and morale, only closing night saved him from a break.

But out of the partial defeat Lee drew a battle plan for the second day as perfect as a painting by Leonardo. Longstreet arrived during the night with the third big corps. While Ewell held on the Confederate left and Hill slightly retired in their center, this fresh corps was to work around Hancock's flank and strike, crushing Hancock's corps and the line behind him against the anvil of Hill and Ewell. Stuart, who had also just arrived with the Rebel cavalry, was to ride round Longstreet, throw out a wing to menace the Union supply trains around Fredericksburg, then turn in behind Longstreet against the Federal rear.

Like Leonardo's greatest work, the plan went to pieces through the shifting of the foundation on which it was painted. As expected, Hancock attacked again the next morning, rushing Hill back until Longstreet came in on his flank. The Union division of General Mott was swept away, men coming back through the woods all disorderly, some with weapons and a few without. But they came past Hancock himself. He rallied them in person, shouting "Halt there!" till a brigade from his own reserve and a division from Grant re-established the line. Under the increasing pressure he took up the retrograde indeed, but slowly, in good order, with no real gain to the attackers. Longstreet, trying to press home, went down with a bad wound. His corps took losses it could afford only as the price of crushing victory, and as twilight sifted through the spring leaves, crushing victory, any victory, was still far distant, riding with Stuart.

For Hancock's stand and Longstreet's wound had left Confederate success dependent on Stuart—whether he could coax Sheridan back on the trains, break his connection with II Corps and arrive on its rear with something over 8,000 men. But Stuart, for the first time in his career, had failed to reach his final objective, or any other objective.

He started early on the morning of May 6, in two columns, just at the flank of Longstreet, toward Todd's Tavern, at which point the columns were to pivot north. Ambling easily along, the Rebel horsemen reached the pivot points without difficulty, but there found log breastworks from which they were received with so lusty a fire of musketry that they reported the presence of Union infantry. Stuart weighted his

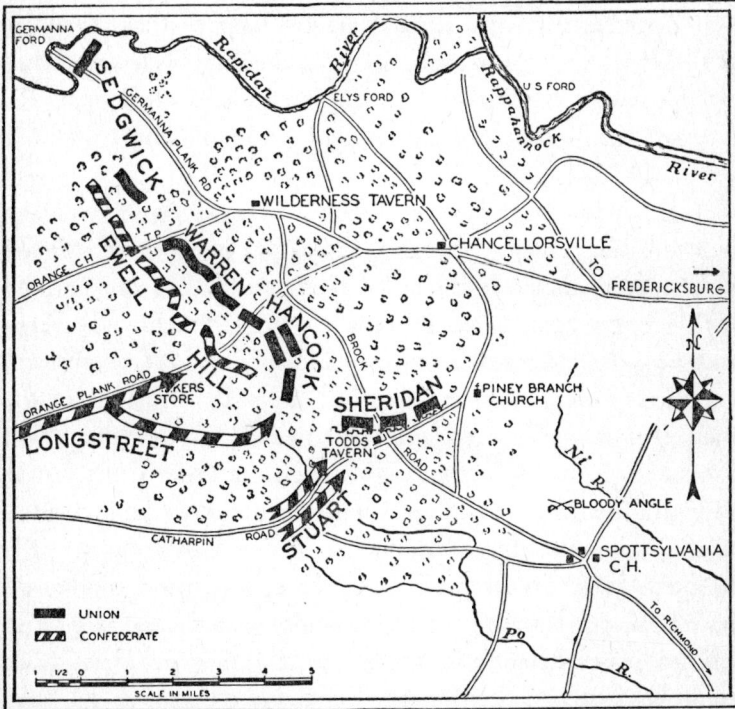

The Wilderness—May 6, 1864

column heads and tried to drive through. He was violently repulsed while the ground shook with Hancock's struggle farther north, could not win an inch, and in the evening reported that Grant must have extended his infantry lines down that far.

It was not Grant, it was Sheridan. Though the fact has been lost to sight in the flare of the giant duel of the infantry, he would not have been there at all had Meade's orders been carried out as written. After crossing the Rapidan, the two cavalry divisions under Sheridan in person had been shunted aside to the left rear of the army, behind Hancock and linking up with the third, Torbert's division, which was seeing the trains through at United States Ford and Fredericksburg. This was a perfectly normal cavalry arrangement for the Army of the Potomac, with the exception that the men were somewhat more concentrated than under earlier leaders, and apparently it was the disposition Lee counted on in making his grand attack.

The night orders Sheridan received on May 5 were to "protect the trains" without specification of method, and the new general took the bit in his teeth. Instead of drawing all his divisions back toward Fredericksburg, he shoved everything up, even bringing two brigades of Torbert's command forward from Fredericksburg to Todd's Tavern. One of the men in that division has left record of the astonishment that ran through the ranks that night when the order came down, "Unsaddle and go to camp," with an order to build breastworks following immediately. It was never so done in Israel before. Always in the presence of the enemy, the Union horse had kept their mounts packed and saddled, sleeping with bridles over their arms, ready for a quick getaway. This time they reached position, the horses were out of it, and they were there to fight.

They did fight; and the report of how and where they fought on the morning of the 6th reached Meade simultaneously with the news of Longstreet's blow at Hancock. Remembering other Lee offensives—Chancellorsville, the Seven Days—Meade could visualize the next step as a Confederate cavalry movement around his rear, between the army and its train at the Rappahannock crossings. He ordered Sheridan to "draw in and protect the trains" and that night the Union cavalry were going back.

Stuart's men followed them in, and on the morning of the 7th, taking this retrograde as part of a general retreat, injudiciously tried a vigorous pursuit of Custer's brigade, the one nearest Hancock. Custer turned on them, counterattacking savagely. Sheridan learned of this almost immediately. At the same time he heard that more Rebel cavalry formations

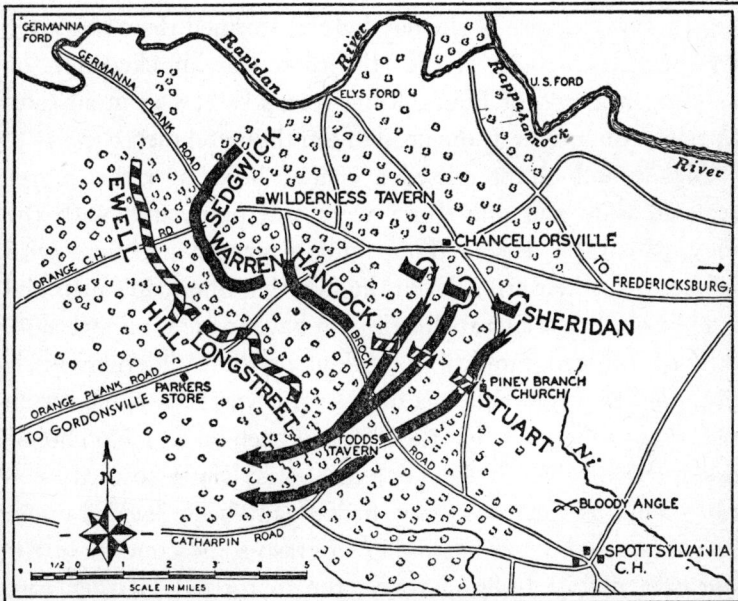

The Wilderness—Morning, May 7, 1864

had been located farther east and got some information from prisoners. The aggregated information brought into focus in his mind a full picture of Stuart's movement—a cavalry advance across a front that grew ever wider as the Confederate formations moved down the radii of a fan.

Once again he ran away with his orders, spun the divisions of Gregg and Wilson sharp round in their tracks, and attacked with all his strength. His closer concentration gave him numerical superiority at all contact points, and the repeating carbines in Wilson's division turned this into something like a two-to-one advantage of fire power. Besides, he was counting on battle and ready for it, his men were nearly all dismounted, operating as infantry against Confederates on tall, vulnerable horses. The Union troops hustled Stuart's men back along every road, carried Todd's Tavern, and beyond it, coming on several lines of field fortifications constructed by the Rebels during their repulse of the day before, stormed them one after another. By twilight of the 7th Stuart was knocked out for a good twenty-four hours, Longstreet's right was in air, and Sheridan on its rear at the head of ten thousand men.

Meade and Grant missed a chance here, or rather never realized they had one. Both were still permeated with the view of cavalry as something fluid, a force which slept with bridles over their arms. Even the fact that Sheridan's men had fought on foot seems at this time to have made no impression. The special geographical conditions of the Wilderness made dismounted action almost a necessity, it was impossible for an observer to discover that the step had been taken from choice. Moreover on the 7th the move to Spottsylvania, toward Lee's right flank by the main army, had already been decided upon; and Grant, who was beginning to grasp some concept of the use of a mobile fighting force, the motorized infantry into which Sheridan had turned his corps, had already ordered the cavalry to lead the flanking maneuver. Once again Meade played the marplot. Wilson's division, now the farthest to the left, and hence to the front of the new movement, went on to Spottsylvania with somewhere near 3,000 men. But Meade in person reached the headquarters of the other two divisions before Sheridan's orders did, and he instantly used both for purposes sharply different from those the Chief of Cavalry intended. Gregg was pulled out of the advance to protect trains (from what?—the whole Federal army was now between those trains and the nearest of Lee's men). Merritt, who had taken over Torbert's division, was held back to accompany and protect the march of Warren's V Corps, guarding infantry on the roads according to the best muddled tradition of the Army of the Potomac. It was night; of course, Merritt's division became mixed with Warren's infantry and wagons on the wood roads. There was a wild traffic jam that stalled both horse and foot. Whenever Meade appeared the cavalry had to yield precedence to Warren, and Merritt emerged from the tangle well behind the infantry he was supposed to lead.

Wilson's single division was of course no match for the entire Confederate corps that presently arrived at Spottsylvania. After some hard defensive fighting it was driven out, and the whole desperate business of the Bloody Angle, with ten days and 14,000 men lost, had to be gone through with.

But Bloody Angle was still in the future when, on the night of the 8th, Sheridan came tearing into headquarters, red, angry, and swearing, not mincing the words he shouted as he demanded to know whether he were truly Chief of Cavalry or only a rubber stamp for others' ideas. Meade snapped back the wearisome old arguments about the safety of trains and columns. Grant listened, impassive as an ox, till both men began to repeat themselves, then turning to Sheridan asked him briefly if, being allowed to write his own orders, he could guarantee the elimination of Stuart.

"Yes," flashed Sheridan.

"All right," said Grant.

V

Next morning Sheridan began concentrating back on the long lateral road that runs from Fredericksburg to Orange, behind the Union right rear. Men and horses had a good night's rest, then started early on May 9, riding south and east at a sober walk in a single column, thirteen miles long, to get right around the Rebel army.

The men, impressed with the leadership of their Little Phil during the hard fighting of the past week, were more impressed now. Under Stoneman, Pleasanton, Kilpatrick, they had moved out on such expeditions at the trot, on parallel roads in tight bunches. When the enemy showed up for a fight, their horses were blown, themselves tired, and the nearest support, also on tired mounts, would be distant across miles of country. Or as we should put it in modern phrases, Sheridan realized that mobility is an evanescent quality, one that can be used for either strategic or tactical purposes, but not both. He was aiming to arrive at the scene of any action with full gas tanks.

Perhaps this is reading more into Sheridan's doctrine than he himself put there. Yet the proof that he had thought the matter through better than any other man of his time lies in that single long column moving slowly on. "I preferred this to the combinations arising from using several roads," he himself said. "Combinations rarely work." With horses at a walk that column did not present the danger it appeared to. A blow at any portion of it would be subject to envelopment from the wings, all the men moving at the full tactical speed that had been preserved to them. . . .

That is, it worked. Confederate Brigadier Gordon located the serpentine column late on the afternoon of the 9th, near Childsburg, already well round the Confederate flank and in the rear, but he dared attempt nothing even against its rear. It seems that Stuart expected to find the Union cavalry off on the other wing of their army, leading the advance. He had the bulk of his men out in that direction, feeling for them till word came through from Gordon.

Now mark the soundness of Sheridan's plan, which brought

him to the North Anna by night. He might turn straight north into Lee's rear, or south toward Richmond. To prevent the first move falling without warning, Stuart had to leave Gordon behind with nearly a third of his own cavalry. To fend off a stroke at Richmond, he had to expend his own mobility in a long, hard ride round the Union head of column, leaving uncovered for some length the two vertical railroads out of Richmond along which Lee was drawing supplies.

That night the Union riders had another surprise. Instead of the all night "stand to" in separate little picket camps which had been the custom during raids in their army, they found themselves in one big camp astride the North Anna, with artillery placed and unlimbered, soldiers getting full bellies and a good night's rest, horses unsaddled. One who was there noted that next morning they began to sing. They were content with their Little Phil. "We saw him daily, whether we were in the advance, at the rear, or the center of the column, and he would as soon borrow a light from the pipe of an enlisted man as from the cigar of an officer. The common soldier's uniform was good enough for him."

That morning, May 10, he sent a brigade of them out east under Custer to Beaver Dam Station on one of Lee's railroad lines. A big supply magazine was burned out; it had held the whole of Lee's medical stores, doubly precious in that army which had to use medicines run in through the blockade. A batch of Union prisoners was released; the trackage ripped up for some distance.

Down in Richmond they had news of Sheridan now, the bells were tolling alarm, home guards were being called out and troops summoned all the way from the Carolinas. The Union column plodded steadily on, slanting toward Richmond. They crossed the South Anna in the afternoon and shot out another brigade, Davies's, which just at twilight touched

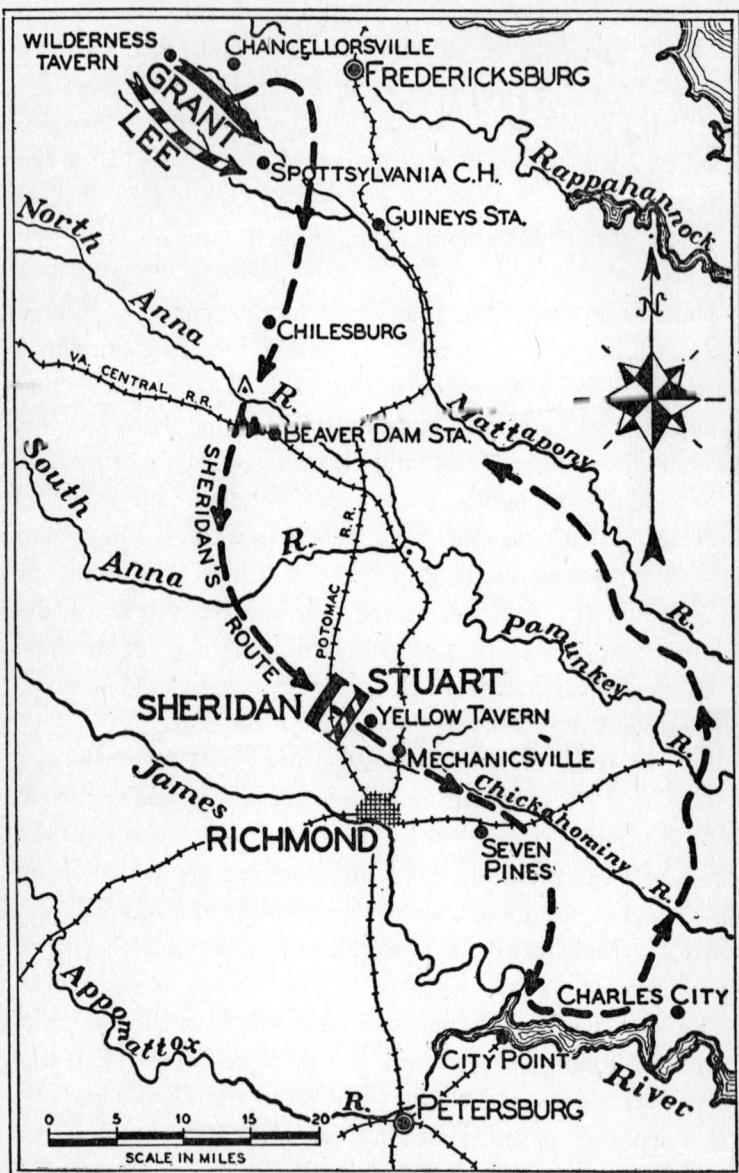

Wilderness to Yellow Tavern and beyond

the second vertical line out of Richmond. Wires were torn down and tracks up; a second depot of stores went. Before midnight both forces had fallen in on the main body, bringing some prisoners.

Sheridan, now as ever his own G-2, extracted from the latter the information that Stuart had arrived before Richmond and was waiting in a prepared position at Yellow Tavern, just north of the Chickahominy. Gordon's brigade had been haunting the Union rear all day. Evidently some measure had been concerted to bring that also into the impending battle. Sheridan had no objection; the whole purpose of his raid was not seize any particular point, but to bring all Stuart's men to action, and to handle them so roughly that they would never again dare one of their great sweeps—as Grant's purpose in the whole campaign was similarly to impose the defensive on Lee.

Merritt's division had the advance in the morning. He found the Confederate line holding a crossroads at Yellow Tavern, facing west across his front; dismounted, and punched through. It was a trap, of course. There was a second line behind the first. As soon as Merritt was involved against it, a battery of artillery opened an enfilading fire from cover, and down from a grove of trees came Jeb Stuart at the gallop into Merritt's flank.

But Sheridan had met trap with countertrap. As Merritt's line crumpled, his men firing as they scattered to cover, George Custer, yelling "Come on, Wolverines!" flung himself into Stuart's flank. There was a violent shock, a tangle, Custer was driven off for a moment, but came on again with the whole weight of Wilson's division behind, and the Confederates went tumbling back, their great leader out of mischief forever, shot through the lungs. Wilson's men swarmed all over the Rebel line, shot down the artillery's support, captured the guns, drove what was left of Stuart's cavalry right away before them.

"Combinations rarely work." Now, when Stuart was down and the defensive line gone, Gordon arrived on Sheridan's left rear in a mounted attack. The Union leader had foreseen that too. Gordon ran into a breastwork of interlaced branches with Gregg's men firing from behind it, was shot dead from the saddle and his brigade driven off northeast on an eccentric.

Sheridan moved on round the defenses of Richmond, got supplies from the fleet in the James, and shuttled back, up across the rivers, to the main army, which he rejoined on May 24. It tells the whole story to say that the Confederate cavalry never molested him again. Infantry tried to stop him once, where the fixed defenses of Richmond reached the banks of the Chickahominy near Mechanicsville. These unconventional cavalrymen rebuilt a broken bridge under fire, crossed it, and drove the infantry off in a combat of which not enough details have survived to permit an intelligent account.

It does not matter. Nothing in the story of this operation matters after the battle of Yellow Tavern, which, hidden from the sight of Northern eyes by the red glare rising round Bloody Angle, inflicted upon Southern morale a heavier blow than the loss of Stonewall Jackson. For Jackson fell in the moment of victory; at Yellow Tavern the Confederacy lost not only Stuart and Gordon but also the legend of its own invincibility in the arm that was the pride of every Southerner. Says Grant: "This raid had the effect of . . . thenceforth making it easy to guard our trains."

No other praise is necessary.

VI

Yellow Tavern thus established Sheridan within the army. To the country he remained merely a corps commander who was doing well, a name among the others in dispatches from the Virginia scrub lands where the fighting was going forward with such bloody indecision. Lee seems fully to have realized the political effect of this indecisiveness on the North and, clutched though he was in Grant's embrace, found means to win minor but morally impressive triumphs in the one field where geography practically guaranteed Southern victory. Or was Early's move to the Shenandoah Valley dictated by the more narrowly military hope of forcing Grant to make large detachments from the forces around Richmond?

No matter. Early was in the Valley with a large corps, Early shuttled to and fro, defeating Federal local guards, breaking up the important supply line of the Baltimore and Ohio. Early crossed the Potomac, smashed a hastily gathered force at the Monocacy, and marched to the gates of Washington, where President Lincoln was under fire. Something would have to be done about Early.

General Wright was pulled out of the Petersburg trenches with his VI Corps and sent to Washington. His operations were sound enough, but futile. The Confederate leader, moving up that fertile and friendly region where he could keep his trains to a minimum, danced away from Wright's lumbering legions. The moment Wright went back to Petersburg, Early came down the Valley. Once more he broke the Baltimore and Ohio and lanced into Pennsylvania, where he laid the town of Chambersburg under $300,000 ransom. There was not that much money in the place, so Early turned the inhabitants out into the summer fields and burned it, every stick.

Throughout the North the papers went wild. A year after Gettysburg the Rebels were burning towns in Pennsylvania! In parallel columns came the news from Chicago—the Democrats had finished their convention; they were going before the elections on a platform declaring "Lincoln's war" a failure, a repetitious bloody agony. Washington telegraphed feverishly to Grant, another in the series of such telegrams that had been flashing along the wires since Early began his raids. Something would have to be done and Grant would have to decide what it was.

Already, some time before, Grant had pointed out that the trouble in the Valley was not one of forces but of commands. As things stood, the Shenandoah and its neighborhood formed the boundary lines of four separate military departments, each with its own troops and officers. Washington agreed with Grant that the whole thing should be under a single head, with a concentrated army "big enough to follow Early to the death," an army particularly strong in cavalry to offset the mobility the friendly country gave to the Confederates, an army that should burn out the Valley granary to an extent where it would no more harbor rats.

But there had been a tug-of-war over leadership. Grant again wanted Franklin, a suggestion which was coldly received. Meade was offered, but the idea was politically all wrong, it would look like the demotion of the commander of the Army of the Potomac, which would be a confession of that very failure the Democrats claimed. Hunter, already in the Valley, was too old and slow; Hancock, too good a corps leader.

This was the situation when the Chambersburg raid caused Grant to react with the speed of a steel trap, as he always did when irritated. "I am sending General Sheridan," he wrote. "I want him put in command of all the troops in the field."

It was a *tour de force* in both directions on Grant's part, for Sheridan himself, approached on the project of taking over what had suddenly become the critical command of the war, was dubious about his own capacity. He would prefer, he said, to command a corps, perhaps the cavalry under some other leader. Grant listened and smoked, his mind probing for the reason behind this unexpected diffidence on the part of an officer who had not hesitated to stand up to the testy Meade. Finally he hit it: the Valley commands were full of old, senior, respected officers—Hunter, Averell of the cavalry, "Fight mit Franz" Sigel, Wright—some of them twice Sheridan's age.

Grant remarked that this was a campaign in which seniority did not count. If the older officers objected to serving under Sheridan he was to relieve them—"Do not hesitate to give command to officers in whom you repose confidence, without regard to claims of others on account of rank." Hunter did object to serving under the junior Sheridan. He was given his walking papers, and on August 7, at Harper's Ferry, the new leader took over his army, with everything in it to do and the political campaign hurrying on.

It is important to any estimate of Sheridan to realize that his new "army" was a motley collection of units, unknown to him and to each other, units that required to be united, magnetized, stamped with the impress of a single personality, before they were fit for anything. The VI Corps, under General H. G. Wright, had a long honorable history in the Army of the Potomac, but, like its general, was distinguished for solidity rather than speed, a unit rather of defense than of attack. The XIX Corps, Emory's, had been doing garrison duty and police work in Louisiana. It had never been assembled as a unit, was unfamiliar with any but guerrilla operations, and could hardly be called a fighting corps. Cook's VIII Corps, the former Army of West Virginia, had seen a great deal of fighting, all of the wrong kind. The men had the hangdog, careless attitude of troops that had never known victory, were spiritless, and were no more used to working in big formations than Emory's men. Two of the four divisions of cavalry, Averell's and Duffie's, were from this same army, with the same drawbacks. They had, moreover, been trained in the prehistoric tradition of "living in the saddle"; regarded dismounted action as something no decent cavalryman would take if he could help it. In the whole army only the other two cavalry divisions, those commanded by Merritt and Wilson,

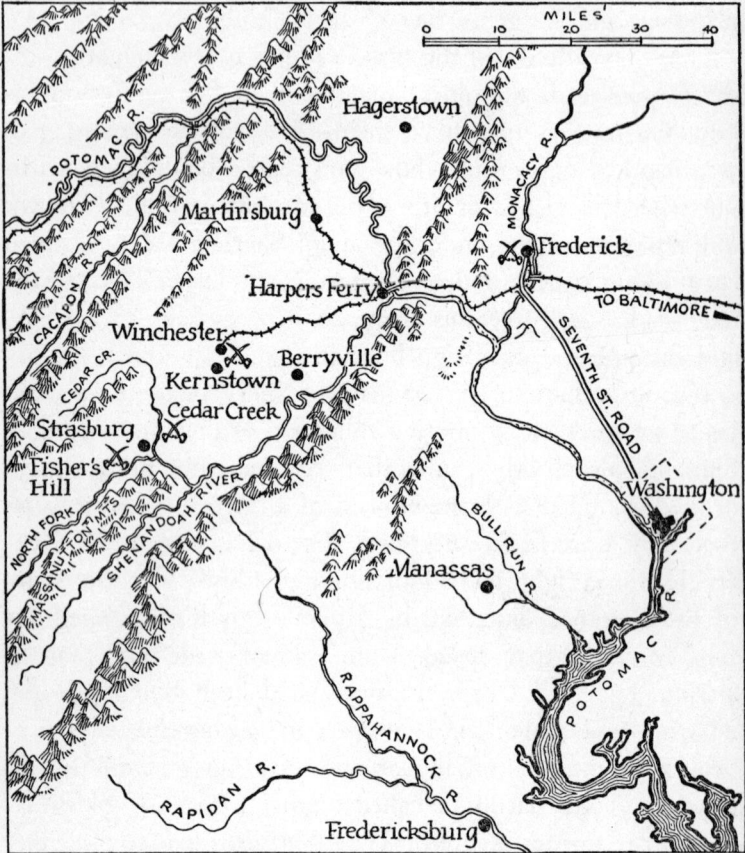

The Valley

knew Sheridan and his methods. They were a small leaven in the mass of 50,000 men.

This then was the force Sheridan had to make into a fighting machine. It had some peculiarities, of which the most striking was the cavalry-infantry ratio of one to four, higher than any before seen on the American continent. Another was that Sheridan assigned no less than nine batteries of artillery to this cavalry, or four and a half times as many guns as he had had in the Wilderness for the same number of horsemen; and this artillery was the best he had, United States regulars.

Early discovered the significance of this in the first and perhaps the most important operation of the Army of the Shenandoah, though it was one crowned by no battle, yielding no newspaper results. When Lee learned that the VI Corps and two divisions of cavalry had been sent to the Valley, he accepted the transfer of major operations thither with evident relief. He reinforced Early with the major portion of Longstreet's corps and Fitz Lee's cavalry division, which brought the Confederate Valley army up to a strength beyond the powers of Sheridan's rag-tag host, at least in the opinion of Grant, who warned his young subordinate to be careful.

Sheridan, who had been well forward toward Winchester, accordingly retired to a position near Halltown, where he could cover both Harper's Ferry and the northbound roads that lead past it on the west, and dug himself in. There was a river on either wing. When Early came up, he inspected the place, and decided it was too strong to be forced, too good to be flanked.

There is more than one way to handle such a situation, and Early worked out an excellent method. He left a division on Sheridan's front, strongly fortified; moved the main body of his infantry up to Shepherdstown, and flung Fitz Lee out ahead to see what he could do about passing the Potomac. If Sheridan advanced against the fortified division, Early would come back and fight the Union leader on ground of his own choosing, but he considered it more likely Fitz Lee's threat would force the Army of the Shenandoah to retreat.

Nothing of the kind happened. Sheridan remained coolly

within his lines. Wilson's cavalry division held the South Mountain passes; Merritt's knifed in between the detached division and Early's rear, feeling for his communications; and Fitz Lee reported that Averell was holding the Potomac crossings in trenches, so well supplied with artillery that crossing would be a bloody business, probably could not be achieved at all without infantry support.

In short, Sheridan had used the mobility of his cavalry as he proposed before the Wilderness—to seize and fortify a series of positions that severely restricted the scope of Confederate operations. Adventures beyond the Potomac had been rendered impossible to Early. But unless his army could adventure there, it had no purpose; could not affect the main campaign physically or morally. It could only go home; and when Grant started the Deep Bottom offensive, Lee called in Longstreet's corps. It was September when they crossed the mountains through the ripe crops, and the Northern elections running on apace. The day Longstreet reached Richmond, Grant sent his commander in the Shenandoah the famous two-word telegram:

"Go in."

VII

When the word came Sheridan had moved a little up the valley to Berryville. Early was camped west of him, before Winchester in a position where several roads came to a nexus among some jutting heights. Stonewall Jackson had won a battle there in '62; perhaps the Confederate commander felt it a place of happy augury to his side. Sheridan, who had visited the town during the early days of his Valley command, thought it radically defective as a military post, refused to put his own army there, and now planned to crush Early in it. At one o'clock in the morning of September 19, the men were roused from their beds, given a meal and hot coffee; at two, the whole army marched. Early had been moving his forces restlessly about during the previous days. Sheridan hoped to strike Winchester while only two of Early's four divisions were there, but planned to inflict a Leuthen on whatever he did find. The main road from Berryville to Winchester, a good metaled highway, runs for three miles through a narrow ravine, then crosses a little belt of plain country and mounts a low plateau, at the far side of which stands Winchester town, with the abutments of Little North Mountain soaring up behind it. A series of tracks, passable for infantry but not much else, roughly parallels the road through the hills south of the ravine. There are more hills, broken and knoblike, north of it, reaching to the very foot of the plateau before Winchester.

The Rebels had a fort at the outlet of the ravine, and their camps lined the plateau behind it, which was not quite high enough to afford a good view over the hills, nor did they have any force out in those hills.

Sheridan's orders put Wilson's cavalry division at the head of the advance. This officer was to use his mobility to the full: as soon as he found himself within the walls of the three-mile ravine press on at the gallop to seize the outlet fort, the only real danger to the movement. Behind Wilson, Wright's VI Corps was to march through the ravine to the edge of the plateau, attack and fix the Confederates there, while Wilson covered their left flank, filing off into some flat country southeast of the town.

The XIX Corps would follow the VI Corps through the ravine, swing right around the foot of the plateau, and deliver an oblique attack on the left wing of the Rebels as they faced Wright. Meanwhile the VIII Corps would take the mountain tracks south of the ravine, strike in between Wright and Wilson on the right wing of the Confederates. Torbert, with the division of Averell, which was already north of Winchester, and that of Merritt, which left during the night to join Averell, was to come down the main Valley pike on the Confederate left rear into the town. It was a combination attack, but one that stood in no debt to time, which makes combinations fail; for Sheridan's main body would be always under his hand for a change of assignments. In fact, all inci-

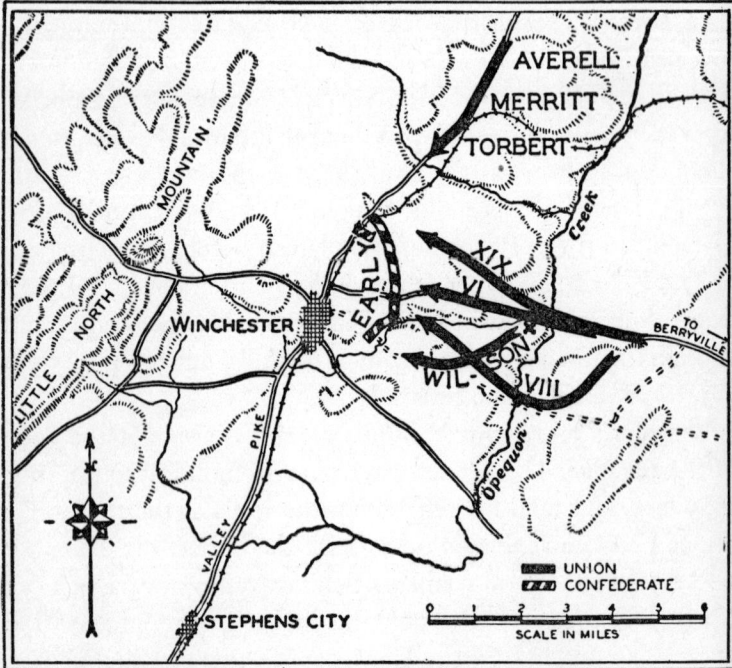

Winchester—Sheridan's Attack Plan

dents were provided against but the one that occurred after Wilson went galloping up the ravine with the first false dawn behind him, and, dismounting his men, stormed the fort. General Wright, that capable but formal soldier, marched on behind Wilson to deliver a surprise attack, with his full equipment of ambulances, wagons, and baggage following the infantry. With breakdowns and bunchings this transport jammed the road through the ravine; the XIX Corps could neither pass nor speed up. It was already noon and the VI engaging the whole Rebel army in a fire fight of the most murderous character when Sheridan in person discovered what was wrong, ordered the teamsters to "get those damned wagons into the ditch," and brought the XIX Corps to the field.

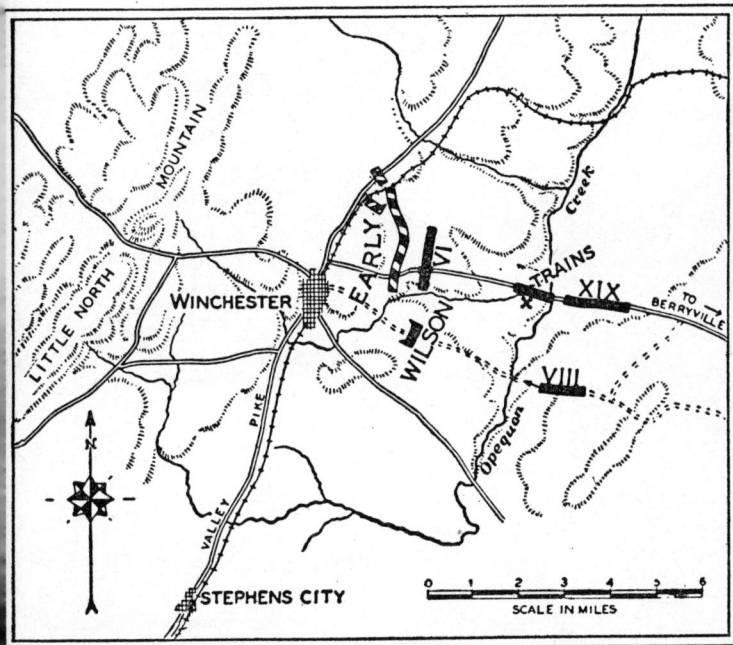

Winchester—The Plan Miscarries

Now it was too late for them to oblique onto the Confederate left. Early had every man up; as the XIX Corps began to reach the field, he flung forward a storming column under his best officer, Rodes, against the right of the VI. One of Wright's brigades went; the attack rushed on till it was halted by a battery of heroes from Maine, who stayed to shoot things out—unsupported artillery against foot. They gained time enough for the XIX to reach the line, marching and firing across the Rebel front, both sides suffering heavily in that open ground where there had been no time to take cover—suffering so much that by one o'clock the battle had sunk to a lull along parallel lines.

But one o'clock brought Crook and his VIII Corps. Boldly changing plans in the middle of action, Sheridan switched it

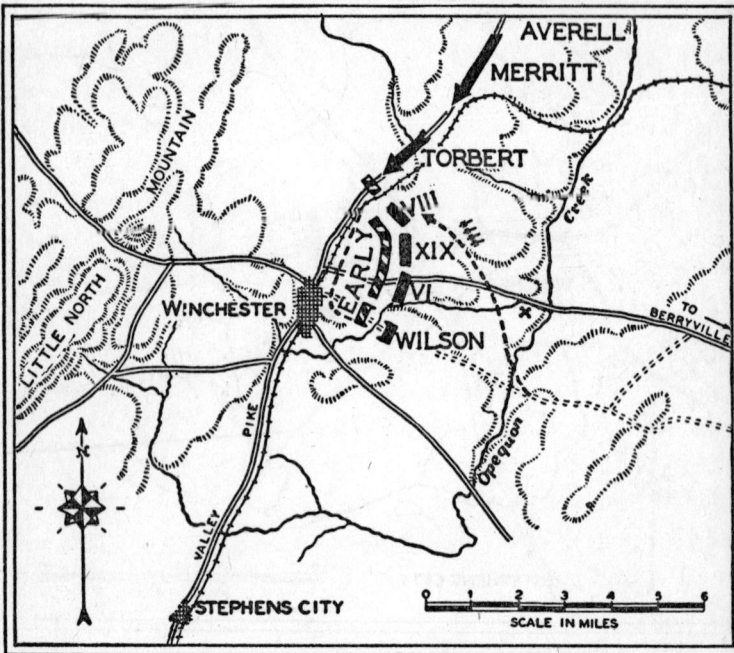

Winchester—Situation at 4:30 P.M.

across the rear of his front around the foot of the plateau to the right of the XIX, through the hills. Crook got his artillery onto a commanding eminence from which it would enfilade the Rebel line. At three he delivered the attack meant for Emory, under cover of the sudden surprise fire from these guns. Among the Confederates Gordon's division was broken and driven in, the XIX and VI Corps took up the forward movement, and it was only some distance back that Early managed to re-establish a right-angled line at half past four.

And now he had found himself in still deeper trouble. Young Wilson had gotten his cavalry division into the saddle again after Wright took over the fort from him in the morning. All day now he had been circling through open ground south of Winchester, great masses of horsemen in full view but beyond gun range of Early's men, reaching for their strategic flank. In the fog of war, where decisions must be based on a glance, Early assumed that this was the whole Union cavalry force. He switched his own cavalry to fend it off, had nothing left to cover the left flank that was floating on air in the Valley turnpike when just at half past four Torbert came riding in at the head of five thousand horsemen.

As they appeared, the Union men set up a whoop. Crook charged, the Confederate line was carried away. "It was sad, humiliating, disgusting; I never saw our men in such panic before," wrote a Confederate officer who was in the wild rout that went tumbling through Winchester in the fading light. "God bless you," telegraphed Lincoln to Sheridan; for a moment all the voices of politics were stilled as this morning star of victory rose in the North, the brighter because it shone on the Valley, Stonewall Jackson's Valley, the Rebels' great road of war.

That night Sheridan sent his tired happy men to early rest. Next morning he had them on the roads with day. At Strasburg, where the Massanutton chain juts forth to split the Valley into twin tunnels, Early had taken his stand. The eastern half of this double valley has bad roads and few from here south. Against an army it is necessary only to watch the other gap, and right across this, behind Strasburg, cuts a deep gorge whose rocky sides are ill work for even an unarmed man to climb, its western beginning being back among the folds of Little North Mountain. Early held a promontory on the far side of this gorge, called Fisher's Hill, and thought the position so strong that he sent his gun limbers to the rear.

On the night of September 20, Sheridan was already in Strasburg and had formed his plan of attack. As the Union troops filed in that evening the VI and XIX Corps were brought up with much parade and skirmishing to take position facing Fisher's Hill across the gorge. The VIII Corps, last in line on the roads, by Sheridan's order delayed its arrival, then came by a long circuit, concealed behind hills from the Confederate signal stations on the Massanuttons. Crook did not join the other corps, but made for the slopes of Little North Mountain. It is all forest there; the VIII men kept well back among the trees, scrambling all day of the 21st and 22nd among the slopes and around peaks till they reached a position, still in woods, behind the Confederate left rear. Even their weapons were wrapped in rags to hide the gleam and clang.

Along the side of Little North Mountain, past the front where Crook's men lay concealed, runs a narrow road. Well back on it Averell's cavalry division was massed to draw the Confederate left as far forward as possible, and to ride in behind Crook after he had delivered his blow. Torbert meanwhile, with the divisions of Merritt and Wilson, was hurried forward up the road of the eastern valley through Luray, a forty-mile march which only cavalry could make at speed. He was to get across the Massanuttons where they flattened at their lower end, seize New Market in Early's rear, intrench it, and hold there. This march was the reason for delaying the main attack; Sheridan meant to make a clean sweep.

By evening of September 22 the cavalry had been given three days for its forty miles. The day had been spent in inconclusive skirmishing and artillery discharges around Fisher's Hill. The Rebels were gathering round their campfires for supper in very good heart when the sun went down. It was a signal; through the long shadows that stalked across the

Valley, eleven thousand men of Crook's command dropped from heaven on the rear of the Confederate line. A shout went up, "We are flanked!" They broke, then began to run. The VI Corps took up the charge, scrambling across the wall-like

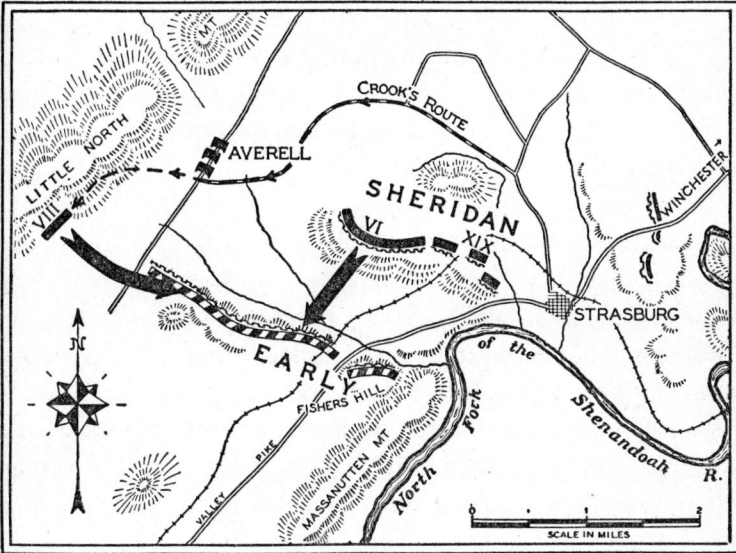

Fisher's Hill

ravine, with Sheridan in the middle of them, shouting "Forward everything! Don't stop! Go on!" whenever anyone asked him for instructions. Everything went forward; in the brief space between sundown and dark Early was driven in rout with the loss of part of his artillery and a big haul of prisoners.

The verdict of Winchester was confirmed. The North went wild with delight, and hundred-gun salutes were fired from every military post, but to Sheridan it was his most unsatisfactory battle. He had planned for destruction; he got only victory. Down the Luray Valley Torbert had encountered an insignificant Confederate force in an entrenched position. He was a good officer, but an infantryman warmed over into a trooper of the old style; though he had seen it at the Wilderness, the new tactic of cavalry charging on foot meant nothing to him. He kept his men in the saddle, uselessly jigging around, till the opportunity passed. At Fisher's Hill itself Averell committed an even worse fault. He waited respectfully for the infantry to clear the road ahead of him, and when they had not entirely done so by dark he went into camp. Sheridan instantly relieved him and gave the division to Custer.

Early, meanwhile, was given no chance to rally. The infantry pursuit held so hot to his heels he was driven to the limits of the Valley. Washington, supported by Grant, wanted Sheridan to follow on and make a campaign against the rear of Richmond, but the latter turned this idea down—it meant long communication lines without any railroad support. Through the next three weeks, therefore, he moved slowly back north, burning out the ripe grain, driving off animals, and answering all protests by the bland statement that loyal citizens could bring claims against the Federal government.

VIII

His operations had caused as much consternation in the Confederacy as delight in the North. It was impossible to repair the physical damage the Army of the Shenandoah had caused, but for the moment this was less important than the question of morale to Lee and the Confederate high command. Desertions were rising at an alarming rate; the men needed the stimulus of a spectacular victory, preferably one that would severely punish Sheridan, since his was the only one of the Union armies that had gained clean-cut wins in offensive

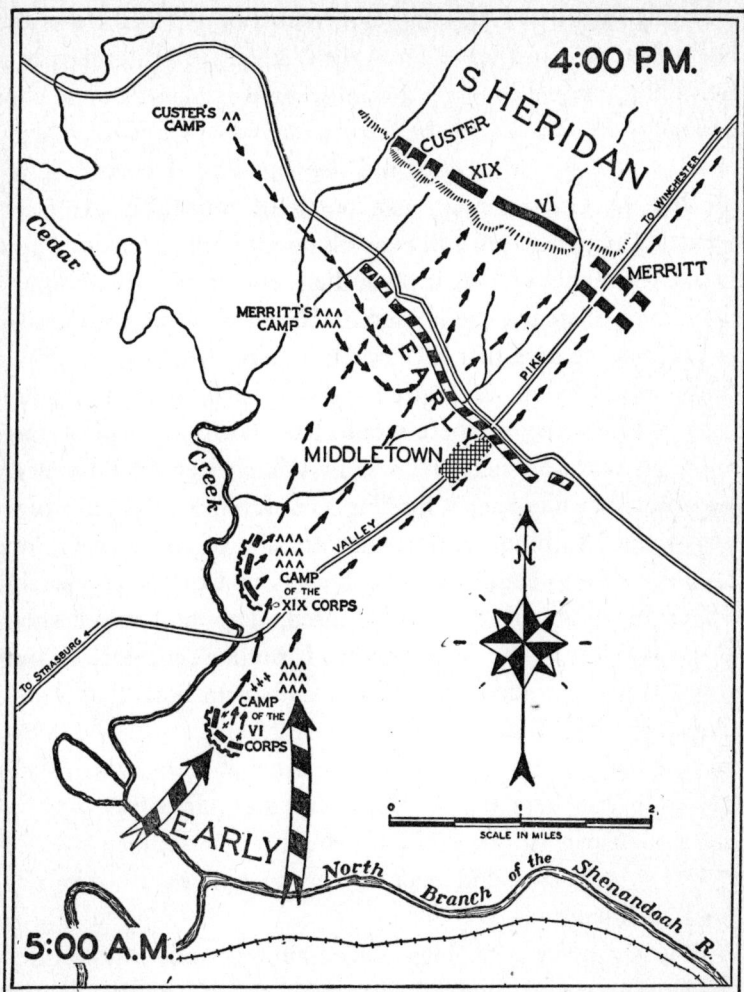

4:00 P.M.

SHERIDAN

CUSTER'S CAMP

CUSTER

XIX

VI

To Winchester

MERRITT

MERRITT'S CAMP

EARLY

PIKE

Cedar

MIDDLETOWN

Creek

VALLEY

CAMP OF THE XIX CORPS

N

To Strasburg

CAMP OF THE VI CORPS

EARLY

SCALE IN MILES
0   1   2

North Branch of the Shenandoah R.

5:00 A.M.

Cedar Creek

battle. Moreover, his work in the Valley was done; the Confederacy was not ignorant of the reports that the bulk of his forces would be returned to Petersburg.

· 151 ·

It was thus that Lee came to detach Longstreet's corps to Early for one more drive down the Valley, the last and greatest. They made a long, fast march. At half past three in the morning of October 19 they were on high hills from which they could look down into the sleeping Union camps along the line of Cedar Creek, just north of Strasburg. At four o'clock a clinging mist hid everything a hundred yards away; at five the Rebel yell went up and an attack from three directions at once struck the horseshoe circuit of Union camps.

We may be sure that if Sheridan himself had been in those camps, with his uncanny gift for discovering an enemy's purpose and movements, there would have been no surprise. But Sheridan was not there; he was in Winchester (not twenty, but fourteen miles back), holding a conference with some bigwigs from Washington. The first division of the VIII Corps, caught in their beds, was swept away, partly taken, partly driven in flight, all its guns captured, without firing a shot. What was left of the corps tried to form line on the XIX, but was taken simultaneously in front and from both flanks and likewise driven into rout without any resistance. The XIX, taken in reverse by infantry, cannonaded in front by the captured guns of the VIII, lasted less than an hour before dissolving, all but part of one division, which fell in with the VI and some of the cavalry and made a stand on a hill overlooking the road, well back.

It was a hasty assemblage, ill-organized, only the cavalry thoroughly sound—which had camped so far from the foot as to be outside the circle of the Rebel attack. Early might have swept it away, but his tired, hungry men could not be torn from the luxurious plunder of the Union camps. At nine in the morning, he got enough of them together to form line of battle and attack Wright, who retreated slowly, in pretty order, swinging out Torbert on his left in a movement that held so much menace that for the time being Early gave up the notion of driving home.

At eleven the Confederate leader had his men in hand and could try again. He came on all along the line, orders had been given for the Union force, the small surviving Union force, to fall back once more, when the discouraged and beaten soldiers heard, far in the rear, that unbelievable and intoxicating music—the cheers of Cedar Creek.

As they stared at each other in amazement, the distant murmur swelled and swelled to a roar. In a few moments more men wearing the Maltese cross of the XIX Corps and the star of the VIII were joining them, not in order, but falling in under any standards or officers they could find. With them came Sheridan. He had mounted his horse at the shock of distant guns early in the morning, riding toward the south until he met the first group of fugitives, whom he turned into a provost's guard by forming them across the road. "Turn around, boys, we're going back," said he. The provost's guard grew to the strength of a company, a regiment, a division, a corps, shouting "Here's Phil Sheridan; we're going back!" and, according to one witness, "throwing up their caps, leaping and dancing in wildest glee" as they hurried back to the battle.

"Where's the VI Corps?" asked Sheridan as he approached the front. There was nothing wrong with that formation; Wright had just stopped Early's last push, was all in line, with Custer champing the bit on one flank, asking every five minutes for permission to go, the other two cavalry divisions on Wright's left along the road, and such guns as had been saved with them. Early, upset by this bold countenance on the part of an army that ought to be in flight, and still more upset by the presence of so much cavalry—his own was weak and had fought badly—was beginning to think of defense. He formed a new line, along walls and rail breastworks, carrying it out left and right to bring infantry opposite those menacing clouds of horse.

While he was doing it Sheridan rode the front of the Union formations from one flank to the other, swinging his old blue campaign cap and shouting, "We're all right. We'll whip them yet."

It would be near four o'clock when he reached the extreme right of the line and there noticed how thin the successive prolongations had made Early's line. There had been time now to get the returned fugitives into some semblance of organization; Sheridan swung them forward in a general attack. It is inaccurate to say that it broke through anywhere; the whole Confederate line rolled right away before that attack, with Sheridan everywhere, urging his men to "Run! Go after them!"

"We can't run, we're all tuckered out," cried a private at him and drew the reply:

"If you can't run, then shoot and holler. We've got the goddamndest twist on them you ever saw."

They kept them going. The overpowering Union cavalry smothered Early's attempts to rally. They recaptured the Union guns that had been taken in the morning; they captured all Early's artillery; all his ambulances; his ammunition wagons, his transport of every kind, and 1,500 prisoners to balance the 1,400 they themselves had lost in the morning. Early went flying up the Valley in such shape that his corps had to be completely reorganized before it could take its place in Lee's lines, and the Shenandoah was out of the war.

The news arrived north with that of the capture of Atlanta. "Sheridan and Sherman have knocked the bottom out of the Copperheads," remarked Horace Greeley—correctly. For Democratic candidate McClellan was forced to repudiate his party's platform declaring the war a failure, and the elections went Lincoln by so large a majority as to constitute *carte blanche* to the President.

IX

Latrine rumor had set the date of the opening of the 1865 campaign for March 29. The day broke cold, wet, and cheerless over the Cavalry Corps, Army of the Potomac, which had done little but outpost duty since Sheridan left last fall. Gregg, whom the men adored, had resigned; Wilson had gone to the West: they did not know the leaders—and it seemed that the war of siege and thickets in which they were now tangled would never end. But that morning a bugle blew sourly through the damp; they saw a guidon half lift and behind there came riding down the line a skinny little man on a big black horse. Little Phil was back; the men cheered and passed the word that things would be humming now.

They were right. For days now Little Phil had been pacing the floor at headquarters conferences, replying to every argument with, "I tell you I'm ready now to strike out and smash them up. Let me go!" He had permission for that date. Before noon the whole corps, now 13,000 strong, was moving through the wet spring woods in the walking columns that meant a long pull with a hard fight at the end of it.

Nominally, it was to be a cavalry slash at Confederate communications—Sheridan's orders were effectively to break the railroads that fed Lee—but actually the assignment was different, reflecting a subtle change in the status of both corps and commander. In the corps it was marked by the fact that only one of the three division leaders was now of the cavalry service—Custer, who had been brought up under Buford, and to the front under Sheridan himself. The others were led by a pair of infantrymen—Devin, Crook. And still more marked was the fact that now the whole corps was armed with repeating rifles and accompanied by that lavish equipment of artillery Sheridan had asked the year before—more artillery in proportion than the infantry itself had.

Obviously, this signified the triumph of Sheridan's theory of cavalry over Meade's. But this is not all. As a subordinate leader whose ideas had gained preference over those of his nominal chief, his position was somewhat anomalous. This anomaly was reflected both in his title, which was "Commander in Chief of the Army of the Shenandoah, serving with the Army of the Potomac," and his assignment in this opening campaign.

For the drive he headed was only nominally against the Rebel railroads. As Grant instructed Sheridan before the move began, the true purpose was to make Lee come out of his trenches and fight. If, after Sheridan had reached the railroad lines, the Confederates threw against him more forces than he could handle, good—he could use his mobility to dodge them and either swing back to the main army, or turn south and hook up with Sherman, who was now thundering through the Carolinas. Meanwhile Grant would take Richmond; for the detachment of a force big enough to handle Sheridan would leave Lee's lines unable to resist assault. If Lee divined the presence of the cavalry corps and opposed it with strong forces before it reached the railroads, good again—Sheridan was to call to his aid whatever infantry corps he found nearest, assume command of it, and fight the big battle right there, under his own direction.

That there would always be one or more infantry corps near enough to help Sheridan was provided for by the remainder of the army orders for the movement. Sheridan's corps was to cross the north-south Hatcher's Run, headed west, then swing north in a vast half-right wheel. Inside his movement, making the same wheel through a narrow circle, Warren's V Corps was to march; and inside Warren, through a circle still narrower, Humphreys with the II Corps.

In effect, then, Sheridan was given a semi-independent command as leader of a vanguard, with as many troops as he needed under his orders. In effect also, the last distinction between cavalry and infantry was abolished except during the period of the approach march. Sheridan's own corps was merely placed at the extreme wing of the turning movement because, of all the corps, it had the greatest strategic mobility, and of all the generals, he had the greatest skill at using speed.

On the afternoon of March 29, it rained pitchforks and nigger babies, continuing through the night and the next day. The country southwest of Richmond is low-lying, densely wooded, quaggy, cut by wide, slow streams that give poor drainage. Under the pounding rain roads became impassable to wheels unless corduroyed, an important element in the military situation. It enabled the Confederates to gain utmost advantage from their South Side Railroad, running laterally behind the front of operations, and unaffected by the weather.

On the 27th, Lee had already learned of the cavalry concentration behind the extreme Union left, and realizing that it portended a raid around his army—though, it seems, he did not grasp the ultimate purpose of the movement—he planned to use his superiority in communications to drive a wedge between Sheridan and the main Federal army, smashing the former.

The night of the 29th therefore saw General Fitz Lee arrive at Five Forks with all the cavalry of the Rebel army. Next morning he was joined there by Pickett, who was to have charge of the operation, and who had brought two infantry divisions with their guns down the railroad. At the same time the Confederate forces in the trenches executed a general slide rightward along their lines, setting free part of A. P. Hill's corps and all of Anderson's for a surprise attack. This blow was to strike in on the extreme left flank of the Union infantry, where their trenches ended near the junction of White Oak Road and Boydton Road, rolling their line up eastward and away from Sheridan.

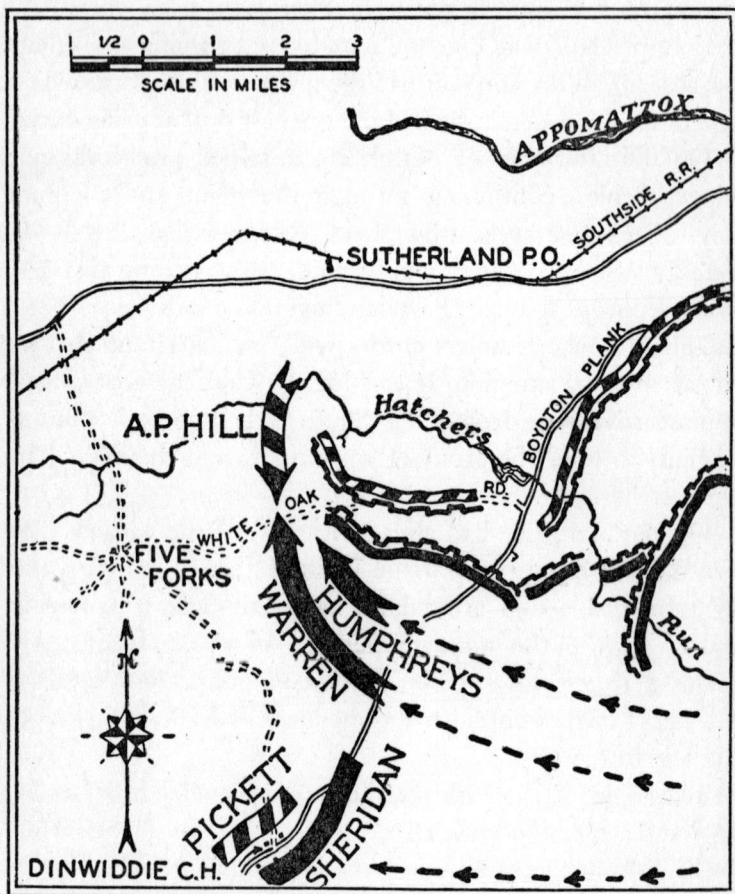

Five Forks—the Move to Position

March 30 was a day of obscure skirmishings in the woods under the rains, Devin's division of Sheridan making contact with Pickett's cavalry vanguard near Five Forks. The same rain and the configuration of the roads delayed the march of Warren's V Corps and forced it in toward Humphreys of the II Corps, at the same time keeping Warren to a narrow front. When A. P. Hill's attack developed on the morning of the 31st it therefore struck the head of a deep column instead of the flank of a line. Warren's leading division was indeed driven in, but the defense impacted along the line of a stream, At noon Hill was stopped; in the afternoon help from Humphreys joined Warren and he counterattacked so vigorously that by afternoon Hill had lost more than his gains and was clinging for dear life to his field works, so lamed as to be unable to take more than a defensive part thenceforth.

Southwest of this battle Pickett had caught Sheridan's columns coming along the several roads into which they had been forced by the rains. With artillery and concentration on his side (Sheridan's guns had been delayed when he pushed on with the horse), he drove the Union cavalry back to Dinwiddie Court House. But here, about the time Warren finished his job on A. P. Hill, Sheridan got all his men assembled in trenches and Pickett also was brought to a standstill.

At this point Sheridan's mission was already a success. Off to the east Grant was asking Meade whether he thought Lee had not taken enough men from his lines to make the final assault of Petersburg possible and he was answering "Yes." But Sheridan was not thinking in terms of the general success alone. He was filled with the spirit of the offensive; when he learned at five o'clock of Warren's success against Hill, he instantly perceived an opportunity to destroy Pickett. His own position, facing a little west of north, meant that the Rebels facing him were nearly east-west, with Warren's corps far in behind their left rear, already across the direct communications between Pickett and Hill. Warren had dealt Hill so rude a stroke as to eliminate him for the time being;

he was therefore free. If now, during the night, he swooped on Pickett's rear with his three divisions—

Sheridan asked for the move. Far in the rear Grant and Meade, reports and maps in hand, discovered the same opportunity and sent Warren orders for the same move. But Warren, always a perfectionist, only replied by telegrams suggesting different routes of march, suggesting that a bridge be built, suggesting a dozen minor improvements in the plan, and while he wrote carefully worded dispatches the night passed. Pickett's scouts brought him word of the danger he was in. At daybreak he drew in his horns, and Sheridan was in no good mood over the missed opportunity as he followed up the retreat.

But now, on the morning of April 1, the weather conditions that had fought for the Confederates shifted their allegiance. Pickett's men had come with trains and guns; even were these sacrificed they could hardly get away from Sheridan's lighter-moving cavalry along the foundered roads. Pickett had to stand for a fight. He chose a position at Five Forks, where some old trenches, hastily improved, gave him chances for defense. His front was a rough crescent covering the road junction, facing south and with the left flank covered by a switch.

Sheridan, as usual in possession of complete accurate information about the enemy, had been following close with his 13,000. His orders brought Warren on the scene from the right and at one o'clock the position solidified. Custer was facing the right flank of Pickett's trench line, Devin was spread along its front. Both were dismounted, along the edge of woods, with instructions to offer constant threats of attack, with the exception of one brigade of Custer's command, which was kept in the saddle working westward, as though to attempt something against Pickett's right wing, and thus attracting Fitz Lee's cavalry to the defense of that flank.

This left Pickett with only that re-entrant angle of trench to cover his left, and against this Sheridan designed to put in the whole of Warren's corps, supported on its right by the independent cavalry division of Mackenzie, which Grant had speeded forward. The attack was to be an oblique with a tremendously reinforced right wing, to throw the Confederates away from their main army. Of Warren's three divisions, that of Ayres, the weakest, was deployed to come against the Five Forks lines from the southwest, linking up with Devin on its left and engaging the attention of the Rebels at the angle. Crawford, the heaviest of the three divisions, would dress on Ayres, slide past the end of the refused angle of trench, and cut around to take the line in reverse. Griffin, with the third division, was to follow Crawford in column, lending intolerable weight to his push, Mackenzie to ride beyond Crawford and cut the Rebel retreat.

But Warren drew his sketch for the operation wrongly, placing the limit of Pickett's trench line too far east. The consequence was that Crawford, with Griffin following, missed it entirely. Ayres, with whom was Sheridan himself, suddenly received an intense fire of musketry from his left, where his troops caught the blast from the angle.

Sheridan himself rode to the skirmish line, helping Ayres half-wheel the division leftward, bringing up the reserve brigade to prolong the line out to the right. His staff rode off to keep Crawford and Griffin going on the line they had already taken, striking far around behind, across the direction of the Rebel retreat. Little Phil labored like a demon, got everything into position, carried two regiments out till they lapped round Pickett's trench line, and then personally led a whirlwind charge, riding his big black horse with a guidon in his hand. Pickett's flank burst; Devin swung in as the attack reached his front and the Confederate line was rolled up. Griffin and part of Crawford arrived from the woods to destroy the last rally; Pickett lost 4,500 prisoners, all his guns, most of his trains, and Lee's striking force, the

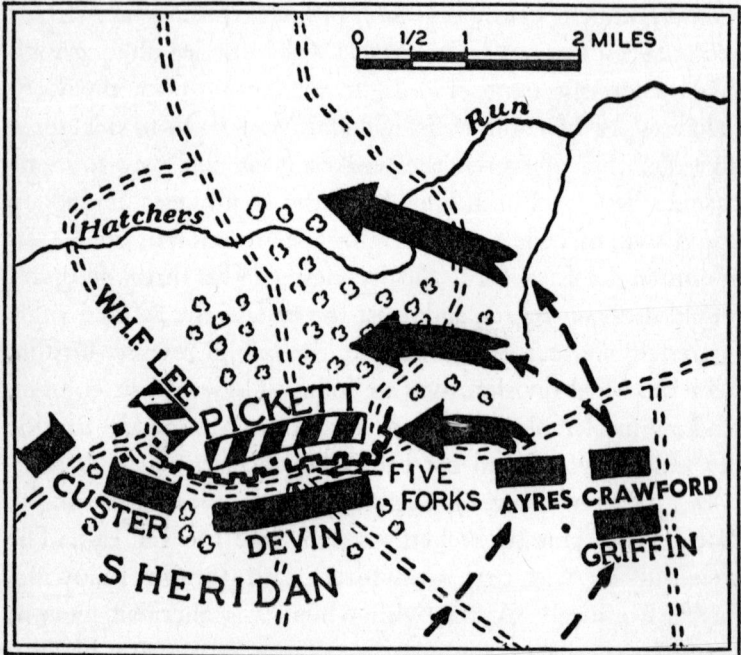

Five Forks—the Attack

only one he had for offensive operations, was destroyed.

Where was Warren while this was going on? He had been near when Ayres was struck by the first flanking fire. When that broke out he rode off into the forest to change the direction of divisions Crawford and Griffin, but in the tangle of woods missed them too, and did not again reach the front till it was all over but the pursuit. There was one thing Little Phil Sheridan could never forgive in any man— unwillingness to get to the scene of action. Now Warren had twice in two days been missing when he was most wanted. Sheridan peremptorily removed the hero of Little Round Top and gave his corps to Griffin.

X

Now the lion of the South was wounded to death, no more men left for any offensive blow, and along the Petersburg lines Wright and Parke attacking him. They won a lodgment, a trench, a whole line of trenches, they were in during that twilight when Pickett's last stand before Sheridan so disastrously broke. Next morning Jefferson Davis was summoned from church to flight; another morning and Weitzel's men of the XXV Corps were marching into Richmond under smoky pillars of destruction.

The pursuit started that April 3, Sheridan leading, with the cavalry and V Corps under his orders, Meade following fast with the II and VI Corps, and Grant bringing up the rest of the army. Lee's assembly point was Amelia Court House. Both Grant and Sheridan guessed it would be near there. The moment the Petersburg lines were won Sheridan had been rushed forward to get across the Danville Railroad between Jetersville and Burke's Junction. He reached position on April 4, before Lee was fully assembled. The same night the V Corps was entrenched at Burke's Junction and one of Crook's brigades lashed out along the line of the South Side Railroad toward Farmville. It was this brigade that caught and burned Lee's headquarters train the next morning, where it had been sent on ahead of the flying army.

Meade did not arrive ahead of the other two Union corps till the 5th. Lee got his men fully in hand that day, and though the troops were dog-tired and starving, dared not stay with Sheridan's formidable force already seizing positions along the only line of retirement now left open. He marched by night, in several columns with the trains north of them and to their right—a change from his original plan, which had been to send the trains ahead, clearing the roads—a change forced by Sheridan.

In the morning Meade went toward Amelia Court House in attack formation and found Lee gone. But Humphreys of the II Corps caught the tail of one Rebel column and his cannonading helped turn the whole army in the right direction. Besides, Sheridan, reaching far north on the extreme left wing of the Federal army, had already attained so great a distance that the Confederate columns had been unduly crowded toward their right, in on their own trains. This slowed them up badly. Crook's cavalry division was granted time to slip between two of the formations and attack trains so energetically that Anderson's Confederate Corps had to stop and form line of battle to drive Crook off, just west of Sailor's Creek.

This halt also stopped Ewell, who was behind Anderson on the roads; Wright's VI Corps caught up the latter and forced him to stand on the banks of Sailor's Creek. Meanwhile Sheridan brought the rest of his division up to help Crook hold Anderson's force. The latter was now in a line of hasty field-works; Sheridan fronted it with all his corps but Crook, who was shifted round Anderson's front to close the only road of retreat. Ewell sent to Anderson, proposing they unite and drive this cavalry off, but before either general could do anything about it, Wright's artillery opened and at the same moment Crook led a dismounted charge into Anderson's flank and rear.

Anderson was blown right away, with half his command taken prisoner, and the advance rushed on to surprise Ewell, who surrendered with what was left of his corps before evening. The trains all went, too. But though Lee had lost nearly half the men he had on March 29, he had now gained a lead on the whole Union army with the rest.

However, there was still Sheridan; there was always Sheridan in this campaign, reaping the fruit he had planted at Yellow Tavern, when the Confederate cavalry service was struck down forever. As soon as the fighting round Sailor's Creek was over, he turned southwest, spending his mobility without stint to get round the Confederate column toward Lynchburg. Behind Sheridan the V Corps was moving west on the roads south of Appomattox River, and south of the V Corps, Ord with the XXV Corps had marched far and fast, taking no part in the move toward Amelia Court House.

On April 7, while Humphrey's II Corps was pecking at Lee's rear guard near Farmville and the Appomattox crossing, Sheridan was gaining, going right past Lee to the south. On April 8, in the morning, he turned north to Appomattox Court House. There he caught Lee's trainloads of provisions, and the poor Rebels went to hungry beds that night. Next morning Fitz Lee and Gordon were appointed to fray a passage through Sheridan. They tried; there were a few shots fired and some little movement, but for once the greatest fighting leader of the Union did not fight. Sheridan's cavalry merely moved right and left like a parting curtain, and allowed the Confederates to see the solid lines of Ord, rank on rank.

"Then there is nothing left to do but go and see General Grant," said Lee.

XI

After the war Grant, who had come to lean on Sheridan as his man of all work as he had leaned on Sherman in the west, remarked that Little Phil was the one man he could trust to lead an expedition without going off on a private war of his own. "I rank him with Napoleon, Frederick, and the great commanders of history."

At the time there seems to have been general agreement, but since then Sheridan's fame has been somewhat obscured by that of Sherman and of Grant himself. Partly, this is no doubt due to what may be called the atmosphere of modern military thinking. The method of Grant and Sherman, strategic attack combined with caution in the tactical field, is apparently more in accord with modern conditions of war than Sheridan's free offensive.

Sectional feeling also plays an appreciable if minor part in the relative decline of Sheridan's renown. In New England, where the best and most numerous studies of the Civil War have been written during the last generation, Sheridan has always been seven kinds of a scoundrel for removing the chivalrous Warren in the very hour of victory. Grant's own reason for his appreciation of Sheridan furnishes another partial clue—Little Phil did not go off on private wars. To anyone reading the orders he received, with a record of subsequent events, his contribution is apt to appear purely executive. His full influence does not develop till one examines the part he played in having the orders written, as well as the documents themselves.

Yet in the long run, it is Sheridan's very success that has deprived him of more complete appreciation. The eye of the beholder becomes irresistibly fixed on the spectacle of the mad scramble up Missionary Ridge, the ride from Winchester, and the rally at Cedar Creek, the little man jumping his horse over the barricade at Five Forks. It makes him look like a leader of happy improvisations, of whom it could be said, as of Logan: "Everything he did on the spur of the moment and in the heat of battle was sure to be right; everything he did on mature reflection was wrong."

This would not be too heavy an accusation, even if it were true. No nation and no army were ever in more need of such moral stimulus as brilliant improvisation can supply than the United States and its forces in the summer of 1864. No man was better fitted to supply that stimulus than Sheridan, who showed a gift of arousing enthusiasms paralleled in American history only by Jacob Brown.

But the accusation is not true. We should not let the fact that none of Sheridan's great battles was fought out exactly as planned blind us to the other fact that he could plan a battle as well as fight one. Something nearly always happens to disturb battle plans—the obstinate refusal of the enemy to behave as expected, if nothing else. The rare thing about Sheridan, the quailty that lifts him to several thousand feet altitude above the ordinary commander, was the ability to recognize in the midst of action that a change of plan was necessary. At Winchester he planned to break down one flank; it became impossible, but he instantly and successfully broke down the opposite wing. At Five Forks the failure of his original plan only led him into another, far better.

It is this quality of flexibility of mind, of being able to do anything and everything, that makes Sheridan difficult to classify or even to appraise. He had no military specialty, like Thomas' counterattacks, or Stonewall Jackson's flank sweeps or Sherman's clutch-and-circle. He did whatever the occasion required. At Perryville he counterattacked; he entrenched at Halltown, cautiously; at Missionary Ridge he was bold to the point of recklessness; worked a surprise attack at Boonville; ordered two gigantic sweeps at Fisher's Hill, and a frontal assault at Winchester. The limits of his talent were never reached; perhaps there were none.

Grant apparently thought so, and if his testimony be thought biased by association, one need only turn to the archives of the French Empire. There is a report there from Marshal MacMahon, a not unqualified judge, dating from 1866, when Sheridan went to the Texas border with an army corps to help the French make up their minds to clear out of Mexico. "It might be worth making a fight," says this report in substance, "if Grant were their commander. But not against this man."

This is not the kind of opinion one expresses with regard to a mere improviser, and the more one studies Sheridan's career, the clearer it becomes that behind his improvisation there was steady, careful planning, based on intimate knowledge both of the enemy and of geographical conditions. It is not the type of planning that aims to eliminate chance, but to leave sufficient reserves of force to overcome chance.

Even Cedar Creek, the least planned of Sheridan's battles, the one in which he was planned against, corresponds to this rule. His camping arrangement placed the cavalry so far from the infantry during the night that the two camps could not be comprehended in the same attack. That cavalry formed the reserve in a sense, when he began the battle again in the afternoon. It won the fight, though the infantry did the physical work, handled the contacts. For it was the threat of the cavalry that prolonged and thinned Early's lines in preparation for the infantry action, as the threat of cavalry paralyzed Pickett in preparation for infantry attacks at Five Forks, as the threat of cavalry halted Anderson and Ewell in preparation for infantry attack at Sailor's Creek.

In fact, it is this constant use of the mobile force as a threat that more than anything else characterizes Sheridan's technique and perhaps holds the key to the recovery of the lost offensive by armies of the future. Sheridan's cavalry as cavalry, mounted, charged into the thick of a fight just three times—at Boonville and Winchester (Torbert's), where the charges came altogether as surprises, and at Yellow Tavern, where the horsemen were operating against an enemy also in the saddle, who had lost momentum. In the rest of Sheridan's campaigns cavalry merely threatened to charge, and by this threat dislocated the enemy mentally and physically, induced him to alter his dispositions and prepared the way for the decisive advance of the infantry. This happened at Cedar Creek, Winchester, Five Forks, even in a sense at Fisher's Hill, where Early kept watching Averell. At Sailor's Creek alone was the threat made good—but then by cavalry metamorphosed into foot.

Yet when all is said and done these are details of something one is not permitted to examine in detail. There are no details of Sheridan's career. It is one, and that one inimitable, from the day he tried to spit a cadet sergeant on a bayonet to the day when he ramped victoriously across the fields of Appomattox. Between the two he had won the greatest moral victories of the Civil War.

GEORGE H. THOMAS

The Rock of Chickamauga

I

THE ABILITY OF DEMOCRACY TO DEFEND ITSELF IN THE modern world, and so to survive, may be said to rest on the skill of its soldiers in handling counterattack. Any government indifferent to the wishes of its citizens can easily set up a military establishment that will guarantee it a series of victories against the best-equipped and most successful democracy—if for no other reason, because a powerful military establishment demands the sacrifice of normal ways of life from a greater proportion of citizens than are willing to undertake it except in the face of immediate danger.

The point has nothing to do with international morality. Democracy can be as aggressive as any other polity—as the Athenian democracy was against Syracuse or our own against Mexico. But even in such cases the people of a democracy regard military service as an interruption of the routine of life rather than as a part of it, and prepare for battle while battles are actually in progress. When democracy is itself the object of an attack, it is nearly always forced to achieve that passage from defense to offense which Napoleon described as the most difficult operation in war.

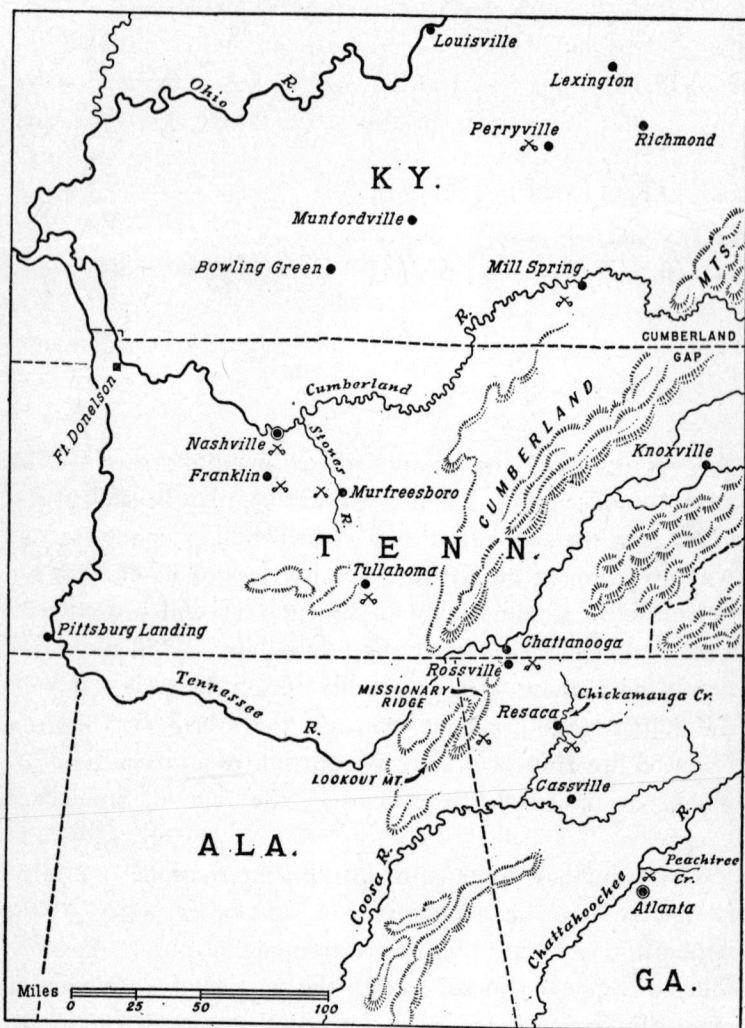

The Western Theatre—1862–63

But before the strategic counterattack can be undertaken, there must obviously be at some point a defensive victory achieved through tactical counterattack; before France is invaded, there must be an Alamein; Stalingrad is the indispensable preparation for the battle of Berlin; Foch's 1918 offensive develops out of Mangin's counterattack at the Second Marne. In fact, an examination of the history of two world wars will show that although the pure offensive achieved many spectacular victories, the battles which produced permanent decisions were those of counterattack.

This may be merely a reflection of the fact that both conflicts were won by the democracies, whose constitutional disposition toward counterattack as a form tends to make it part of the mental habit of their military leaders. Still it is a fact; and a fact which may have the other explanation that modern technology has outlawed the system of Napoleon in favor of one which looks toward striking the enemy at that moment when he is striving to gather dwindling resources for one more effort to drive home an offensive that has almost but not quite succeeded.

"It is those campaigns in America that we must study," said one of the most acute of German soldiers. Here, as in so many other cases, the American Civil War was the first modern conflict. It produced one man who, unconscious of and unconcerned with the long-range ideas with which he was dealing, worked out the correct answer through pure ratiocination, considering each problem as it arose in the light of its own surrounding conditions—after the manner of Nathanael Greene, three-quarters of a century before. A man ahead of his time is often neglected when the time comes, but it is still rather odd that so little attention should have been given to George H. Thomas, the old gray mare of the Union.

Partly this is no doubt due to the reputation for being a solitary which surrounded him from his first days at West

Point, and this in turn to the circumstances of his appointment, which came from the dynamic and bad-tempered Mr. Mason of Virginia. When young Thomas called to thank him: "No cadet from our district has ever yet graduated," said Mason. "If you do not, no more will be appointed and I never want to see your face again."

It is only necessary to add that the Thomas family valued its position and that Mr. Mason was a social and political lion of the type whose frown made flies tremble on the wall, to see why Thomas obtained and deserved the reputation of being a grind of the most stodgy sort. The fires were banked; they called him "Slow-trot Thomas" and observed only that he was deliberate in speech, in movement and reaction. The high grades he made in mathematics brought him an appointment to the 3rd Artillery on graduation.

Exactly a year later Thomas had a brevet for gallantry, gained in the Seminole War, for the personal capture of 28 braves. He is next heard of in Mexico, being mentioned three times in dispatches and receiving the brevet rank of captain for the handling of his battery at the battle of Monterey. At Buena Vista in February, 1847, he won the unprecedented honor of a third brevet rank—to major. "Without those guns we were lost," reported General Taylor.

The war was one in which volunteers and political generals received most of the credit, but the three brevets brought Thomas a considerable reputation within the service, and what was more important, the personal attention of that other notable West Pointer, Mr. Jefferson Davis. When the latter, as Secretary of War, organized that famous 2nd Cavalry regiment with the cream of the Southern-born officers (it has always been thought in anticipation of the irrepressible conflict), he summoned Thomas from duty at Fort Yuma to be one of the majors. The date was 1855; Thomas was attached to his regiment in Texas when the elections five years later turned the world upside down.

II

At the time, Major Thomas, coming through Louisville on leave, had been in a railroad accident and was lying in a hospital, whose resident surgeon told him he would probably never be able to walk again. The news that Virginia had seceded proved a specific; he staggered from bed, sought out a magistrate, and repeated his oath of allegiance to the United States of America. In the South they said later that his wife, a northern girl, influenced him to the step. She denied it, with the remark that any effort on her part to apply influence would have driven him in the opposite direction.

Perhaps this is true; the important point is that in repeating that oath of allegiance Thomas was taking the more difficult way. Secession was an accomplished fact and a fact in which the Buchanan government was appearing to acquiesce to a degree that would prove binding on the incoming administration. The general opinion was against the idea of a war. But war or not, Thomas was cutting himself off from his family, his friends, his home, all the associations that make life agreeable and comfortable. To Virginians he was a traitor; one little remark to an officer who said something about the effect on his feelings of breaking all the old ties shows how keenly he appreciated this. "I have had to educate myself not to feel," said Thomas, and going to his room, closed the door.

There were certainly no professional advantage to be gained by staying with the Union. Whatever reputation he possessed was in the service, in that tight little 2nd Cavalry circle of friends and associates who had learned there was a brain behind the glacis of slow movement and difficult speech. The colonel of that regiment was Albert Sidney

Johnston; its lieutenant-colonel, Robert E. Lee; the other majors were Hardee and Van Dorn. Twelve of its officers became generals in the Confederate service, and Thomas could certainly count on better treatment there than with the Union, which was fairly sure to suspect the loyalty of a Virginian.

Yet he believed his duty was to keep that earlier oath of allegiance and he "went North." The Confederacy might better have spared Lee; for it is possible to maintain that both the spiritual and the physical justification of the Southern system ultimately shattered on the Rock of Chickamauga. He showed it was possible to possess that special nobility of character which has always been so much admired in Lee, and yet be loyal to the Union; and in the strictly military field he posed an unanswerable question. One of the indirect but fundamental claims of Southern apologists has always been that the Confederacy was somehow better and finer because its generals achieved much without superior numbers like Grant, or superior mechanical equipment, like Sherman. The name of Thomas is seldom brought into these discussions—and it had better not be.

III

Shortly after the oath of allegiance Colonel George H. Thomas' sick-leave was revoked, and he was ordered to Carlisle Barracks to reorganize the 2nd Cavalry, the loyal members of which had just come north by boat.

He was found there by General Robert Patterson, a bee-keeping old militia keepsake from the Mexican war, who appointed him to command a brigade consisting of his own new regiment and three of Pennsylvania militia. The new colonel had barely time to set up his brigade organization and assemble a staff, before Patterson and his corps were ordered forward to cover the flank of McDowell's march on Richmond. The

Washington strategists (probably Scott had some hand in this though Secretary Cameron was the main operator) directed Patterson into the upper end of the Shenandoah Valley, presumably because a Confederate force was already operating there under General Joe Johnston.

Thomas protested the order and Patterson endorsed his protest on to Washington. If the corps crossed the Potomac at Leesburg, operating east of the mountain chain, he said, it would protect Washington quite as thoroughly as by a direct advance against Johnston. At the same time it would place the Pennsylvania corps where it could either strike in on the flank of the main Rebel army or cut the communications of Johnston's force by driving rapidly through one of the passes.

The plan was too bold for Cameron; "the venerable Patterson" moved into the Valley and followed Johnston's retreat in the manner to be expected from an aged bee-keeper and banker, with the result that the Confederates slipped away from him in time to show up on the plateau of Manassas and send McDowell flying from the First Bull Run.

Of course, a demand for official heads followed the loss of the battle, Patterson was obviously nominated for the role of sacrificial goat. The Virginian defended his general with vigor (it would be interesting to know on what grounds but all we have is the fact it was done), which caused the rivulet of suspicion round his own loyalty to widen into a pool, on the theory that no one but a traitor would defend an incompetent. Fifty-four men were promoted past Thomas to brigadier general. Indeed he might have remained a mere colonel for the rest of the war, but for the intervention of Major General Robert Anderson.

That hero of Sumter had just been appointed to the command in eastern Kentucky and Lincoln had told him it would be desirable to choose his four brigadiers from slave-state loyalists, because of the delicate political situation in the state. Anderson agreed and placed Thomas first on the list. Faint echoes of the towering row that followed come down to us; even Lincoln was doubtful about the Virginia colonel, but Anderson made his own acceptance conditional on that of Thomas. Since Anderson was too important to be spared, he got his man.

The new general went west in the fall of 1861, with orders to organize a division, and found everything at sixes and sevens in the camp. There was no mustering officer; he had to muster in most of his own privates. There being no quartermaster service, he had to offer his personal credit for necessary groceries. The place was full of politicians who entertained the unruly recruits with speeches every evening after colors, the proceedings always closing with the division shouting for various officers to come out and talk to them. On one occasion they called for Thomas. "Damn this speech-making!" he bellowed, then retired to his quarters for twenty-four hours; for, like that other testy Virginian, George Washington, he thought losing his temper as bad as losing a battle.

Anderson was replaced by Sherman and Sherman by Buell as the task of organization went forward. The Southern leaders had their plan now, drawn by Albert Sidney Johnston. The part calling for a defense line across central Kentucky is remarked in every history book, but not so familiar is the Confederate leader's intention of staging an invasion of the North around the right of the line, through the territory Thomas was covering. Thomas, however, was not thinking merely of covering this line; he submitted a plan for cutting through Cumberland Gap, marching down the valleys to Knoxville in Unionist eastern Tennessee, and then taking position facing northwest on the mountain slopes. It would flank the Rebel line across the west and place him astride their vital supply railroad from Nashville to Richmond; this would force the Confederates to attack against the natural bastions of the Cumberland Mountains. The Union itself was forced to attack these summits later and found it hard enough work, but—plan rejected: we cannot spare the men, they told Thomas.

The result was that Johnston got his defenses set up and pushed General Zollicoffer across the Cumberland River into eastern Kentucky, with orders to strike for Lexington and Louisville. Zollicoffer crossed the river without difficulty (the officer Thomas sent to the spot forgot to put out pickets!), entrenched a strong position on the north bank opposite Mill Springs, and began to feel his way forward.

It was the turn of the year, the weather was bad, and the roads in a mire, but Thomas moved out to stop Zollicoffer. Uncertain by which of two roads the Confederates would come, he did what he would not have done later—divided his forces, sending Colonel Schoepf with a strong detachment eastward down one road, while he took the other himself. A wide creek lay between him and his subordinate. When it came on to rain the afternoon of January 18, the stream swelled to spate. Zollicoffer, who had perfect information in that land of divided loyalties, came hurrying forward to knock Thomas out while the tumultuous creek kept his lieutenant from closing.

The Union general was posted near a place called Logan's Cross Roads, where a string of low hills was crossed by the road down which the Confederates were advancing. Most of the hills were scalped on top for farming, while the slopes and gullies were wooded. Thomas had two infantry regiments with a battery of artillery well forward at the southern edge of a clearing. A regiment of cavalry (Wolford's) was forward in the woods of the slope. These troops were dismounted and spread out in pickets so strong as to constitute patrols— an extremely odd tactical arrangement for 1862. The main-

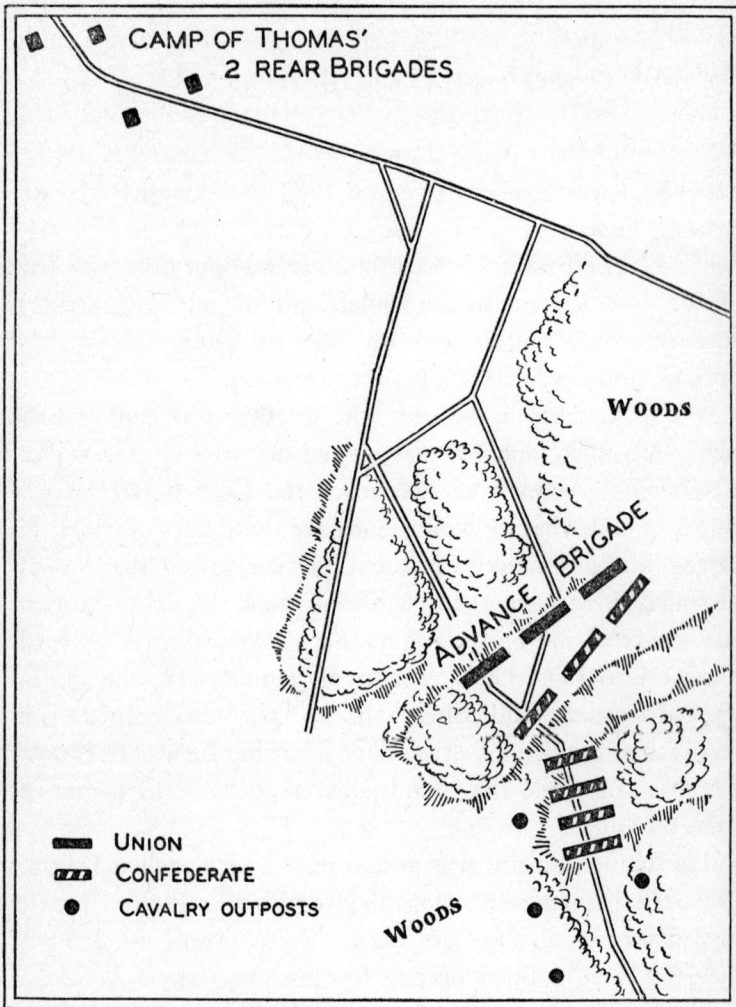

CAMP OF THOMAS'
2 REAR BRIGADES

WOODS

ADVANCE BRIGADE

WOODS

▭ UNION
▭ CONFEDERATE
● CAVALRY OUTPOSTS

Mill Spring—First Position

guard, two brigades, was back at the next hill with more artillery. The whole force aggregated perhaps 5,000 men; the Rebels, pushing toward them through dark and rain, were half again as many.

At six in the morning, still in road column, Zollicoffer struck Wolford's outposts. The cavalry, fighting dismounted, executed "fire and retire," slowing up the Rebel advance and forcing it into a deployment much cramped by the trees. Yet half-hearted as this deployment was, it took time; when the Rebels mounted to the clearing, the line of Thomas' advance brigade was already drawn across it, the rear regiments were hurrying up, and a messenger riding to call Schoepf in.

The Union line received Zollicoffer with a fire more noisy than damaging, and got better than it gave. The Confederates came swinging on into the clearing, extending toward their right, where the ground was clearer, to turn a flank. Both advance and extension were held up by Union fire, mud, the jam on the road, and the constant nagging of Wolford's men around the head of the column. Before the turning move was half complete, Thomas was on the field, riding around as conspicuous as Goliath of Gath. One of his brigades was up; this formed at an angle across the wing of the hopeful Confederate flanking body, flanked it in turn, and hurt it badly with a blaze of fire. A regiment of Minnesota lumbermen came up to sustain the center and their fire killed Zollicoffer. Just as the Rebel line began to shake under these blows, Thomas brought the 9th Ohio around behind his line of battle and threw it with the bayonet into the Confederate left flank, which had achieved almost no deployment.

The Rebels went to pieces. Thomas put his fresh troops (including Schoepf) onto their track with most of his artillery, which had not even unlimbered. Before twilight he was outside their lines at the entrenched camp of Mill Springs. There he directed the placing of his guns and shelled the place all night. In the morning he found it empty except for a few companies which surrendered.

"We were doing pretty well," said one of the captured officers, "till old man Thomas rose up in his stirrups and we heard him holler, 'Attention, Creation! By kingdoms, right wheel!' Then we knew the war was over." It was, for Zollicoffer's army; the casualties were only about 800, but the pursuit and night bombardment had been so relentless that the force was broken up, dissolved into stragglers, and could not get together again.

Mill Springs was more than the destruction of a minor Confederate force. In the North it was received like a gift of flowers—admirable but not important—but Albert Sidney Johnston, a man who ought to know, took it to heart. "If my right wing is broken as stated," he wrote to his president, "the country must be roused to make the greatest effort they will be called on to make during the contest. Our people do not comprehend the magnitude of the danger that threatens us." The shadow of what would follow the Chattanooga battles already lay across his mind. When Johnston found the reports of Zollicoffer's defeat not exaggerated, he made preparations to abandon the Kentucky line, even before Grant broke it again and for keeps at Donelson.

IV

After Grant's thrust, Thomas and his division were drawn into the general swing forward of Buell's army toward Pittsburg Landing. When Halleck came down to take over after the desperate battle at that point and kicked Grant upstairs into an anomalous post of second-in-command, he gave the latter's wing to Thomas. A coolness sprang up between Grant and Thomas over this, emanating apparently from neither man so much as from the staff officers of both, who felt there should be resentment and, without actually carrying tales, pushed advocacy to the irritation point. The two generals got on very well when they could talk to each other; it was only when they had to convey ideas through intermediaries that misunderstanding resulted.

For the time being, Thomas passed into a period of district commands, during which he established himself by imperceptible degrees as the operating brain of Buell's Army of the Cumberland of which he commanded a wing. He was in charge of many operations but these were minor. The next time he emerged on the center of the stage it was August, 1862, and he was trying to persuade Buell that the unusual Confederate activity out toward the strategic left portended a drive north by Bragg. Where? Up the central one of the three great corridors into which the West is divided by the Tennessee River and the Cumberland range, said Thomas. Buell would not believe; pointed to Forrest's famous raid westward, insisted Bragg was trying a wide flank sweep to cut the Union army from Nashville and drew Thomas in on that base. On the last day of the month Thomas captured a courier and sent the dispatches to Buell without comment. They told how Bragg had watered his horses in the Cumberland a week before and was marching on Louisville and Lexington with all speed and a week's start.

Buell, still not more than half convinced, wired Grant to borrow a division, ordered it in on Nashville, and leaving Thomas there with three more, started north through Bowling Green. Halfway to Louisville, his line of communications north suddenly went dead. Bragg had got as far north as he wished, turned west to Munfordville, where he captured 5,000 men and a depot, then swung across the only road line Buell could use, and took up a strong position on jutting hills.

The Federals, in these last days forced into an eccentric march that meant two miles to the Rebel one, came tramping up on September 19, footsore, hungry, and short of ammunition. Everything was cheerful as Christmas in the Rebel camp that night. For once they had a Union army outnumbered, and the Damyanks would have to attack uphill against a prepared position. Bragg thrust forward Buckner's division to provoke a battle that could hardly have more than one outcome, but Buell pulled in his outposts and refused to fight that day.

Toward evening the Confederate commander went out to the skirmish line in person to see what could be done about starting trouble in the morning. Just as he reached it, torches began to be carried through the Union camp, and there was faintly borne to his ears the sound of shouting. This seemed such strange behavior for an army that ought to be dispirited that the Confederate commander canceled a plan for a new move by Buckner and began fishing for information.

His patrols presently brought in the dismaying news that Thomas, without orders, had gathered up the 20,000 men in Nashville and marched to Munfordville in a single jump—one of the longest, fastest marches of the war. Bragg had sent General Kirby Smith, with a part of his own army, off on a raid, and the addition of Thomas to the other side placed the preponderance of numbers most prodigiously with the Union. There was another day of hesitation in which Kirby Smith did not arrive and Buell began to show a disposition to attack; then the Confederates slipped from the path, Buell went on to Louisville, and Munfordville became an unfought battle, a bloodless Union victory that deprived the Confederates of any fruit of their invasion.

But Buell had run the thing too fine; too narrowly missed defeat. The command was offered to Thomas and he refused it. Whether he was justified is a nice question in military ethics. His loyalty to Buell and his modesty would certainly have received extravagant praise if he had been on the other side; and even where he was, it brought him a good deal.

The question of whether it did not really constitute a kind of disloyalty, on the highest plane and from the purest motives, is probably only important in evaluating that Virginia code which Thomas shared with so many officers who wore the gray. The practical side of the question was settled by retaining Buell in command. He promptly fought the battle of Perryville, gained a half-victory through the brilliant work of young Sheridan, and missed a whole one through an incorrect estimate of the situation.

That was the end of Buell, who stood revealed as a sound corps commander, but one who could not form the large conceptions necessary for the handling of armies. Secretary Stanton fought hard to have Thomas in his place, but even Lincoln was now against the Virginian, whom he described as a man who had refused his chance and did not deserve another. "Well, you have made your choice of idiots!" snapped the secretary, as he signed the commission naming Rosecrans to the Army of the Cumberland. "Now you can await the news of a terrible disaster."

V

They very nearly had it. Perryville left Bragg suspended at the end of a dangerously long line of communication, with Union armies clouding all round him; he swayed back to the Nashville area, and there clashed head-on with Rosecrans during Christmas week. For two days the forces, nearly equal, lay with the little stream of Stone River separating them at the town of Murfreesboro. On the final day of the year Bragg and Rosecrans started movement to carry out complementary plans of battle, each arranging to hold with his right on his own side of the stream, take a heavy left wing across, and crush the other's right.

Arthur McD. McCook, of six generals McCook, had the Union right with three divisions. Crittenden with his own

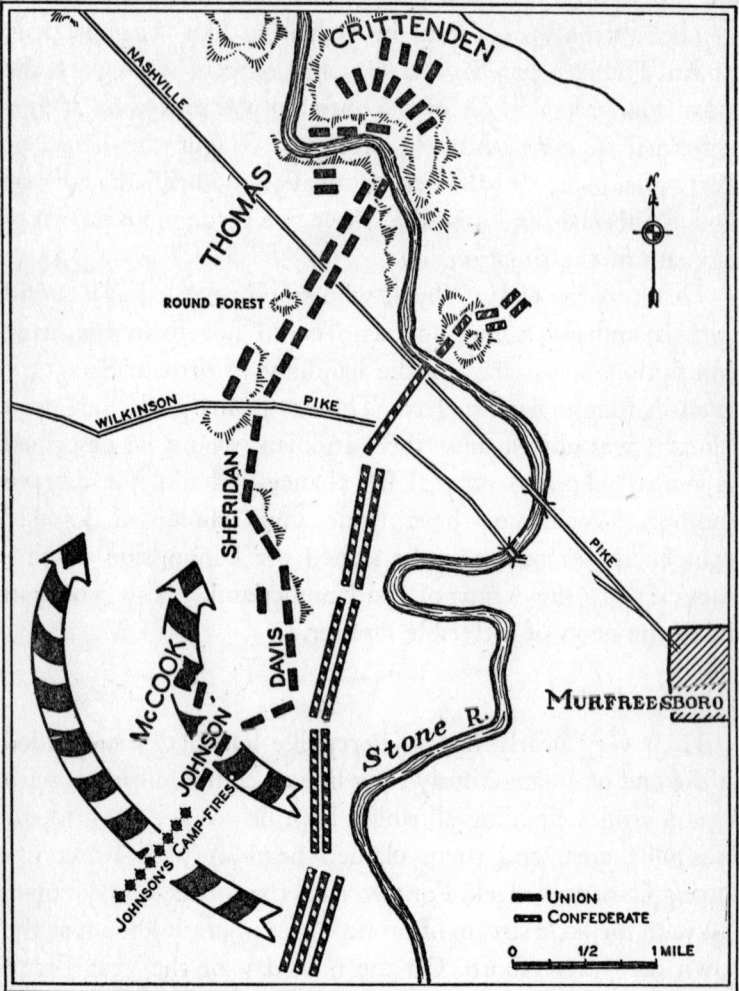

Stone River—First Position, and the Confederate Attack

three divisions and one borrowed from Thomas was given the attack mission. Thomas held the center with four of his original five divisions. The left of this center reached into a loop of Stone River; its front was penetrated by two roads (Wilkinson and Nashville pikes) through rolling country starred by brush and groves. McCook's right, the tip of the Union line, was held well back from the stream.

At the conference of corps commanders on the night before the battle, Rosecrans pointed out that the success of the whole combination depended upon McCook holding against anything that came toward him for three hours. He calculated this to be the time it would take Crittenden to gain a line of heights on the other side and there deploy his own and Thomas' artillery to blast the stuffing out of the Confederate army with an enfilade.

McCook said he could hold but he does not appear to have inspected his lines to make certain; and Rosecrans, being busy with the details of his attack, did not bother either. Neither general was aware that Johnson, the commander of the extreme flanking division, had prolonged beyond his own wing a line of campfires to give a spurious impression of strength in that quarter. The result of the trick suggests the thought that although camouflage is useful in concealing the strength and dispositions of an attacker, it may be a positive detriment when used to hide the weakness of a defense. In this case it deceived the Confederates; but it deceived them into prolonging and greatly strengthening their attacking left wing.

Bragg had set his movement an hour ahead of the time Rosecrans had named for the Union attack; when it came on, led by Hardee, it was already beyond Johnson's most extreme position. There was no one in command where the attack fell, for the local Union division commander had placed his headquarters two miles behind the line because there was a comfortable house there. The Federal regiments were mopped up in detail under a frontal and flank attack of overwhelming numbers. The big Confederate left hook turned in on the next Union division, Davis', took it front, flank, and rear all at once, and demolished it in turn, though Davis had been granted time to reach the line of the Wilkinson pike. Sheridan, next in line, beat off two assaults and only stopped a third by a last-gasp countercharge that wrecked his division.

When news of the attack on Johnson came to Rosecrans, it was with no tale of rout, only that the flank had been attacked. The Union commander treated it as interesting but unimportant. (Had not McCook been positive?) It was two or three hours later, Johnson and Davis had been broken, Sheridan's division pounded to shreds, and the Wilkinson pike lost, before he realized what had happened. When he did realize it, he ordered a couple of divisions back across the river from Crittenden, but things were then so bad that the men jammed in the loop of the river would have been cut to pieces like the Romans at Cannae, if the line, now back to the Nashville pike and cramped at a frightening angle, gave way.

It did not give way; Thomas held it. Before anyone else he realized what was happening; perceived that the Rebel attack could sweep McCook's wing back for a long distance without serious damage, but that if the point where the Nashville pike approached the river were lost, everything was lost and Crittenden cut off. He rushed nearly all the artillery of the center to this point—a cedar clump on a hill, the Round Forest. Sheridan, falling back from the Rebel masses, was ordered to direct his own guns thither; the cannon of Negley's and Van Cleve's fresh divisions were hurried out to the new right wing, where another bit of high ground gave them an enfilade into the flank of any force crossing the Nashville pike. The infantry were arranged under the general's own eye just as the Confederates came across low crests in six-deep waves, yelling with the consciousness of certain victory, three to one at the point of contact.

There is a legend of Thomas quiet and dignified in the hour of emergency; on the testimony of at least one soldier who saw him during the crisis at Stone River it was certainly not

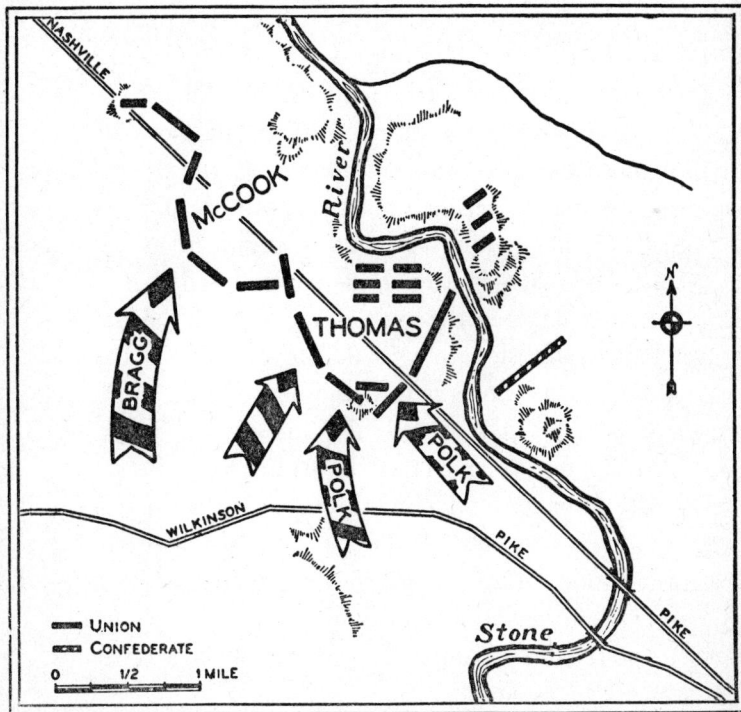

Stone River—Thomas's Stand

true there. He always had an eye to the value of formal effects, and as usual when a battle was toward, that morning had climbed into the nearest thing to a full-dress uniform that the camp afforded. Now, all togged out like a Christmas tree, he rode along the line, bellowing in a voice audible to every man within a hundred yards that help was coming, all they had to do was keep down and shoot low. "Fighting under

Thomas," said one of his soldiers, "was like having a stone wall in front of you or a battery to cover you." He was the most conspicuous object on the field; and hardly any man, perceiving how he rode untouched through the storm, but lost some of that sense of personal danger which makes troops break. Nor was personal courage all that Thomas offered by his presence; if a spot were really weak, the appearance of the general was infallibly followed by reinforcements.

Bragg's attack was driven back along the line of the Nashville pike, and a second, third, and fourth likewise, all of them delivered with furious enthusiasm. At the Round Forest eight of Sheridan's guns had been lost, but not until they had taken such toll that one Confederate regiment lost 207 men in 402, another 306 in 425. Polk commanded there for the Rebels; he recognized the spot as the key of the battle and asked another division to win it. Bragg, satisfied that there was nothing to be done against the new Union right, where Negley's artillery had stalled him and cavalry menaced his floating wing, sent the men to Polk. At 2:00 P.M. Polk pumped in the first brigades, concentrically against the angle held by Thomas; they lost. At four Polk tried again with two fresh brigades leading the swing, the original pair in support. Again Thomas beat them off, and as the tide began to ebb, flung out his weary troops in a counterstroke that shattered the attacking formations.

That ended the day's fighting. Rosecrans, a man whose brain was far better than his nerves, called a council of war for the night, at which officer after officer spoke of losses, disorganization, shortage of bullets. There seemed only one thing to do; Rosecrans turned to Stanley of the cavalry to ask him about covering a retreat.

Thomas, whose physical mechanism, like that of a clock, required periodic rewindings, had come out of the battle so wearied that he dozed off, but that final word penetrated his half-consciousness. "Retreat?" he said suddenly, drawing every eye in the room as he slowly pulled himself to his feet. "This army doesn't retreat."

"By God, no!" cried Sheridan, and they all began to talk at once. The Union army did not retreat, but spent New Year's Day waiting for ammunition from Nashville; and the

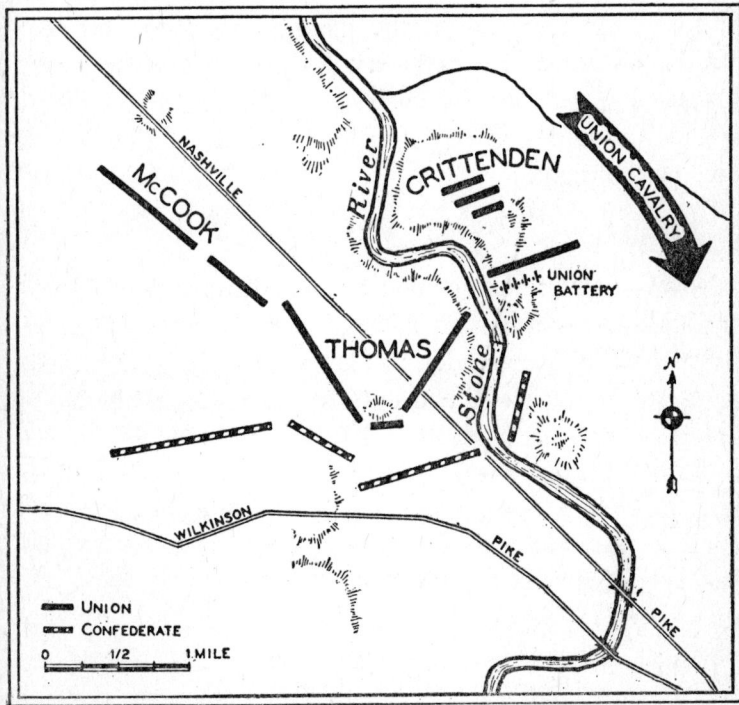

Stone River—The Victory

Confederates, who had had so heavy a dose of Thomas on the first day, spent the second reorganizing.

On the morning of January 2, Bragg discovered that Rosecrans had sneaked a division across Stone River during the night and established a battery on some hills to enfilade his right. He ordered an attack that was temporarily successful, but got caught in one flank by a terrific counter from one of Thomas' brigades and in the other by the fire of the battery. The attacking division went to pieces, the Union cavalry began to reach for Bragg's line of communications, and he pulled out quickly. The battle had cost each side over 10,000 men, and it ended Bragg's opportunity to invade the North—the Gettysburg of the Cumberland, as Perryville had been its Antietam. And narrow as the margin was to be between victory and defeat on Cemetery Ridge, Stone River saw a dividing line still finer—namely, that Thomas stood in the Round Forest during the afternoon and sat at the council table in the night.

VI

Now winter came in earnest on the Army of the Cumberland and was spent in reorganizing into three corps—Thomas', McCook's, and Crittenden's. Throughout the spring there were nothing but raids and outpost skirmishes, while Bragg wrangled with his generals and Rosecrans with his government. The Union general wanted cavalry; by the end of June he had received it and moved out in the campaign known as that of Tullahoma, the best piece of work he did during the war, but a perfect example of the futility of pure maneuver uncrowned by battle.

Bragg's advance base at Tullahoma was captured in the early days of July, and Rosecrans took a month's pause to bring up rations and organize the train for a new thrust toward Chattanooga, the key of the mountains. Do we trace Thomas in this halt? Perhaps, for he was a man careful to see his soldiers had full bellies, being more mindful of the matter than most officers, since his personal efficiency depended so largely on physical comfort. We cannot surely say; but Rosecrans leaned heavily on the Virginian in matters of organization and detail, and tended to hold aloof from such daily problems and to concentrate on more sweeping issues.

Rosecrans did have a grip on wide strategic matters that Buell never achieved, and came down against the mountains protecting Chattanooga on so wide a front and behind column heads so strong that Bragg's forward elements were driven in without being able to obtain any sure information of the Union movement. "Those mountain ranges are like a wall full of rat holes," the Confederate general said despairingly to a subordinate. "Too many rats pop from too many holes. Who knows what lies behind those peaks?"

The subordinate was Longstreet, who had come from Lee with Hill's corps, just as 15,000 reinforcements arrived from Mississippi to join Bragg. The war horse of the Army of Northern Virginia replied that whatever holes the rats popped through they must ultimately come to the pantry of the Chickamauga Valley. Concentrate there, he advised, and knock the rats over the head as they come out of their holes, one Union corps after another. Victory would be certain and crushing; for the reinforcements gave Bragg three to two of the whole Union army. He could probably take its scattered corps piecemeal and need not fear its united strength.

Bragg's first plan was that of throwing his full force on Crittenden, who was out east of Chattanooga on the extreme Union left. The scheme misfired when that stout fighter but indifferent strategist, General and Bishop Leonidas Polk, took up a defensive position opposite Crittenden and asked for men to hold it. Bragg rode off to squabble with his lieutenant; while he was about it both Thomas and Rosecrans independently divined danger in the suddenly stiffened front the Rebels offered, and both judged a blow at the center would be next. Thomas held that center; Rosecrans ordered both wings in on him, while "Old Pap" blocked every road and pass on his front with felled trees. Behind these obstacles he repeated the Mill Spring preparation on a huge scale, covering his whole front with cavalry to delay the enemy by dismounted fire from cover. Sure enough, Bragg struck in the center at Thomas; but obstructions and the skirmisher fire of the horsemen slowed his punch to the deliberation of a slow-motion picture. Crittenden and McCook rallied on the Union center and there was nothing left for it but a parallel-order battle.

The form taken by the battle was the interaction product of Bragg's ingenious grand tactic and Thomas' elastic defense. In Chickamauga Valley the creek of that name skirts the eastern mountain wall; west of it, beyond a hummocky lowland, stands Missionary Ridge, with numerous passes running through it to Chattanooga Valley, down which flowed the main road of Union supply, parallel to Rosecrans' front. Bragg planned a powerful right wing, which should cross the creek far down toward its mouth, sweeping up the valley onto the Union left, each division of his own extended center and left joining in the movement as the ford or bridge by which it would cross was uncovered during the progress of the drive. As the Northerners were driven from the roots of the passes, Bragg would fling a force through them, seize the road to Chattanooga, and cut his enemies from their base.

On the morning of August 19, the dismounted cavalry spotted a Rebel brigade on the west side of the Chickamauga and in a loop of the stream. Thomas, now holding the left of the army since Crittenden had fallen in rightward of him, thought it a local maneuver, and reached leftward with the division of General Baird to break it up. Baird struck through the brigade opposed to him, and behind encountered the big Confederate right wing, massed to attack. He pulled back to a refused flank, began to dig in, and notified Thomas of what he had found. It was the Virginian's first sure knowledge of Bragg's movement or plan, but he saw through the scheme instantly, rushed the four divisions he had into position to cover the passes through Missionary Ridge, and sent for help.

Bragg's wing spent a long time getting through the forest tangles, and Baird's unintended counterattack had caused further delay, but he sought to make up for the loss of momentum by an increase of mass, pulled more troops from the center and went in on Thomas. For a time the Rebels carried everything before them, right up to the road through the main pass, McFarland's Gap. "Old Pap" showed up among the infantry of the firing line, sure sign he was hard pressed, and got things stabilized just as Sheridan, the hardest hitter in the armies of the Union, arrived with two fresh divisions. Thomas put him in in an immediate counterattack. The Confederates were caught unorganized and carried right back to the stream, with many men lost as prisoners.

Bragg tried a blow at the Union right upstream in the afternoon, but had drawn so many troops from that wing for his movements on the other flank that the thrust had no force or result; then took one more crack at Thomas after dark, also in vain. The armies lay on their rifles for the night, with prospects for a heavier battle in the morning. Rosecrans, a great man for working things out in committee, called a council of war. There was no question of retreat as there had been at Stone River and Thomas frankly went to sleep listening to the argument over points of detail. Every time they nudged him to wakefulness he repeated, "I think the left wing should be strengthened," with the iteration of a parrot which has only one phase, and then dozed off again.

Nobody could suggest a better idea than strengthening the left and waiting to see what the Rebels would do. Rosecrans finally ordered Negley's division of McCook to report to Thomas and sent his small reserve corps under Granger to hold Rossville Gap, the pass lower down the valley beyond Thomas' left. It was fortunate the disposition was made thus;

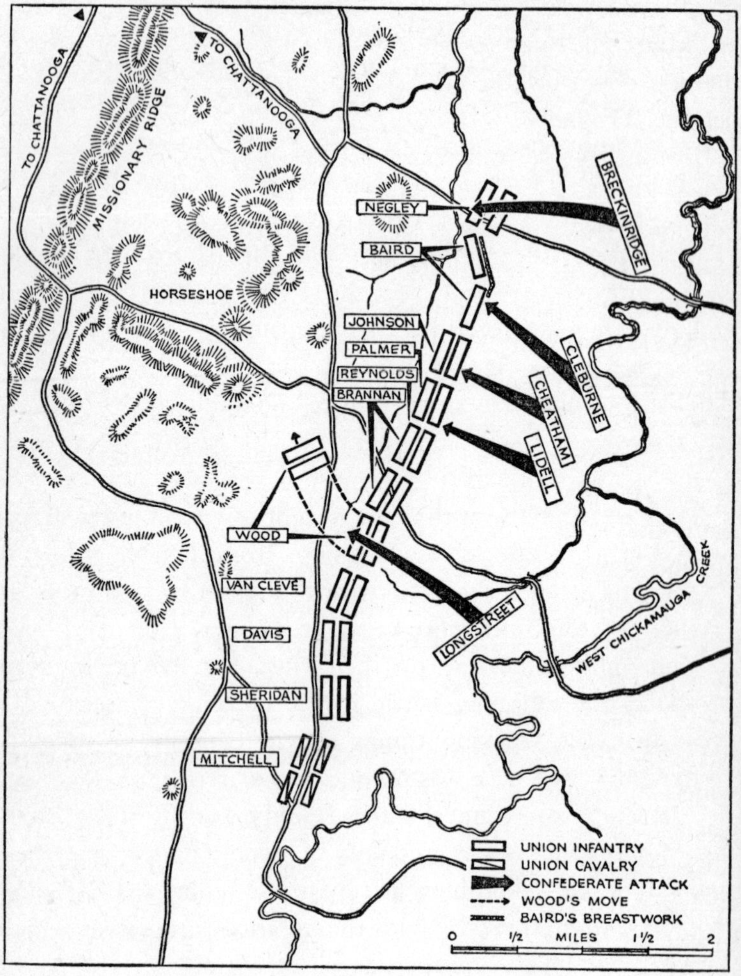
TO CHATTANOOGA
MISSIONARY RIDGE
TO CHATTANOOGA
HORSESHOE
NEGLEY
BAIRD
JOHNSON
PALMER
REYNOLDS
BRANNAN
WOOD
VAN CLEVE
DAVIS
SHERIDAN
MITCHELL
BRECKINRIDGE
CLEBURNE
CHEATHAM
LIDELL
LONGSTREET
WEST CHICKAMAUGA CREEK
UNION INFANTRY
UNION CAVALRY
CONFEDERATE ATTACK
WOOD'S MOVE
BAIRD'S BREASTWORK
0 1/2 MILES 1 1/2 2

The Second Day at Chickamauga

Bragg had worked a slide rightward during the night. Still intent on carrying through his original plan, he had ordered an attack to encircle and crush Thomas' left wing, each division down his line falling on as the one to the right of it became engaged.

Breckinridge on the extreme Confederate right started at dawn. He had expected to outflank Baird, but found Negley in front of the latter and parallel to his own lines. The morning woke under fog and the Rebels were able to deliver a close-range massed assault that was altogether too much for Negley, who broke before 8:00 A.M. Baird, next in line, should by the rules have been flanked and routed. But on the previous evening, before the council and before Thomas had received Negley's division, the general himself had inspected this part of the line. Fearing a flank attack, he had sharply refused Baird's division, ordered trenches dug, a log breastwork set up, and emplaced all the artillery he could gather to hold the point. Breckinridge, his lines disordered by the costly victory over Negley, hit this Gibraltar and got a repulse so stunning he was through till late afternoon. Bragg was present; instead of trying to press on here, he switched his right-wing reserve farther upstream and tried to thrust between Thomas' wing and the Union center, attacking so fiercely that Thomas was forced to call again and again for reinforcements.

Meanwhile Braggs's divisions had gone into action against center and left; Longstreet had found the famous gap left by the muddled order of Major Bond and General Wood's cranky obtuseness; and the whole Union center and right, taken in flank, had been broken, dissolved, and flung off at wild tangents out of the battle. Rosecrans' headquarters went, and with it the parked artillery; the commanding general was carried from the field in the mass of flying men, never halting till on the outskirts of Chattanooga. There is a famous story told by Garfield, the only staff officer who remained to Rosecrans as he drew rein on the road with men pouring past through the dark:

"Do you think there is any chance?" asked Garfield—it was unnecessary to say chance of what. Both dismounted and placed their ears to the ground. They caught the low distant grumble of cannon that told of a fight still in progress somewhere.

"Ride to the front," said Rosecrans, speaking like a man who had been punched in the solar plexus. "Find General Thomas, if he is still alive. Tell him to cover the retreat with Granger's men. I will wire to have Cincinnati and Louisville put in order for a siege."

It had come to that at Chattanooga, a vision of Cincinnati under siege, all the gains of Vicksburg lost and perhaps the war with them, for to the Union a draw would be as fatal as defeat. The same vision danced before the eyes of the Confederate leaders that afternoon as they stormed into the gap in one more effort to win the important pass, McFarland's Gap, from Thomas.

That general had dispatched one of his calls for reinforcements just before the rout of the center; an aide told him that men were coming from that direction but he thought them Confederates. Thomas rode off to confirm this impossible news; did so, and ignorant of everything but that some frightful disaster must have occurred to bring the Rebels onto his right rear, instantly withdrew to the horseshoe-shaped ridge behind his morning position, still covering the Gap. Here the artillery received his especial care. He posted it high on the spurs of the ridges, not too far forward; and from there it had to bear the brunt of the first disorderly rush of the Rebels who had broken the Union center.

It was now afternoon. In a renewed effort to get around Thomas' flank, Bragg threw Breckinridge's reorganized troops forward, far out on the slope of Missionary Ridge.

Too far out, as it happened; Breckinridge lost liaison with the next Confederate command, Cleburne's, did not after all get around Thomas' line tip (which had been withdrawn), and took a bloody repulse in what turned into a frontal assault against artillery. Thomas noted the gap, flung forward Baird in a counterstroke against Cleburne, took him in the flank, and completely broke up his division. The battle was all over here by 4:00 P. M. and Bragg was beaten.

But what happened on the Rebel right no longer mattered; the south face of Horseshoe Ridge, where Longstreet led the attack, was now the center of events. Here was the hardest fighting of the day, of the battle, and many think of the whole Civil War; here the 19th regulars lost every officer down to a lieutenant; here the Rebels gained a commanding ridge perpendicular to the Horseshoe, and were expelled only by a desperate bayonet charge in which General Steedman bore forward the colors of a Michigan regiment. Longstreet's assaults were beaten back; he sent to Bragg for reinforcements and received the reply that on the Confederate right were none but troops so mauled "that they would be of no service to you."

Yet it was still far from dark of that summer afternoon; Longstreet had three brigades in reserve and the best chance of destroying a Union army since the second day of Gettysburg. He need hold out nothing, and he was the best battle captain of the Confederacy. He reorganized for a final assault, put his fresh reserve in the lead, mixed brigades following, and came on through the twilight in a rush.

Just then General Brannon rode up to Thomas with the appalling news that the ammunition train had been carried off in the rout, and that there were only about two or three rounds per man left. The Rebel rifles were now flashing along the lower slope in the preliminaries of another attack. "What shall we do?"

Thomas glared down from his six feet. "Do? Fix bayonets and go for them."

There is no greater moment in our military history than that. Thomas went to the front. Longstreet's last charge was hit hard by the artillery, and then met with a cold-metal countercharge, at one point delivered with such energy that a regiment tore through the Confederate line. When charge and countercharge were over, the battle was over and the Union army was saved.

VII

Bragg followed the Federals up, and there had to be a siege of Chattanooga. On the besiegers' side, this operation was marked by a lack of realism which demonstrated that the essentially doctrinaire quality of Bragg's mind was the reason for his repeated failures. On the Federal side, it showed how little Grant appreciated the true quality of the man who inevitably received the command of the Army of the Cumberland after the necessary removal of Rosecrans. The Confederate leader had won a textbook victory; he failed utterly to realize that it had been Pyrrhic. "After Chickamauga," said D. H. Hill later, "the élan of the Southern soldier was never seen again." Having closed off the bread lines to Chattanooga, Bragg sat down before the town, convinced that nothing could happen but the textbook surrender of the army within.

Almost everything else happened, beginning with the appointment of Thomas, and Grant's wire to him not to give up the town. When the soldiers heard who their new general was, they broke ranks on parade and cheered wildly, crowding around the beloved leader, who rode through the press with his hat pulled down to his whiskers to hide the fact that he was blushing. "We will hold the town till we starve," Thomas wired back to Grant and, characteristically, launched the maneuver that kept it from starving. This operation was the capture of the oxbow loops of the Tennessee by silent surprise and the establishment of the "cracker line" across them, half road, half ferry. The next happening was the arrival of two corps from the Army of the Potomac with Fighting Joe Hooker to lead them, then came a corps from the Army of the Tennessee, with Grant and Sherman. The whole avalanche fell on Braxton Bragg in the battles of Lookout Mountain and Missionary Ridge, knocking his army out of the campaign and himself out of its command.

With these events the war was over for the year; the curtain of the spring lifted to find Thomas playing the old part on a new stage. Nominally he is a star with a company of his own, commander of the Army of the Cumberland; actually that army forms but one of the three great wings of Sherman's 90,000 who are striking for Atlanta. That campaign was Sherman, all Sherman. For the first time Thomas was under a leader who thought things out for himself, yet the first contacts of the two men are of more than passing interest, for out of them apparently grew that legend of Thomas' excessive slowness which was to dog him to the last.

Sherman opened his campaign by stripping his army for its work—one wagon allotted to a regiment, no tents even for officers, no baggage, and no kitchenware. He would sit by the roadside, fishing in a tomato can for lumps of meat with a pocket knife, and bandy arguments with privates who trotted past making derisive remarks. He had not seen Thomas for years, or since both men's habits had become fixed in the mold of time; he found him prematurely aged, portly, deliberate of speech, unable to function well without those creature comforts "Uncle Billy" despised—the big tent, always scrubbed clean, the negro striker, a good cook, and silver service.

"Thomas' circus," Sherman called this caravan, and may, naturally enough, have deduced military conduct from per-

GLENDALE COLLEGE LIBRARY

sonal habit. We do know that during the Resaca maneuver, the first of the campaign, Thomas' force was held in position at the cost of some confusion, while McPherson's army made a sweep across his front. McPherson's wing proved both too light and too slow of movement to achieve the designed result of breaking Confederate Johnston. The subsequent Cassville operation, in which Thomas saved a defeat by remorselessly driving before him the strong containing force Johnston had left behind, seems to have opened Sherman's eyes to the measure of his chief subordinate. Yet there was little opportunity to test that measure to the full until the Chattahoochee River had been passed and the Atlanta campaign was in its final stage.

That stage was announced by Sherman's crossing Peachtree Creek, which flows due west, north of Atlanta. Thomas had the right wing, with three corps; his mission was to push south and ahead, pinning the Confederates to the line of defense north of the city, while Schofield turned in from the northwest with one corps and McPherson with three made a wide sweep toward the city from the east.

Hood, who had replaced Johnston, divined Sherman's plan, though not the length and strength of McPherson's movement. He knew the ground by inspection—a series of high, finger-shaped hills reaching toward the Peachtree, scarred with difficult ravines. The stream itself flowed between quagmire banks and was crossed by few bridges. Lateral communication between the Union column heads, working along the roads that followed the backs of these fingers, was almost impossible. Hood planned to throw two-thirds of his army in a wedge between Schofield and Thomas, split the latter off, and throw him back to destruction in the stream.

The day of execution was a sweltering one in July, the 20th, and Hood's plan was aided by the fact that Thomas had been given a bad map, which showed Peachtree Creek shorter than it was, so that the Union right went too far out from its center. Thomas' XIV Corps was so far in this direction as to be out of action; Howard, with two divisions of the IV Corps, was making a rearward circuit to connect with Schofield. Only the XX Corps with Hooker's and Newton's divisions of the IV Corps were across the Peachtree and on the finger hills when the assault came.

The position thus favored the attack, the more so since Newton was echeloned well forward on Thomas' left so the assault struck his left flank and rear. To make matters worse, all three divisions of the XX Corps had been forced to cross by the same bridge, and to scramble through the ravines south of that stream to their positions. This had the result that only Geary's division, the one occupying the hill at the bridgehead, had been able to bring its artillery; the others, unable to get their guns through the ravines, had left them north of the Peachtree.

Late in the afternoon while the men were bivouacking, the attack came, headed by Hardee, and like all his, both fast and furious. Newton was violently thrown back, and to one experienced officer present it looked as though he were about to be broken. The Confederates stormed into the gaps between Geary and the divisions on either side of him, but there met check. Geary had his guns; he had also crossed the creek on the previous evening, earliest of all the divisions, and his front was fortified. He easily beat off the frontal effort with rifle fire; and then turned his artillery into the flanks of the Confederate columns surging past to work round the neighboring formations.

Yet the determining feature of the battle was not there; it was far back at the creekside, where Thomas had ridden forward to the sound of the guns. In an instant he perceived the situation as an artillerist's dream—heavy columns in close formation coming forward along deep-rutted valley bottoms, in the face of the artillery of two and a half divisions. Thomas brought the whole mass of guns into action at once, without any support but what they could give themselves. Nothing more was needed; the supports of the attack on Newton were blown out from under it. At every point the Confederates were caught in a cross fire of musketry from flank and cannon from ahead, and hurled back under losses frightful for the numbers engaged—over four thousand casualties in less than two hours. Hood would not admit he was beaten—so near to driving Newton out!—and prepared for another try later in the day, but McPherson was crowding him so rapidly on the eastern defenses of the city that he had to give up the idea. It is not likely the second attack would have come off better than the first.

In the later moves around Atlanta Thomas played only the part of a corps commander, except for the occasion when Sherman, desperately anxious to hurry a flanking movement, took the Gothic step of sending the dignified general galloping across country with a message. It was doubtless comic, but it is out of such things that quarrels grow up between old friends and it speaks volumes for the mutual respect between the two that Thomas was not offended nor Sherman amused. Indeed, when Sherman reached the Carolinas he paid one of the finest possible tributes to the man he had begun by doubting. "I wish I had old Tom here!" he cried one day, when some move was not performed with the efficiency he liked. "We always pulled differently, but we pulled well together."

VIII

Sherman was to pay "Old Pap" a higher tribute yet—the tribute of action, of selecting him to hold back Hood with scraps and patches of an army while the march through Georgia took the flower of the forces. "Thomas will take care of Hood," said Sherman with such conviction that Grant, who had smoked and doubted when the plan of the march to the sea was put to him, gave way; and even Thomas himself asked that he might have some other assignment unless he were the man essential to the task.

He *was* essential; the only man Sherman felt he could trust in such a case. Twenty-two thousand troops of the right veteran sort were all he could have—the IV and XXIII corps under Schofield, with those of Sherman's army found unfit for the Georgia march. There were 9,000 unorganized casuals and 5,000 horseless cavalrymen in Nashville. On their way to the same place were a large number of recruits and a corps (XVI) from Missouri under Andy Smith, but that also included many green men and nobody knew when it would arrive. Hood was rolling up through Alabama 45,000 strong, with 10,000 horsemen led by the incomparable Forrest around his flanks.

The problem before Thomas was basically that of a containing action by covering force to gain time for the organization and equipment of his army at the concentration point, Nashville. The detail of the movement he left to Schofield with his two corps and some cavalry under Wilson. Schofield was helped by the series of natural barriers given by the west-running rivers south of Nashville, as well as the November weather, which would inevitably drown the roads in mud. The battle of Franklin, which brought Hood up to Nashville already severely hurt (the Rebel general admitted 7,500 rank-and-file casualties in that fight, not counting his walking wounded) belongs to Schofield's story, and in it Thomas has no part beyond urging his subordinate to delay the Confederates as long as possible.

Andy Smith, with the 12,000 men of his corps, pulled into Nashville on November 30, one day before Schofield's retreating corps arrived. Thomas had been there for nearly two weeks, whipping the casuals, convalescents, and recruits into an army. But the day all the forces were united, there was a telegram on hand from Grant, so vigorously worded as to constitute a peremptory order to attack Hood; Washington feared the Confederates would slip away south or swing past Nashville in another invasion of Kentucky like Bragg's in 1862.

Thomas flatly refused to attack under the conditions, and to the threats that he would be relieved, replied calmly, "I feel conscious that I have done everything in my power to prepare, and that the troops cannot have gotten ready before this, and if you order me to be relieved I will accept it without a murmur." Inwardly he was far from the imperturbability thus indicated. "The Washington authorities treat me like a schoolboy," he told Wilson, "but if they'll let me alone, I'll lick those people yet."

His excuse for not moving was a lack of horses, which Grant found insufficient reason. We can agree as to the insufficiency, without seeing in it, as Washington did, a causeless policy of delay. Is it not just possible that the Virginian had a deeper reason for withholding his stroke, one difficult to explain over the wires, or to justify before an army body? Civil War staff work was notoriously bad; Thomas was on the eve of a battle which he wished to render decisive, and he knew how none of his troops except those of Schofield's corps would behave. The hypothesis that before attacking he wished to learn more about the men under his orders is lent color by the fact that he ultimately shuffled his corps into an arrangement far different from that they were in on December 2, the day of Grant's order.

In the final plan the provisional division of casuals and recruits, under Steedman, was placed on his extreme left; Wood, with the IV Corps, was brought into the center. Smith's XVI Corps was placed to the right of Wood, and Schofield was marched around behind the whole army to be the hammer

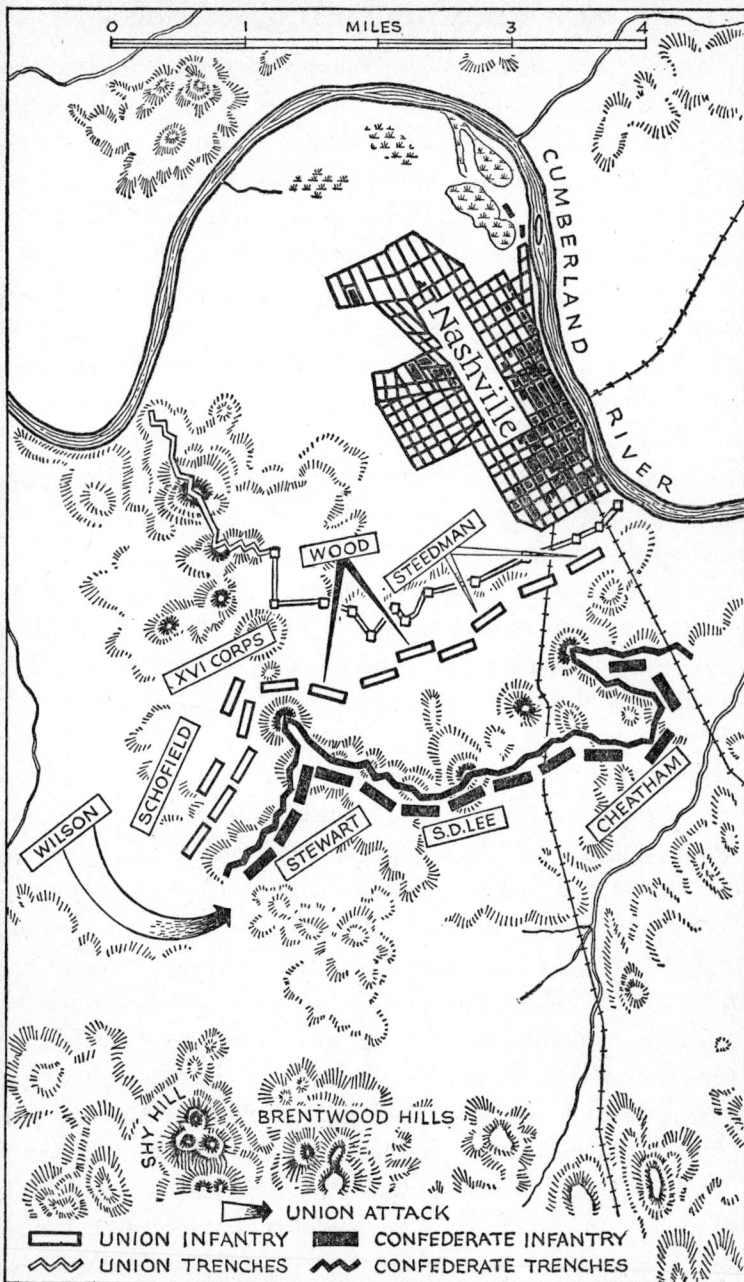

MILES

CUMBERLAND RIVER

Nashville

WOOD
STEEDMAN
XVI CORPS
SCHOFIELD
WILSON
STEWART
S.D. LEE
CHEATHAM

SHY HILL
BRENTWOOD HILLS

UNION ATTACK
UNION INFANTRY
UNION TRENCHES
CONFEDERATE INFANTRY
CONFEDERATE TRENCHES

Nashville—the First Day

of a wide flank sweep, with Wilson's cavalry riding out beyond Schofield.

Yet this same series of moves is capable of quite another explanation. Hood lay entrenched on the spurs of the Brentwood Hills, just south of the city, his right, under the command of Cheatham, his best fighting officer, thrown well forward in a cramped angle on some of the summits. Here he expected to beat off the attack by the Federal left which was the obvious Union move, both because of the ground and because Schofield, with the bulk of the Union strength, had been reported as lying in that quarter. Thomas planned to destroy the Confederates through their own battle plan, using their knowledge of where his heaviest concentration was placed by shifting that concentration to the other wing.

The reason for Thomas' plan does not matter except in relation to what history says of the general's mind; the important fact was that a storm of sleet came up before Schofield could begin his swing, frosted the ground in ice, and prevented all movement. Grant lost patience and temper, and on the 13th ordered Logan west to replace Thomas. On the 16th the new general stepped out of a train in Louisville, just in time to find that it would be no use for him to go farther. Thomas had struck and there was no Rebel army left to fight.

The weather for which he had waited so long broke on the night of the 14th. Early next morning Steedman's provisionals, with all the militia and quartermaster's men who could be gathered, came out under a fog and made a noise on Cheatham's front. The diversion nailed that commander fast to his entrenchments—for how could the Rebels know but this was Schofield, since one man in blue looks much like another in a battle? Wood fell on next and gave the Confederate center enough to do; Smith hit the angle where Hood's center turned into a refused left. Meanwhile, the whole of Schofield's corps, more than 10,000 strong, had been on the march since before

5:00 A.M.; it was afternoon before he finished his circuit and came in against the scattered cavalry posts and redoubts that covered Hood's left rear, but when he did he burst right through without loss to himself.

To check this menacing rush which promised to wipe out his flank, Hood pulled men from the nearest spot, the left center. Smith had not ceased his pressure; now he broke through, stormed the fortified hill crests, captured half the Rebel artillery, broke down their whole wing, and began to roll along the line.

It was dark by this time. The Confederates could find no better resource than a rapid retreat some two miles south to the next line of hills, where they took a position with both flanks refused. Most of the night they had to spend digging trenches, and by dawn they were in bad physical shape. Hood got his right solidly posted on a high and round summit, Overton's Hill, with a good line, but the anchor of the left wing was a place called Shy's Hill. It was the only eminence high enough to afford a hold, but he had to fight for it half the night against some of Wilson's troopers. The result was that the fortifications were neither well built nor along a good line.

With the first light of day a couple of Schofield's brigade commanders spotted the fact that the Rebel trenches followed a right angle, and brought up artillery to enfilade them along both sides of the angle. Thomas had planned during the night to combine another sweep by Wilson's cavalry round the Rebel left with pressure by Wood and Steedman against Overton's Hill. Wilson was off before dawn; the general himself was with Wood watching the progress of the movement on the Union left.

By noon it was clear that though Wood was making progress, further gain would be at such cost that another spot might be better for attack. Thomas rode west along his line, arriving opposite Shy's Hill just in time to see some Confederate artillery in action with much evidence of hurried and perturbed movements. The Rebels had reason for their excitement; the artillery fire that had drenched the angle since

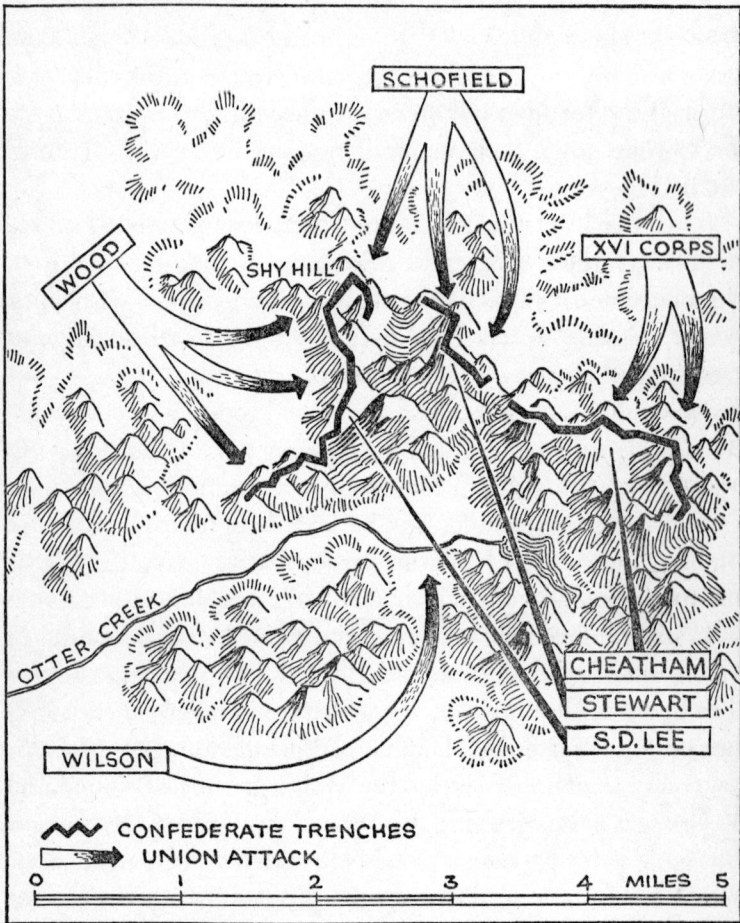

Nashville—the Second Day

morning was hard to bear and Wilson's horsemen were now clean around their rear. Hood had been forced to draw first a brigade, then a division from his extreme left to hold off the cavalry, who were advancing persistently as dismounted skirmishers. This made extension of the rest of the line necessary; it became thin at the angle just about the time Thomas arrived.

The Union general had a battery of heavy rifled guns in reserve; he ordered them up, outranged the Confederate cannon on Shy's Hill, and silenced them. Almost at the same moment Wilson came galloping up on a tired horse. Tense with hurry, he cried, "For God's sake, order an attack. My men are in Hood's rear."

With maddening deliberation Thomas lifted his glasses. He could see right across the flank of Shy's Hill, how there were smoke puffs among the thickets in the Rebel rear. "You may attack, General," he said gently to Schofield. Wilson turned rein, but before he had ridden five hundred yards, half of Schofield's corps swept forward in one long cheering line. There was a single disorganized volley and the Confederate army collapsed like a kicked melon.

No one is quite sure of what happened during the remainder of that afternoon. Hood, in prolonging his lines to parallel his adversary, had put in his last reserve; there was nothing left to cover a retreat or to stop the sweep along the line into which Smith, Wood, and Steedman swung with Schofield. The Confederate brigades caught between Schofield and Wilson were captured entire; all the artillery went, all the equipage, and when night came down Thomas hurled Wood and Wilson into the best pursuit in American history. It kept on for a week; and when Hood finally rallied the fragments of what had been an army behind the Tennessee River, he had less than 9,000 men out of the 55,000 who had begun the campaign, no guns, no ammunition, and no train.

IX

So George H. Thomas rides out of history in the night, to meet young Wilson on the muddy dark road after the battle and to shout at him, "Dang it to hell, Wilson, didn't I tell you we'd lick them?" He went to California after the war and died of apoplexy at the Presidio in 1870, while writing a reply to some criticism of his career. The date was too early for his own fame, for he was able to take no part in the great printed military debates of the eighties, which did so much to establish for the various commanders the places they were to occupy in the story of the war. Grant's, naturally, was the controlling voice in most of those debates; it followed that the officers who were partisans of his view repeated and elaborated upon the theme of Thomas' slowness until it became a legend.

At a casual glance there seems something incompetent in the strategy which flung Schofield forward to hold up thrice his numbers under Hood, while his commanding general remained behind at Nashville, totting up reports of strength. Yet the very critics who lodge this charge allow that Nashville was a victory of truly Napoleonic proportions.

There is something inconsistent here; one cannot have Thomas stupid on Monday and a genius on Tuesday. But the inconsistency fades when the Nashville campaign is examined as a whole, and vanishes when Thomas' career is taken in one piece. For the further such an examination proceeds, the more one is impressed by the fact that the Nashville campaign is nothing but a large-scale repetition of Mill Spring, which was an essentially defensive battle, culminating in a crushing counter-stroke. In the one as in the other a Union advance force was thrust forward to be driven in; caused the Rebels some loss, slowed their advance, and allowed time for Thomas' striking force to swing round the rear of his whole army and destroy the Confederates by smashing their flank and rear while a containing attack held their right in place.

It is the same in every battle in which Thomas took part. His steadiness at Stone River and Chickamauga has been much praised; but Rosecrans showed as much resolution as he, and mere staying power would not have turned the tide in either battle. An attack that has been merely brought to a halt can always rally and come on again, or at the worst, the attackers will escape without being hurt, as the Confederates demonstrated at Chancellorsville and Gettysburg. But when an attack against Thomas began losing its sting, he never once failed to deliver his punch into the reflux. Chickamauga is the most brilliant instance. Thomas' stand there was magnificent; but what really saved the Union army was the fact that in the afternoon, "Old Pap" discovered the hole between Breckinridge and Cleburne, and as soon as the Rebel charges let up, threw Baird into the gap. That move broke Bragg's right wing, and used up his reserves, so that Longstreet could get no reinforcements for the final and decisive movement in the evening. And even in the last movement Thomas was there with the infallible counter—"Fix bayonets and go for them." Peachtree Creek is, in fact, the only battle where Thomas made no attack; and in that struggle Sherman had already arranged for the riposte.

Mention of Peachtree Creek brings up another feature of Thomas' mind, striking in its modernism—his appreciation of fire power in an age when nearly all generals were still thinking in terms of the Napoleonic shock. If it was a happy accident that gave him personal command of the corps artillery at Peachtree Creek, he seems deliberately to have repeated that accident at Nashville, placing the biggest and best guns, the rifled battery, under his personal orders. Never once do we find him ordering a cavalry charge; repeatedly—at Mill Spring, Chickamauga, Nashville—he employs cavalry as a means of carrying rifles rapidly to a desired position. Similarly, throughout his career, he never once sends infantry against artillery, or even against a solid line of infantry. His attacks are invariably delivered at moments when the enemy's fire power has been disorganized by advance and when they have overreached the support of their own artillery.

But if counterattacks are the only kind worth trying in a world of mechanical weapons, is not war reduced to the paralysis of M. Bloch, with both parties waiting interminably? It is doubtful whether the question occurred to Thomas; but he answered it in advance at Nashville, which if strategically a counterstroke, was tactically an offensive. He answered it with deception, as Sherman and Jackson answered it with mobility and Grant with surprise. Each of these methods partakes of the others, but there is a basic difference between the technique of the jujitsu expert who draws his opponent off balance before the blow and that of the boxer who hits so hard and quick that the parry cannot keep pace.

The thing Grant failed to realize about Thomas was the same thing the uninitiate fail to understand in jujitsu—the force of its compulsions, which are invisible, psychological, working on the mind and morale of the opponent. There was no visible military reason why Hood could not slip away south from Thomas at Nashville; and the Confederate general has left record of having just begun to consider such a step when Thomas hit him. There was no visible military reason why Hood could not have reinforced or extended his left wing on December 15, 1864; he had Cheatham's corps available, which fired hardly a gun that day. Thomas was merely certain that Hood would do neither the one nor the other; he had fought against this Texan before, knew that he always accepted retreat with reluctance and as a last resort. More than this: he encouraged the Confederate's delusion of strength by remaining almost excessively quiet in Nashville during the two weeks of preparation, just as he encouraged Hood to expect an attack on his right by posting in that quarter Schofield with the *Stosstruppen* of the Union army. Information of that arrangement would be certain to reach Hood; the more essential information that it was a temporary disposition remained locked in Thomas' mind till the day of the battle.

Seen by this light, psychology becomes the master key of the military art, for the choice of the proper moment for counterattack is also a question of psychology. But the success of Thomas in everything he undertook cannot be explained by any formula, even a psychological one; for the deception practiced on Hood at Nashville through design was no more than a repeat of the deception practiced on Zollicoffer at Mill Spring, largely by accident; a happy improvisation on a single instrument caught up and repeated titanically through the full orchestra of war. The genius of Thomas is, in the long run, the same as that of Frederick the Great—the genius for reproducing on the largest scale whatever has turned out well on the small.

JAMES H. WILSON

The Man Who Got There First

I

A GOOD DEAL HAS BEEN MADE OF THE CAREER OF NATHAN
Bedford Forrest, and not unreasonably. He represents
at their nth power all those aptitudes which Americans like to think of as peculiarly their own in connection
with the art of war. He was without formal education of any
kind, a civilian who sprang to arms when the bugles sounded;
yet West Pointers like Lee and Sherman rated him among the
ablest commanders in the field; he was impatient of control,
gifted with abounding common sense; full of quaint expres-
sions; the inventor of a technique which carried the freeboot-
ing individualism of the West to the level of serious military
operations affecting the course of campaigns. The man and
his doings have irresistibly drawn the attention of every
American student of the Civil War.

Foreign military critics have been somewhat more hesitant
about according him the highest rank, pointing out that there
were few occasions on which his raids achieved major results.
Even so, it is rather odd that both here and abroad so little
regard has been given to the Union opponent who was present at the decisive moment when Forrest was missing and
who ended the war by beating him thoroughly.

There are always two sides to a conflict, and it is quite as important to understand why one army won as why the other lost. The biographers of Forrest slide over that final campaign with the remark that he was outnumbered. So he was; but to no greater extent than the Confederate commanders opposing Ben Butler on the James and N. P. Banks on the Red River. Those Union officers were opposed by generals of nowhere near Forrest's ability, but they never inflicted on anyone so crushing a defeat as was administered to Forrest at Selma. Nor was Selma Forrest's first setback at the hands of the twenty-seven-year-old major general who outmaneuvered him there; as it was not the first time when the riding and raiding cavalry of the Confederacy found itself unable to deal with James H. Wilson—an officer who believed that the difference between infantry and cavalry was that the latter could deliver more fire power on a given point in less time.

The theory is about as widely different from that behind the Confederate method of handling horse as it could be, even though it may be viewed as an extrapolation of Forrest's own famous remark about getting there "fustest with the mostest men" into getting there first with the most bullets. In that extrapolation, in changing the emphasis of combat from weight of men to weight of metal, lies the story of the modernization of war. Wilson was the first to prolong the curve.

He was also a figure out of legend—the youngest army commander in American history, one of the youngest in any history (only Napoleon and Alexander the Great led armies at an earlier age); yet living on to be one of the oldest generals of record and dying at eighty-eight after service in four conflicts.

II

James Harrison Wilson was graduated from West Point in the class of 1860, a young man with a high-bridged nose and a long sharp chin, on which he immediately sprouted an imperial to give him a fictitious appearance of maturity. His academic rank was sixth in a class of forty-one, which entitled him to a brevet in the Topographic Engineers and an assignment to then unsurveyed Oregon, where he spent the best part of a year in surveying the route from Puget Sound to the Columbia River. While on that duty he did a great deal of reading, and developed several notable ideas, one of which was that the business of combat intelligence should be handled by a special reconnaissance battalion in each division.

The plan has a surprisingly modern sound when one remembers that only a year later McClellan was getting his intelligence from Pinkerton detectives and they were deceiving him badly. Wilson got nowhere with it at the time, but one of his other ideas he put into immediate personal and practical application. He set down in his diary that military officers are political figures whether they wish it or not, and himself kept up correspondence with his congressman, his home-town pastor, and even the governor of his state—with the result that he was one of the first officers to obtain the desired recall from the Northwest and assignment to active duty in 1861.

The duty was as chief topographical engineer for the expedition to Hilton Head and Port Royal in South Carolina under General T. W. Sherman. It was not quite as important a post as it sounds, since Wilson remained a brevet second lieutenant. He was one of those young men who can never be still a moment, and increased the value of his appointment by activity—ran up all the inlets in a boat to map the whole area, invaded the quartermaster department to invent a new method of rapidly loading a transport, and ingeniously snaked some heavy guns across a wide salt marsh for the siege of Fort Pulaski when the other engineers said it could not be done. General Sherman gave him a highly favorable report, and General David Hunter (who relieved Sherman early in

1862) gave him a still better one. Wilson was not impressed with either officer; set them down as intolerably supine, and began bombarding Washington with requests for a transfer.

It came through in August. Arriving in Washington, Wilson found the demand for engineer officers so far beyond the supply that he could practically write his own ticket, and he wrote one for Grant's command in the armies of the west. There were details to be cleared; in the meanwhile he went as a volunteer aide to McClellan's staff for the Antietam campaign, then just beginning. Wilson has left of record his bitter disappointment when the attack that began in an atmosphere of confidence and energy petered out on the battlefield into disjointed effort, gloom, timorousness. He asked to be relieved, "and taking leave of my messmates at nightfall, I covered the entire distance of about 75 miles to Washington by sunrise the next morning." On November 7, 1862, he joined Grant as chief topographical engineer, and with that event the story really begins.

It is evident to anyone who examines Wilson's own narrative and diaries that up to this time he had been looking for a leader to follow. He called on every general within reach and committed his frank opinion of all to paper. T. W. Sherman was overstrict in minutiae and lacked combativeness; Hunter too easy-going by half. McClellan, with his dashing air and fluent conversation, failed the test of battle; Burnside was stupid, Sumner irresolute, Hooker wanting in the simple fortitude to fight out a line once laid down. The young man had visited Halleck after having read his *Art of War*, prepared to find in that general the moving spirit of the western triumphs, but fifteen minutes' talk showed him a flabby pedant, who could not possibly have struck so hard at Donelson or turned dreadful Shiloh from defeat to victory.

The man behind it all must be Grant, then; but Wilson's first impression of his new commander was almost as unfavorable as of the others. The general's bearing was hopelessly unmilitary; he might have been the proprietor of a country store. One of the other members of the staff sidled up to the newcomer with the information that Grant would be all right if the staff could keep him away from "bad habits."

On the other hand the general promptly supplied his new topographic engineer with good mounts and an adequate staff of photographers, interrogators, and artists. Wilson decided to suspend judgment on Grant and set to work to make his own department into a kind of G-2 section, the first of its kind in any American army. Indeed, it was something beyond a G-2 section. During his stay in Washington, Wilson had carefully polished the brightwork on his political connections, and among other contacts had established relations with General John A. McClernand. That ambitious and energetic Illinois politico was in the capital to present his plan for raising an entirely new army in the northwestern states and taking Vicksburg with it. Wilson was well-enough informed to have learned that Lincoln and Stanton regarded the scheme with decided favor.

The young man brought all this out at the headquarters conference following Confederate Van Dorn's big raid on the supply depot at Holly Springs in December of '62. The raid had forced the abandonment of the overland campaign down the corridor of high ground to Vicksburg. Wilson now urged Grant to treat the Mississippi itself as his base and line of operations "since it could neither be broken nor obstructed." It is not necessary to claim that he supplied his commander with the idea for the river campaign, but he did provide the somewhat inarticulate commander-in-chief with cogent arguments against the other officers, particularly Sherman and McPherson, who wished to conduct the operation along more "normal" and slower lines.

That conference was a key incident both for Grant and

Wilson. The general had experienced a good deal of difficulty in handling McPherson, who had graduated No. 1 in his class and was so often spoken of as the brains of the Army of the Tennessee that he had come to believe it himself. Wilson's own high standing and quick intelligence made him a valuable makeweight at the council table, and he himself was from this date forward Grant's man. At last he had discovered a commander who was willing to attack, and to do it in a manner not prescribed by the rule book.

III

It was a full year later, and Grant, now in charge of all the western armies, was facing Bragg at Chattanooga, when there occurred the second of the incidents lying behind young Wilson's rapid promotion to high command, which so much astonished contemporaries. Bragg had detached Longstreet's corps against Knoxville, and the War Department was keeping the wires to Grant hot with messages full of apprehension about what might happen to the loyalists of eastern Tennessee. Grant himself was equally apprehensive, but for quite a different reason—to wit, that the commander in Knoxville was Ambrose E. Burnside, in whose judgment and resolution he had very little confidence. Wilson was sent to the city to furnish Burnside with a temporary brain if possible, carrying positive orders that the place was to be held at any hazard. Charles A. Dana, "the eyes of the War Department," went along.

The two emissaries found conditions just as Grant had feared they would be. Burnside understood the strategic situation thoroughly, but his own plan to meet the oncoming attack was a witless scheme for crossing the Tennessee River in a southeasterly direction, with the idea of threatening Longstreet's communications as he came up the other bank against Knoxville. In short, he wanted to take the offensive and distin-

guish himself. Wilson pointed out that in detaching Longstreet, Bragg had so weakened his own forces that he must be
heavily defeated as soon as Grant could complete his attack
dispositions. By crossing the river Burnside was almost certain
to lose Knoxville city and might be thrown off to destruction
among the Great Smokies. What was needed was that he
should merely stand fast; and this was what the orders directed him to do. After a wearisome argument that lasted for
eight hours, Burnside finally consented to sit still when Dana
said that the War Department would undoubtedly take
Grant's view.

The next day Longstreet was reported as having crossed to
the north bank of the Tennessee. Burnside rode to the front
to verify the fact and then changed back to his original plan,
pointing out that at Knoxville he had a good bridge, while the
Confederates would have none for 25 miles in their rear as
they approached the city. This particular line of argument
had been up before, but the matter was being laboriously
beaten out for a second time when word reached headquarters that someone on the engineer staff (it was uncertain who)
had ordered the bridge burned, so that after all Burnside had
to stay in Knoxville whether he liked it or not.

It is possible that he was annoyed, but Dana certainly was
not, and the report he made to Stanton brought a new assignment for Wilson, whose persuasiveness backed by direct action was precisely in accord with the Secretary's own method
of handling difficult situations. Already from Mississippi
Grant had asked that Wilson be made a Brigadier General and
transferred to the cavalry. The Federal mounted arm in the
West was at a low ebb, being especially deficient in scouting;
and Grant, who considered cavalry as primarily an arm of information and screening, believed that Wilson's activity and
experience in intelligence work would make him the right
man to undertake a reorganization.

The promotion had been approved when Dana reported. Now at this time the Cavalry Bureau was in a complete mess, dominated by a group of contractors with sticky palms who did nothing, while all the cavalry units in the field were calling for remounts that never arrived. There would not be much field work for cavalry till spring; why not (suggested Dana) bring in this energetic young man and let him make his acquaintance with his new branch as head of the bureau?

It was done. Wilson reported to Washington in January of 1864, finding Stanton scowling and obviously disappointed at the youth of the new general, but not disposed to back down on the appointment. "My life is worried out of me by the dishonesty of the contractors who supply us with inferior horses, or who transfer their contracts to sub-contractors who do not fill them at all. They are a set of unmitigated scoundrels, and I want you to reorganize the business. I give you *carte blanche* and will support you with all the resources of the department."

The contractors began by offering the new chief of bureau an elaborate dinner; he declined and called a meeting, at which he told all known bidders that regulations would be executed to the letter on contracts for a new lot of 11,000 horses, with no subletting permitted. Apparently they did not take him too seriously. Only one of the successful bidders fulfilled his contract—for 2,500 animals. Wilson instantly had the defaulters thrown into jail for trial by courtmartial, and when yells of anguish began to arise from the contractors' political friends, brought into play his own not inconsiderable influence as well as the formidable Stanton, who thoroughly made good on his promise of support.

The improvement in remounts had a good deal to do with the rise of the Union cavalry in '64, but in the long run it was less important, both to Wilson's history and that of the cavalry service, than another change which he made incidentally. At the time the young general came to the bureau, there had been gathering endorsements for some months a series of reports on a novel firearm invented by one C. M. Spencer, of Massachusetts. Its special feature was that it had a magazine in the stock, from which nine cartridges were delivered to the firing chamber as rapidly as the operator could throw forward and pull back a lever which formed the trigger guard. The infantry's interest in his invention having been mild, Spencer produced his weapon in a carbine version. The first samples had been delivered in October and were tried out by a troop in Buford's division during the futile Mine Run campaign.

Wilson read the reports (noting that all the unfavorable opinions were from older officers), saw the weapon, and fired it himself. It got off nine shots in a minute, and seven of them went into the target. Buford had died during the winter, but there seems to have been a good deal of discussion around Washington about his new tactical doctrine of having cavalry do its fighting dismounted and with the fire weapon. It was a doctrine which Sheridan, as new cavalry commander of the Army of the Potomac, heartily agreed. The anticipated difficulty was that cavalry would be unable to maintain itself long against infantry attack, since it can put in so many fewer men per unit length of front.

This would hardly matter as long as the cavalry remained what Grant expected it to be—a scouting and screening force. But Sheridan was already filled with his new plan of employing the whole cavalry service of the Army of the Potomac as a unit; and Wilson was already meditating the logical but still more radical extension of this idea into employing the massed cavalry as a fast battle wing for the army—a return to the Napoleonic method for the tactical use of heavy cavalry, but with fire power substituted for shock as the means of attack. In this new carbine the young bureau chief saw a means of enabling horsemen to hit hard, despite an inferiority of numbers. His last official acts as head of the bureau were to contract for Spencer carbines as fast as they could be produced, and to order that the 3rd Cavalry Division of the Army of the Potomac be equipped with them.

There was a reason for this special solicitude over the 3rd Cavalry Division; Wilson was going to lead it in the field. Neither Grant nor Sheridan was particularly satisfied with Kilpatrick, whom they found at the head of that command. The former at once thought of his intelligence specialist from the western army, and the latter, who had come into contact with Wilson on the remount business, and knew his views were sound on Sheridan's own favorite subject of the conservation of horse energy, was willing to try him. The new general of division was so junior on the permanent army list that all three of the brigade commanders—Merritt, Custer, and Davies, themselves among the youngest generals of the army —ranked him, and had to be transferred.

IV

He found the division in appalling condition, with only two-thirds of the mounts it should have had. 615 men out of the 3,000 present for duty appeared for drill, and these gave so poor a performance that Wilson's first act was to order one of his colonels in arrest and to give the remainder a dressing-down that they remembered all their lives. The bulk of the command was strung out along a 28-mile picket line, but within sight of the infantry they were supposed to be covering. The assembly of all the cavalry into a body that could act as a mass belongs rather to Sheridan's story than Wilson's; but the young general did his part in it well enough to be placed at the head of the movement across the Rapidan on May 4, less than a month after he had taken command.

In that first fierce clash of the Wilderness, Wilson's division was generally echeloned out in front of the left flank of the

Union army, while Sheridan's other two divisions were eastward to cover the army's rear against Stuart. The new carbine had not been issued to all Wilson's regiments as yet, but the first dividend from that piece of equipment was drawn when only 500 men, under Col. Hammond, were struck by the leading elements of Ewell's Confederate division near Parker's Store.

The Union horsemen fought dismounted and in extended order among trees, delivering so heavy a fire that Ewell reported he had made contact with the Federal infantry, deployed his own men, and conducted an attack in form. The gain was six hours, and Wilson was afterward somewhat bitter because Hammond had not been given the infantry support that would have permitted the establishment of a much better and more forwardly position on that flank than the one that ultimately resulted. The criticism is not very thoroughly justified—the infantry nearest Hammond would have been pulled into a movement quite other than that intended for them—but it shows the lines on which the new division leader was thinking.

He himself was well to the southwest of Hammond's action during the day, where he encountered a brigade of Confederate cavalry and drove it in, in the first attack. Wade Hampton, of Stuart, ultimately forced the Union horsemen back by putting in double their numbers, with infantry support, but the encounter laid the foundation on which Sheridan erected his tactical structure, and Stuart was held far from a major battle for the first time in his career.

The Wilderness fighting went to its conclusion without Wilson's division after that first day. He was used to the left and rear of the army, covering its trains, then pushed out to be the vanguard again as Grant made his first sideslip toward the enemy flank. On the morning of May 8 the division reached Spottsylvania and took it, with 45 prisoners, from

Longstreet's corps. Wilson questioned them in person, learned that Lee had designs on the place he was occupying, and sent to the nearest Union corps commanders for infantry. If they had come, the Confederates were forced into a long circuitous march by the North Anna; but "the custom of outmarching and outflanking the enemy had not yet appeared in that army." Neither Burnside nor Warren (who received Wilson's messages) could see the point, an order from Meade pulled back the energetic cavalry leader, and the terrific struggle of the Bloody Angle had to be fought out.

Meade's order to Wilson was the prelude to the Yellow Tavern raid and the end of Stuart, an occasion which moved Wilson to remark in his diary that the *beau sabreur* of the Confederacy "never fully realized the advantage of operating in mass in close co-operation with infantry." The entry marks the fact that Wilson had now carried to its logical conclusion the doctrine of cavalry employment that began with Buford and came down to him through Sheridan. The young general demonstrated it at the end of May, when Grant prepared for the flanking move across the two Annas by sending Wilson and his division to make a feint behind Lee's left. It was a good and a successful feint; the fire of the Spencer carbines convinced the Rebels that Federal infantry was on the move in that direction, and Grant made his flank march to the opposite wing without interference. But a feint was by no means the move Wilson wished to make; he tried to persuade his chief to use the whole Cavalry Corps in an all-out attack on the rear of Lee's left flank, and Grant, as usual, found the idea too radical.

Wilson's service with the Army of the Potomac was all pretty much of that same character—a tale of opportunities missed because no one but he could see them, and because Grant clung to his concept of cavalry as a scouting and raiding army. Late in June, after Petersburg had been laid under siege, Grant worked out a plan for cutting the Confederate railroad lines supporting Richmond—Sheridan to take the divisions of Torbert and Gregg up the North Anna to break the Virginia Central Railroad connecting with Lynchburg, while Wilson with his own men and the independent division of Kautz ("which was no division, only a badly organized brigade") struck the lines reaching south and west of Petersburg. The plan miscarried when Wade Hampton with the Confederate cavalry got across Sheridan's line of advance at Trevilians Station. Sheridan won the battle, but heavy forces of infantry began to move in his direction and he abandoned the raid; Lee rapidly switched Hampton to the south bank of the James, where Wilson had progressed some 100 miles from support.

The young leader was badly outnumbered, and was hard put to it to save his division, getting out only after losing all his wagons and some artillery. He was ever after critical of Sheridan's performance, maintaining that that general should have pinned Hampton north of the James. It is hard fully to agree; for one thing, Lee was adroit enough to have used infantry against Sheridan and withdrawn his cavalry anyway, and for another thing, raiders must expect to get hurt.

But this was soon behind and forgotten, for Grant's next move was to send Sheridan to the Valley of Virginia with that splendid group of young generals—perhaps the youngest that ever led a major American army. Wilson had one of the three divisions of horse. It was a golden opportunity, but he was not allowed to make the most of it. Even while he was riding through the ravine to the Opequan and the first of those three ringing victories that changed everything, the wires were humming between City Point and Atlanta. Sherman wanted a new cavalry commander: "My present cavalry need infantry guards and pickets and it is hard to get them within ten miles of the front." Grant answered: "I have ordered General Wilson to report to you. I believe he will add 50 per cent to the effectiveness of your cavalry"; and gave the young leader his major general's stars at the age of twenty-seven.

V

The situation found by the new Chief of Cavalry for the western command was as discouraging as it could possibly be. Sherman received him cordially enough, but for some reason the two men never got along particularly well, and they circled each other like a pair of strange cats. For one thing Wilson was not at all clear about his duties and the limits of his authority. He was officially Chief of Cavalry for the Military Division of the Mississippi, but there was no uniformity in the interpretation of the title among the various armies.

There was also the condition of the cavalry force itself; the new chief found 50,000 men on the rolls, but less than 10,000 present for duty, and these scattered from hell to breakfast, on the bad old system that had obtained in the eastern army till Sheridan made his concentration. They were armed with a wonderful collection of weapons that made the service a museum on horseback. "Their engagements were nearly always at the outposts or on raids; they were hardly ever in camp long enough to make returns and rarely long enough to make requisitions. The mounted service was looked upon as futile and discreditable." The opposition to this scattered and disorganized force was Forrest and Wheeler, whom Sherman himself considered the best cavalry leaders in the world.

The remount situation was bad; Sherman was full of the projected great march to the sea and would talk of nothing else. Finally, the divisional and brigade commands were filled with respectable old generals of great seniority, who had made failures elsewhere—Garrard, Stoneman, Elliott, Grierson. Wilson had a natural aversion to these ornamental seniors; back with the Army of the Potomac, he had advised Grant that the best means of improving the army would be to get a good Indian chief, furnish him with a scalping knife and a gallon of bad whisky and send him out to remove the topknots of all the major generals he could find.

To test his position, he accordingly asked for the relief of all the heirloom officers. It was promptly accorded, while for his own part Sherman said frankly that although Kilpatrick was a crazy damn fool, he was just the sort of man to command the cavalry on the march through Georgia. Would Wilson be willing to go back with Thomas and take personal command of his cavalry arm?

He would; and a reasonable basis of co-operation was established. Wilson assembled the scattered troopers, gave all the best mounts and equipment to Kilpatrick, and shipped the dismountees back to Nashville, whither he ordered enough Spencer carbines to supply the whole of the mounted force that was gathering there under Thomas. The cavalry commander himself went up to Nashville at the beginning of November and found things fairly tense. Thomas had assembled only 22,000 infantry at that date and Hood was approaching with almost twice that many. Forrest was with Hood, at the head of a cavalry force that had never been stronger, for he had drawn in formations from all over the Confederate west, while Wilson himself had mounts for only 5,000 men, and was not very likely to get more with the railroads under such pressure to carry supplies.

To cap this, an instantaneous and bitter row developed with Andrew Johnson, the patriotic, but highly political governor of Tennessee and vice-president-elect of the United States. While Wilson was still in the Cavalry Bureau, Johnson had wished to enlist 12 regiments of volunteer Tennessee cavalry for one year's service, and Wilson had prevented it. The succeeding head of the bureau had not been so hard-hearted; here the regiments were on the muster rolls and in Federal pay, scattered through the state where they would be nearest their homes and make the most votes for Johnson. " A bunch of drunken rowdies," Wilson described them; his first act on reaching Nashville was to scatter the men among northern regiments and to court-martial several of the field officers for being absent without leave.

Johnson's feelings can be imagined, and they were by no means improved when Wilson secured from Stanton authority to requisition all the horses south of the Ohio River and let the owners sue the government later. The authority was interpreted literally; Wilson took the horses that pulled the Nashville cabs and streetcars, and ended by attaching Johnson's own fine stable of riding and driving horses. There was an interview between the two men, with the politician sullenly angry and the cavalry commander impertinent; it ended with Wilson telling the governor that he had once thought him worthy to be president of the United States—"but now I have changed my mind."

As for the horses, they joined the cavalry and the cavalry went down into the Duck River country, where Schofield, with the XXIII Corps and part of the IV, was retiring toward Nashville, under orders to slow up Hood's advance as much as possible.

That the Union commander was able to accomplish his mission so well was partly due to the weather, which delayed Hood a good deal on muddy roads; and partly due to Forrest, who thought he could hamper Thomas' concentration by a long cavalry raid up toward the Cumberland River. The move was a success in one sense, since Forrest destroyed perfect mounds of stores. But it was a success purchased at the price of strategic failure, for Thomas was far too downy a bird to scatter men in pursuit of Forrest when he had a battle with Hood on the agenda; while Hood was left almost without cavalry to cover his march, and Wilson was able to slow it considerably by forcing the Confederate column to use the single main turnpike up through Columbia and Franklin.

The Rebel raider fell in on Hood on November 27, just south of the Duck. Schofield was holding the line of the stream, and Hood (who liked to think of himself as a second Stonewall Jackson) worked out a plan for a wide-sweeping flank attack across the up-river fords to reach Spring Hill and cut off the retreat of the Union force. Some artillery was emplaced on the south bank opposite Columbia to make an appearance of forcing a crossing by frontal attack there, while Forrest went upstream to gain the fords and lead the turning maneuver.

The Confederate cavalry leader was two to one of Wilson and easily gained his crossings; infantry began to pass over, but not until Wilson had gained a clear idea both of the force and the direction of the drive. As early as one in the morning of the 29th, Schofield was in possession of the fullest information and of Wilson's suggestion for an immediate retreat.

That was the setup behind the famous tangle of Spring Hill, in which the blunders of one side so beautifully canceled those of the other. Schofield blundered first; impressed by the Confederate artillery on the south bank and by his orders to cede as little ground as possible, he did not begin his retreat till the afternoon of the 29th. On the other side, Cheatham, commanding one of the Rebel corps, delayed his march for a reason no one ever explained, while Hood quarreled with some of his juniors and, instead of pressing forward, sat still to have a row with them. When the Confederate vanguards reached Spring Hill, they found the Union army already filing through, past barricades and artillery which halted any attempt to cut the column.

When Hood found the Yankees had slipped past him, he sent for Forrest and asked him to throw his cavalry across the Federal head of column and force them to deploy while his own main force gained on their rear and brought them to action.

But Forrest was in no shape to do anything of the kind. When Wilson had been driven from the fords of the Duck on the preceding day, he kept his cavalry well together, retreating not westward toward Spring Hill, but along country roads directly toward Franklin. Forrest was compelled to follow him, or to leave the Union horsemen in position to fall on Hood's flank and rear as the Confederates main body made toward Spring Hill. The country was densely wooded; Wilson went back very slowly, his brigades in turn being deployed dismounted and using their carbines from cover against opponents who had to put in three or four times their strength to oust them from each successive position. The consequence was that Forrest had been involved all day long in a harassing, if not particularly costly, fire fight, and when evening brought Hood's request to stop Schofield, he was obliged to report that he was out of ammunition, too far from the trains to obtain more before morning, and could do nothing.

Thus Schofield reached Franklin and dug in. Hood was now in a perfect fury with his corps commanders and gave the order for that furious frontal assault of November 30 which cost his army so heavily in morale and casualties. Forrest's force was split that night—an arrangement which its commander would probably never have made for himself—one of the brigades being used on the Rebel left in the assault against the fortified town, while the other two moved up the Harpeth in a new effort to gain fords and come down on the Federal rear.* Wilson was concentrated to hold the fords,

* The terms "brigade" and "division" cause much confusion in the Civil War because they were applied to organizations of different size and character in two armies. The Confederate brigade was normally something like three-quarters the strength of a Union division, and it was so in these opposing cavalry forces. But Forrest's big brigades were sometimes called divisions, even by the Confederates themselves; in fact, in the Selma campaign the latter term was always used.

whose position made it likely the enemy would attempt a turning movement. He had kept his men in the saddle most of the day, waiting for orders or the approach of the Rebels, and it was falling twilight when Hood's assault was launched against the town, Forrest's men simultaneously trying for the river crossings.

Wilson thought he had the whole Confederate cavalry force to deal with, twice the size of his own, but he knew it would go hard with Schofield if the Rebel horsemen broke through, and "I lost no time in pushing all the troops I could dismount against the enemy." It was a fire-power counterattack against opponents still mainly mounted, as the latter came up out of the stream and tried to ride down the Union lines. A battle without tactics, almost as fierce and close as that of Franklin itself—and it ended with Nathan Bedford Forrest taking the first real defeat of his life, every man but the dead and prisoners rejected to the south bank.

Hood was too hard hit to interfere further with Schofield's retreat to Nashville, where Thomas at last united his command. There the armies stood face to face until the dark December day when General Logan, en route to relieve Thomas, stepped off the train to learn that the man he was to replace had just won the most crushing victory of the entire war. It was Wilson's hand that guided the thunderbolt on both the battle days, but only as a hand; Thomas made the key tactical decisions, as it was Thomas who refused to fight till Wilson had his remounts and the cavalry could be used as the young general had insisted it should be used—a fast-moving wing to deliver a terrific weight of fire power on the enemy's flank and rear. "The damn Yankees loaded up their guns in the morning and shot at us all day," said one of their dismayed opponents.

Remembering that the Nashville maneuver was precisely the move Wilson had wished Grant to make at the North

Anna, it is probably not too much to assume that he had something to do with planting the idea in Thomas' mind, though neither commander has said so. The heart of the victory lies in the attack of the cavalry corps—not only because the decision to wait for remounts provided Thomas with his striking force, but also because the delay, which so much irritated Grant that he wanted Thomas relieved, had quite a different effect on Hood. The Confederate leader became imbued with the legend of Thomas' sluggishness; fortified his own left flank and sent Forrest off on a raid to Murfreesboro, where he was when Thomas struck.

The old and the new theories of cavalry were never more perfectly contrasted than on December 15, 1864, when Forrest tore up six miles of railroad track while Wilson was tearing up the left flank of the Rebel army.

VI

Down to the war with the Nez Percé Indians (who have received inadequate publicity for one of the best-conducted fighting retreats of record) there was no pursuit in American history to equal that which drove Hood's fragments beyond the Tennessee without guns or wagons. The reasons that brought it to an end were largely logistic; Wilson was pushing through used-up country which contained neither food nor forage and his transport could not hold the pace. In the meanwhile the battle of Nashville and Sherman's arrival at Savannah had brought a reconsideration of western strategy, both in Washington and at Confederate headquarters.

On the Rebel side, two of Hood's "corps" (together they could not have amounted to much more than 6,000 men) were shipped to the Carolinas to oppose Sherman's northward rush. The remaining infantry, with Forrest's command, which had not fought at Nashville and was still in fairly good shape, went down into Alabama, where it fell under the departmental command of General Dick Taylor.

Grant's original plan was to send Thomas marching to the sea at Mobile as Sherman had gone to Savannah, starting at once. But Thomas would face the same logistic troubles that had brought Wilson's pursuit to an end, and did not think his heavy columns of infantry could overcome them on a winter march. His army was accordingly broken up, part of the infantry going by sea to join Sherman, part being sent down the Mississippi to furnish weight for an overland operation from New Orleans against Mobile. It was planned that Wilson should take all the cavalry on an "expedition" that would be a prolongation of his pursuit of Hood, a raid down into Alabama toward Selma, the last important arsenal remaining to the Confederacy.

Wilson established a concentration point near Florence, Alabama, drawing in detachments that had been guarding the rail and river lines, as well as nearly a division that had been sent up to Louisville for remounts. Grant wanted the expedition to start early in February, but Wilson was not satisfied with his organization, and besides, had developed his own cavalry doctrine into something so different from the raiding concept that he and Grant were hardly talking the same language. "Cavalry is useless for defense," the young leader wrote. "Its only power is in a vigorous offensive. Therefore I urge its concentration south of the Tennessee and hurling it into the bowels of the South, in masses that the enemy cannot drive back."

That is, he was talking about an independent, self-sufficient cavalry army, in terms that might have come from De Gaulle or Guderian or George Patton. This was the type of force he proceeded to build among the pine barrens, while the spotlight was so thoroughly turned in other directions that no one noticed it. By mid-February he had six divisions in camp, 27,000 mounted men, all trained alike to march on their horses' feet, but fight on their own. (One must go back to Genghis Khan to find so many horsemen serving a single command.) The divisional leaders were young and active—Long, McCook (this is Edward M. McCook, the youngest of that fighting family), Winslow, Emory Upton; the last an infantry specialist, but Wilson had asked for him, and Grant seldom refused the requests of his favorite staff officer.

One thing, however, Grant would not concede, and that was the desired permission to use this whole force for the Alabama expedition. Detachments were made for the New Orleans command; for the army before Richmond; for trans-Mississippi operations. When Wilson set out to push south on March 23, 1865, he had only the three divisions of Long, Upton, and McCook, 12,500 mounted men. Behind them came a train of 250 wagons, with a guard of 1,500 dismounted troopers, who seem mostly to have ridden the wagons during marches. The supplies carried consisted solely of small rations and ammunition, for Wilson expected to cut loose from communications and live off the country as to bread and meat.

Forrest's total strength he estimated as nearly equal to his own and the enemy would have elaborate knowledge of the country as well as considerable help from local militia. The Union general catalogued his own advantages as his mobility, the armament and training of his horsemen (which permitted them to meet infantry in a stand-up action), and the fact that Forrest did not know precisely where he was bound.

The last turned out to be the decisive strategic factor; the Rebels adopted what was essentially a linear defense, which would have proved valid only had Wilson been conducting a raid, as they thought. Forrest and Taylor had Chalmers' division of cavalry at Columbus, Mississippi; Jackson's at West Point, Mississippi (he was called "Mud Fence

Jackson" to distinguish him from Stonewall), and most of
Roddey's at Montevallo, Alabama, but with one detachment
at Tuscaloosa. There were a couple of brigades of cavalry at
Mobile and several infantry commands of no great individual

Wilson's Selma Campaign

strength at various points. The main concentration was toward
the border line of the two states, with strong wings on the
main routes along either flank. The rivers along this line
flow generally southward, and they were in a spate sufficient

to make lateral movements difficult—a fact on which Wilson counted.

He fanned his three divisions out along as many different roads, expecting their advance to be reported and that the reports would keep the Confederates in ignorance of his real line of attack. All three were brought together at Jasper, where Wilson learned from his own scouts that there were signs that the Confederates had begun a concentration toward their strategic right, Chalmers' division having moved eastward. As the Union leader meant to turn this wing, it was important to anticipate the Rebel move. He dropped his trains, shot a brigade of McCook out toward Tuscaloosa, and with all the rest of his force set out at the best possible speed for Montevallo.

Forrest believed that the Yankees were coming down in a number of separate raiding detachments, which he expected to beat in detail. He identified McCook's brigade as one of these detachments and ordered Jackson's division up from West Point to deal with it. The force making for Montevallo he imagined to be another detachment; went to that point himself and ordered up one of the brigades from Mobile, while the infantry was to be brought together at Selma to handle any raiders who broke through.

The consequence was that Wilson easily passed the barriers of the rivers on his front and struck Montevallo on March 31, with nearly his whole force against one weak Confederate division. Forrest instantly attacked his advance elements; was violently counterattacked by Upton and driven from the field, so disorganized that he could set up no effective rear guard. That night the Union head of column bivouacked 14 miles south of Montevallo, and the encirclement of Forrest's right wing was effectively accomplished.

On the field Wilson captured a file of the enemy's dispatches, with information that located practically every man they had. Forrest himself, with the defeated men of Montevallo, was east of the Cahawba River, which is unfordable except along its upper reaches. The division of Chalmers was at Marion, still west of the Cahawba; Jackson was near Tuscaloosa; the Mobile brigades and the infantry still en route toward Selma. Wilson sent the remainder of McCook's command to gain possession of the only good bridge across the Cahawba, at Centerville, thus covering his right flank; with the other two divisions he pushed straight on toward Selma.

The Rebel commander had dug in at Ebenezer Church. Long's division attacked him there and took a momentary repulse when one regiment tried to ride down a battery and was countercharged by Forrest in person. But Upton was close behind Long; the weight of his dismounted attack broke the Confederates and sent them tumbling into Selma, leaving three guns and 300 prisoners. Forrest had ordered Jackson and Chalmers in on the city as soon as the Montevallo defeat made it clear he was dealing with something more serious than a raiding detachment, but the Union horsemen followed so fast that they were all round the place by early afternoon of 2 April, before the Rebel divisions had passed Marion.

There was an effort to man the works with old men, boys, what infantry had arrived, and the fragments of the twice-beaten cavalry, but Wilson dismounted his men and stormed the lines in three places at once. Forrest himself cut his way out with a small escort and escaped across the Cahawba; but 3,000 of his men were taken and the Confederacy had lost its last source of arms and ammunition.

Moreover, one of Forrest's divisions had been wiped out, those of Jackson and Chalmers had suffered so severely by attrition and overmarching that Wilson could hold the Cahawba line by dropping McCook's division. With the other two he turned east, expecting to fall in on the flanks of Sherman's army, but it was only a week after the fall of Selma that U. S. Grant stepped out on the porch of the McLean house and lit a cigar after accepting the surrender of the Army of Northern Virginia. Wilson's move resulted in nothing more than the capture of Jefferson Davis in poke bonnet and crinoline.

VII

For a variety of reasons the Selma campaign has received little attention from military students. There was Wilson's own record. He came north at the end of hostilities to find Andrew Johnson, an unforgiving man, had become President of the United States; and Johnson not only refused Grant's request to give the young general command of the military district of Georgia, but deprived him of his brevet rank and ordered him, as a captain of engineers on the permanent establishment, to report to his corps for duty. The upshot of this was that, after a short assignment on the inland water-ways, Wilson left the service, not to return to it until the Spanish War. Lest he be drawn into the whirlwind of controversy that presently gathered around Johnson, he took no part in the memoir writing and debating of the seventies and eighties, when so many of the general concepts of the War of the Rebellion were fixed in semi-permanent form.

The Selma campaign took place far from the main centers of interest and the numbers involved were small compared to those in the armies of Grant and Sherman. There was no great battle as a focus of interest, and in the three minor engagements that took place, Wilson was so overwhelmingly superior on the field as to remove the element of contest and invite neglect of the whole performance.

But it should not be overlooked that if Wilson's numbers were superior at points of contact, and if the fire power of his forces was even more superior than the numbers indicated, the latter was due to his intelligence in arming his troopers with the Spencer carbine, as the former was to his skill in feinting Forrest out of position. "It was not by his battles that Napoleon destroyed his enemies, but by his unheard-of marches," said a German critic once, and the same remark will apply here. The total forces under the Confederate general's command were not so very inferior to those of Wilson, and Dick Taylor would have supplied him with more infantry if there had been any logical place to station them.

The point is that in the Selma campaign Forrest was dealing with an opponent who had developed a new theory of mobile war, one not seen again till 1940; and it was a method with which the older system of handling cavalry, though carried to the highest peak of perfection, was ill fitted to cope. Forrest himself, an honest and an intelligent man, acknowledged as much when he met Wilson after the surrender. Doubtless he would have picked up the idea of using cavalry as a fast battle force, just as he armed his own headquarters troop with repeating carbines as soon as he could get his hands on them. But wars are only fought once, and victory usually goes to that leader who can introduce a viable variation into a familiar pattern.

CHARLES P. SUMMERALL
Sitting Bull II

I

A CURIOUS STREAK OF CHURCH RUNS THROUGH AMERICAN military history. Nathanael Greene was a devout follower of George Fox before being ejected from the latter's church for having become a still more devout follower of George Washington. Jacob Brown labored in the same vineyard until friendship with Hamilton aroused in him an un-Quakerly interest in war; Leonidas Polk held the incompatible ranks of bishop and general; Stonewall Jackson lectured in theology and prayed on the field; and the city of Washington during the Civil War was delighted by Secretary Stanton's ability to step into the pupit for a sermon in the best fire-and-brimstone manner of the Connecticut dominies. It was, therefore, less in response to personal idiosyncracy than to historical process that Charles Pelot Summerall, son of a long line of preachers, and himself intended for the pastorate, should turn out a soldier and a general and should look less like a bombardier than a bishop.

He often behaved like the latter; by which it is not meant merely to direct attention to the gift of self-expression which made his little speeches before battle celebrated in the A.E.F., and his reports the most pungent official reading since Joseph

O. Shelby used to introduce passages from *Marmion* into his. Nor has the combination of faith and fighting spirit been new since the crusades. It is rather that his ecclesiastical background imparted to the general's mind certain special characteristics which aided not a little in making him one of the most remarkable figures in the American forces during World War I.

No officer but Bullard soared through the hierarchy of command more rapidly; none succeeded better in every task assigned to him; none displayed greater inventiveness; and none was more beloved by the rear-rank private. Not all of the general's characteristics as a commander can be referred to his churchly background, but there are enough to render fruitful an inquiry into what this background gave him.

The most striking of these gifts can perhaps be described as that of subordinating the minutiae of discipline to the essentials of duty; for the ecclesiastical mind, though unswerving in its demand for the latter, looks upon it from the heart rather than the head. The difference can perhaps be illustrated by remembering how N. P. Banks complained of the "wanton indiscipline of this troop of ragged guerrillas" Sherman had sent him for the Red River campaign. The day of battle came; Bank's own beautifully uniformed regiments saluted punctiliously and ran away, while the ragged guerrillas worked out a victory against half again their numbers.

On this point there is a tale of Summerall making an inspection trip through the snow, mud, and night of the Toul sector.

"Any drinking in your command?" he asked.

"Some drinking, sir, but no drunkenness," replied the captain to whom the query had been addressed, and hardly got the words out of his mouth before a door was flung open, and out staggered a cook who had served with the general in the Philippines. "My old captain from the Philippines!" he shouted gleefully, and collapsed into the snow. The explosion the horrified staff expected never took place. Instead the general, who does not himself take any liquid stronger than coffee, took the man off with him, gave him some light punishment, and made him his headquarters chef.

The incident was not without honor among the men, and doubtless helped in assuring to Summerall his singularly perfect control of the moral factor which Napoleon estimated as four-fifths of soldiering.

II

But this is outrunning the story. General Charles P. Summerall was born in 1867 at Lake City, Florida, missed a college course preparatory to the Episcopal ministry through that impoverishment that lay like a blanket on the post–Civil War South, entered West Point in 1888, and was graduated in 1892, twentieth in a class of sixty-two. Within a year of graduation he had reached the 5th Artillery and remained uninterruptedly with the regiment until the Spanish War, through which he passed as aide to the general commanding the Department of the Gulf.

The outbreak of the Philippine Insurrection brought him back to the regiment and sent the regiment on active service in the islands, where Summerall earned a brevet and (what was more important) learned how much artillery could help infantry when used in close support. Essentially the insurrection presented a problem in minor tactics—how to keep attacking infantry from being sniped to death as it moves in— and the trouble was over as soon as this problem had been solved by the free use of artillery in close co-operation with the foot. The observation of this fact was to be important to Summerall's later history, but it was not immediately important, for he was called away to China with Reilly's battery to serve in the Boxer Rebellion.

In the attack on the Forbidden City he performed a deed of valor that made him a marked man then and for long after. The battery was opposite the gate, not shooting too accurately, or at least not accurately enough for Charles P. Summerall. He dashed forward straight into the blaze of Boxer fire, and standing calmly, chalked a big cross on the gate as an aiming point. The guns spoke up; they hit the cross, the gates went down, and the city fell. Summerall got the Certificate of Merit which was then the only American award for courage besides the Congressional Medal.

His story between the Boxer Rebellion and World War I is normal for the service and of no particular interest except to himself. He located and planned Fort Seward in Alaska; spent six years at the Military Academy, three as Major of the 3rd F.A., at San Antonio, and three more in the Militia Bureau in Washington. The last three were the years in which all the guns of Europe let go; there were naturally some pretty lively discussions on the technical aspects of the European conflict among the officers stationed in Washington. Major Summerall, with memories of the manner in which his own guns and the infantry had co-operated in the Philippines, was both vigorous, and according to then current opinion, heretical, in his insistence that the infantry-artillery team was being grievously misused.

The doctrine that had emerged from trench warfare was that of proportioning the number of guns to the lineal frontage to be attacked or held, with the character of the ground furnishing an insignificant modifying factor. Summerall protested that to accept this was to reduce all cannon to pieces of position. The primary function of artillery (he said) was to protect the infantry so that it could keep in movement; to neutralize the forces which attack infantry in movement. Shells expended for any other purpose might as well be dumped into the ocean. Guns, therefore, should not be proportioned to linear front, but to the number of infantry in action.

But what had happened in the World War? Along the Western Front, especially on the British-held portions of that front, there had been allotted "guns enough to cut the wire," with the expectation that they would also be enough to pulverize the defense. Infantry was then packed in ahead of the guns as close as it could stand and assigned no function but that of occupying ground conquered by the artillery.

As a result of this shift in perspective from the true doctrine, "no attack of the World War before 1918 was supported by half enough artillery to protect the men," according to Summerall. This not only insured frightful casualties; it also guaranteed resultless battles, for it erected artillery to the major arm while keeping it static by so breaking up the ground before an attack as to make artillery advance impossible. The more brilliantly an infantry attack succeeded, the farther it got beyond the zone where it was protected by its own guns. There was also the not unimportant detail of practice that artillery, as the new primary arm, showed signs of emancipation from infantry control. This reduced to a minimum the difficulties attendant upon liaison, it is true, but it was not satisfactory to the infantrymen being shot to pieces by the enemy's machine guns.

The deep defense of 1917 still further accentuated all these characteristics of the war of trenches then current. But in 1917 experienced Franco-British Western Front officers were hearing Summerall's remarks on artillery with the same polite amusement they accorded General Pershing's observation that the rifle was being used for nothing but the handle to a bayonet. After all Pershing had not fought in this modern war, and Summerall was a quite junior and newly appointed general of the National Army, commanding the 67th Artillery

Brigade of the 42nd Division. The gap between him and a position where he could make his theories felt in practice was not, however, as wide as it might look.

"Stick wit' us, guns, you're de only guys dat knows what it's all about," said a Bowery-born sergeant of the Rainbows out of the side of his mouth, as the infantry swung past a spot where Summerall's brigade had turned out to clear a road. The man in the infantry ranks is probably the world's best authority on the effectiveness of artillery; and the high command agreed with this man sufficiently to assign Summerall (in December, 1917) to the prize artillery command of the A.E.F.—the 1st Artillery Brigade of the 1st Division, just about to take its place in line along the Toul sector. His code name was "Sitting Bull"; the war correspondents clucked with delight when they heard it, and gave it to him for a permanent nickname.

III

The materials from which the inner history of that period of the war will one day be written still lie, dissociated fragments, scattered through official files and the memories of men who have not yet written them down. It is impossible to reconstruct the reasons that led General Pershing to push this junior artillery brigadier into a major-generalship and command of one of his two divisions of seasoned regular infantry on the eve of the first major offensive undertaken by the American forces. Summerall's control of morale undoubtedly had a great deal to do with it, for by the spring of 1918 he was one of the best liked as well as the best known officers in the army, already famous for assembling the men under his command before any important operation and addressing to them a little speech in which he explained the business in hand and what was expected of the soldier.

An examination of the First's record on the Toul front also

SITTING BULL

reveals certain details of operation which must at the time have impressed the high command. Perhaps the most striking of these was Summerall's emphasis on re-sealing the marriage between artillery and infantry. "When the sector was taken over," says the division's official history, "the communications net was found to be entirely inadequate." Analysis of the statement shows that the inadequacy lay principally in the connections between the two arms. Summerall had a complete set of communications wires installed to connect the forward infantry positions, through a switchboard at artillery H.Q. direct with battery, and sent down a standing order that requests for artillery help were to be routed through instantly. On March 19 the system received its test. The Germans tried a dress-shirt, surprise raid, a whole battalion of storm troops coming over behind a box barrage. Summerall's guns, silent till the storm troops started, clapped down on them in one of the quickest and most accurate shoots of the war, and destroyed the raiding party with the loss of all its officers and nearly half its men before it got more than ten yards from the jumping-off point.

In April the division moved up to Cantigny to hold the German drive. The lines were disconnected shell holes, the problem one of defense in open warfare. In view of the lack of trenches the French reinforced Summerall's brigade with two battalions of their own 75's and a considerable number of old fortress howitzers, pieces of limited range but heavy caliber. For the first time since he had come to France, Sitting Bull had enough artillery to show what he could do about protecting the foot. He assigned double crews to the old heavies and kept them croaking right around the clock, registering on every machine-gun position reported by infantry reconnaissance at a pace that made sleep in the sector impossible except for those who sought it in deep dugouts. But he also made more than sleep impossible for the Ger-

· 251 ·

mans. After four days of this pounding the enemy command reported that their machine-gunners were becoming unreliable; in the brief drive that eliminated the Cantigny salient their front went all to pieces at the first shock, and one of the captured German officers underlined the effect with, "My God, your artillery must be crazy! All they do is shoot; my men couldn't get any rest or work on the trenches or lay their guns properly."

Of course, there were disadvantages, too. It took lots of ammunition, and as soon as the salient-straightening operation was over, the French pulled out some of their heavies to halt a new German drive at Compiègne, with the result that the enemy artillery concentrations that had been attracted by Summerall's activity were free to shell the American infantry, which suffered a good deal of loss.

Evidently General Pershing believed the advantages outweighed the disadvantages; on July 17, when General Bullard of the 1st Division was moved up to a corps, Summerall received command of the division. The next night, amid a storm of almost tropical violence the 1st went in to take part in the great Soissons offensive. Summerall's new division, with some Moroccans and the American 2nd, were to be the spearhead of the attack.

As usual the general was dissatisfied with the quantity of artillery allotted to him—plenty by the standard of the division front, but nowhere near enough by his own standard of the number of men in line. Years before he had read a monograph by General Skobelev, of the Russo-Turkish War of 1877— "Troops under fire from directly in front will not reply on an oblique," said the key sentence of it. In the night, with the storm whirling round and the troops dogging up through the mud toward the jump-off, that sentence came back to Summerall with the force of an inspiration.

He rapidly prepared a change in operations orders; a slight

change in appearance, but one of major import. Only the 18th Infantry on the right of his division was to attack at the original jump-off time. The 16th, 26th and 28th were to greet H hour with intense rifle and machine-gun fire, then follow the 18th at half-hour intervals; and the entire divisional artillery was to cover each regiment as it moved to the attack, firing from the oblique.

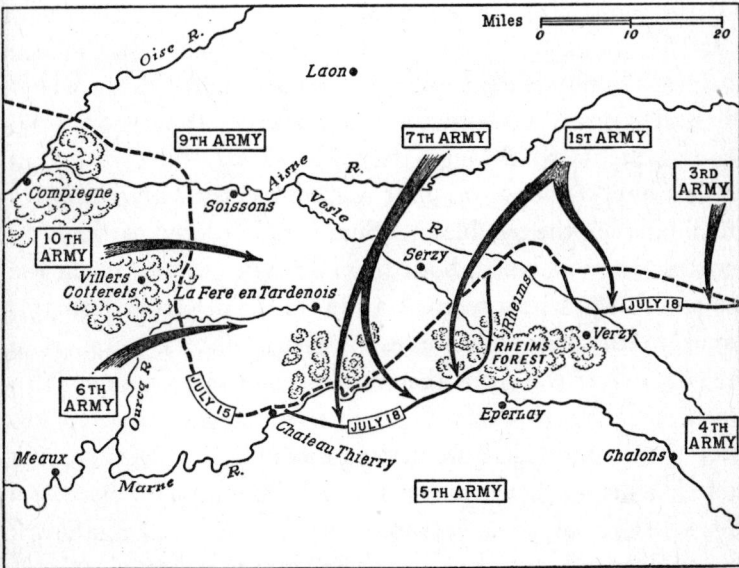

Soissons Attack

The country for the advance was as bad as it could be, broken ravines and marshes impregnated with mustard gas by constant shelling, but the 1st went right through, outpacing the Moroccans on the right, the French on their left, reaching their second objective before evening of the first day. At the heights of Chaudun, German batteries were captured that gave eloquent testimony to the effectiveness of the new method; their personnel had been wiped out in the concentration Summerall's guns put down. The division took heavy casualties, it is true; but they came mostly from a complex of ravines on its flank which the French had failed to clear. The Germans, fired on from straight ahead, replied straight ahead, as Russian Skobelev predicted, and took their beating. But there was trouble in keeping the guns up with the advancing infantry; the second day of the attack did not go as well as the first and the last two days worse still.

IV

The difficulty is the capital one in a form of warfare where all attacks are frontal—that of the infantry-artillery team becoming separated through its own success and slowing up against impacted opposition. It was apparently with the object of eliminating the trouble that Summerall ordered particularly careful reconnaissance, both from air and ground, when the 1st took over a new sector on the St. Mihiel front just previous to the big push there. Artillery officers were taken carefully over the maps that resulted and in the preparation fire for the attack every German machine-gun position "received the undivided attention of one heavy or two light guns," which direct firing was to be discontinued only when the schedule of advance should have brought the infantry beyond the point where the machine gun was located.

Already this is a long step from the somewhat aimless steam-roller barrages of 1916, whose purpose was the obviously impossible one of delivering a shell onto every square inch of front; but more was to follow. Not only were the maps studied for German defensive emplacements, but also with reference to the movement of the guns, and firing along the routes selected for pushing them forward was avoided unless the infantry specifically asked for it during the attack itself.

In the attack as delivered the German resistance was somewhat less than expected, but so were the 1st's casualties, particularly those inflicted by machine-gun fire. Within four hours from the time the advance began, the artillery was well beyond the original jump-off spot and firing a barrage for a renewed advance, and the 1st, with the longest distance of any unit to cover, did its work in the least time. "We could have gone right on and taken Metz," said Summerall later, a trifle mournfully.

Perhaps it was well that the division did not lose much at St. Mihiel, however, for it was about to make the translation from what Liddell Hart calls "the battle of a dream to the battle of a nightmare"—from St. Mihiel to the Meuse-Argonne. The 1st was put directly into the offensive along the line of the Aire on October 4, without having had time to do the preliminary scouting that had been so valuable at St. Mihiel, against a country of tall and steep hills, their slopes bare, their crests densely wooded, ideal for defense.

Montrefagne was the big barrier, a fortress of nature; and the Germans installed there had orders from their own high command to hold it to the last. An ideal observation center toward the Americans on the south, it also dominated the hills of the Argonne eastward, where the Germans had their heavy artillery positions and communication lines for a wide stretch of front covering everything up to the gap of Grand Pré. Von Gallwitz, in whose army groupment the sector lay, had crowded the mountain with machine-gun nests and backed it with all the artillery he had; already American attacks had twice broken in bloody foam at its foot.

To make matters worse, Summerall had against this prepared position of immense strength only his divisional guns with one bare regiment of French; and orders from above forced him still further to scatter these resources by assigning two cannon to go up with the infantry advance of each regiment as accompanying guns. "That is not to neutralize the enemy's fire, but our own," he commented; "a 75 as an accompanying gun is nothing but a target."

The pep-talk he administered to the division the night before the battle is still remembered by some of its veterans as the best they ever heard. It was probably not so important as his care in arranging double liaison lines from each element of the advance to the artillery, for, with other features of his support technique rendered impossible by the character of ground and battle, everything depended on placing gunfire just where the infantry wanted it.

The battle that started next morning saw some of the most furious fighting in the history of the A.E.F. and the war, for if the resistance at St. Mihiel was less than expected, here it was greater. Summerall had his regiments attacking in succession behind the barrage of the whole artillery brigade as at Soissons; but quite early in the game the resistance became so stiff they could not follow the curtain of fire. As he had arranged, the control of the guns passed instantly to front-line infantry commands; they fired on observed strong points, pushing clear forward to the original jump-off. At places, and those not few, the combat was hand-to-hand; but by evening the left wing of the 1st had won most of the Montrefagne, with a salient a mile deep into the German line there.

Eastward the ring wing had crossed a ravine and stormed the hill beyond, then stalled at the foot of another high hill (Hill 212) with a deep ravine running between it and the Montrefagne, down which as through a tunnel came torrents of German fire. At the north end of this tunnel was a doubled mount, very steep, with a beautifully organized position known as the Ariétal Farm. Von Gallwitz had received Prinz Eitel Friedrich's division of Prussian Guards in response to his call for reserves. He determined to pivot on the Ariétal Farm position, slash into the flank of the First's salient and bite it off with a counterattack at the first light of morning.

This sensible procedure was attended by an inconvenience; namely, that Summerall also had planned an attack for the morning, so that dawn saw barrage crossing barrage and assault meeting assault, head on. All morning long there was desperate battle along the slopes of the hills, with no one able to tell who was winning. But about noon a smart sergeant of the 26th managed to work through cover behind Ariétal farm with his squad. His brigadier sent help; and now Summerall's care in doubling and tripling his infantry-artillery communications suddenly weighted the scales in his favor. For the Germans had but a single line of wire, running along the edge of a wood, right through the spot where the sergeant and his squad had arrived. He cut the wires; the runners who presently came down the line he gathered in; and along the constantly changing front the Teuton artillery began to miss, for any observation other than front line was useless in so tangled an affair. Summerall's own guns, firing off the map at 1,200 yards to perfect observation in spite of the fog, did terrific execution—and by twilight the whole Montrefagne was American, Ariétal as well and all the other commanding heights, with von Gallwitz confessing defeat by firing mustard gas into the lines he had lost.

Eitel Friedrich's division was so used up that it was valueless for the rest of the war. Three other divisions were sent in against the 1st during the week, two of them on the succeeding days when the Americans did nothing but hold on, but they could not shake the regulars loose. The 82nd came up behind them and cut into the Argonne, and the Germans were thrown back to the Kriemhilde Line, their last defense south of the vital lateral railroad from Metz through Sedan and Mezières to Valenciennes. On October 11 the 1st came out of line, leaving behind it 196 officers and 7,324 men, after the hardest fighting it would be called on to do; and that same day Charles P. Summerall, who had gone to Europe as a new colonel, was advanced to the command of a corps.

V

His corps was the V, consisting of the worn 1st Division, which immediately went into reserve, the 32nd, 42nd and 89th, with the 2nd Division coming in later. The 42nd and 32nd took over the line of the corps front at once, the former relieving the 1st; and Summerall instantly expressed his opinion of the prevailing artillery arrangements by sending the 1st artillery brigade back to help the 42nd's shoot things out with the Germans. There were local offensives along the front on October 13, 14, 15. Then it quieted down briefly while preparations were made for the November 1 battle, the biggest and best in American World War I history and the one in which Summerall played the most prominent part.

The 2nd Division passed into line to the left wing in his attack; the 89th formed the right. Behind the 2nd, the 42nd was in support, behind the other wing the 1st, with the 32nd in corps reserve—an assemblage under one command of four of the five most experienced divisions in the army, with one big new strong unit that had done especially well at St. Mihiel. The job before this force was to break straight through the Kriemhilde Line, crossing the steep ridge of Barricourt, and to work down the slopes toward the Meuse. If the attack succeeded the Germans were done.

Now, as a corps commander, Summerall had at last all the artillery he wanted, sending the guns to position and collecting ammunition for them for October 22 on, then bringing the artillerymen back to rest billets for a few days before the drive. The guns of the 1st and 42nd were added to those of the two combat divisions for the task; the corps artillery was brought forward till 608 pieces were lined up on the two-division front, as against the 108 the same officer had had to cover his one division on October 4.

To every German machine gun was assigned a 155 or two 75's as at St. Mihiel; to every German battery, two or more heavy howitzers. The barrage was to reach the depth of 1,200 yards—75's firing H.E. at 150 meters ahead of the men, 75's with shrapnel at 350 meters, 155's with fragmentation at 600 meters, and beyond that heavies. Moreover, the 155's were brought into positions before sacred to infantry. "Whenever we saw one of those damn 75's," General Mc-Glachlin, the chief of artillery, has said, "we decided we weren't far enough forward and we moved on." Yet there were still enough guns left to have several batteries detailed to fire only at the call of the infantry, and the liaison net was stretched tight so they might make calls easily.

Behind all this concentration of fire the reserve divisions were to follow close on the heels of the attack units, ready to jump in should unexpected obstacles develop. One final instruction: During the October 4 offensive, Summerall's men had run into heavy machine-gun fire at the very start of the movement, where the Germans had pushed little knots out beyond the curtain of preparation fire, close up to the American line, to lie in wait for the attack as it started. This time, when the preparation fire began, the attacking elements were directed to retreat 200 yards; the Germans would be given time enough to get these forward machine guns in position, and the barrage laid down on the old American front line.

As the general explained these preparations to the war correspondents at his headquarters the night before the attack, some of them noted that certain usual arrangements were missing.

"What about the counterattack?" they asked.

"Gentlemen, there will be no counterattack."

Like the annals of a happy people, those of the November 1st offensive were brief, consisting mainly of the monotonous repetition of "We have reached the objective. Losses small."

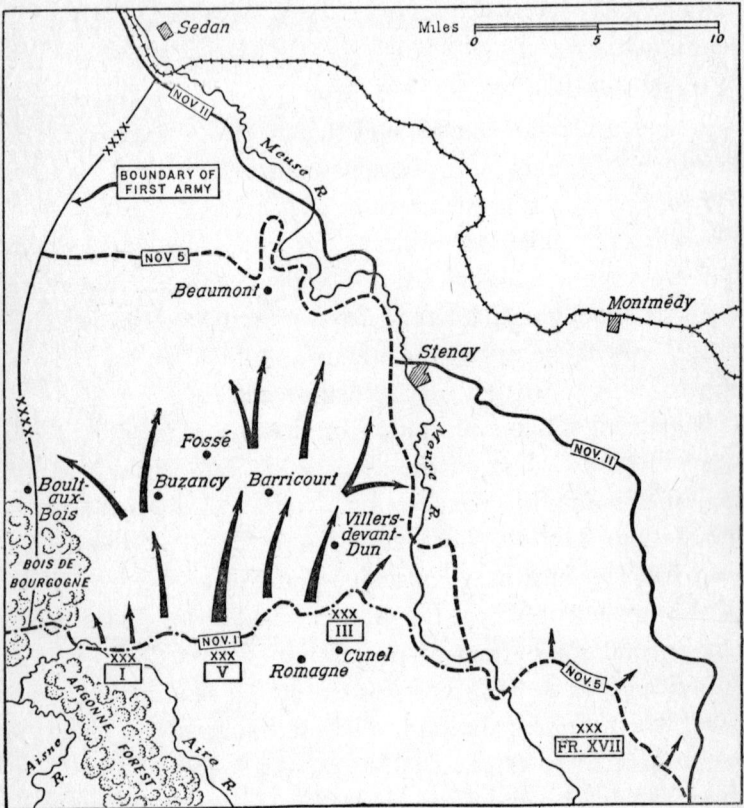

November First Attack

The famous Kriemhilde Line was smothered. On the first morning three German artillery regiments were taken complete; two nights later one of the German divisions opposing the advance (15th Bavarian) came out of action with only 277 rifles left. By this time von Gallwitz had brought up the last reserves he could scrape from his impoverished resources. Reconnaissance reports showed he was trying to build up a new line around a succession of posts, well back, but still forward enough to give him time for an orderly withdrawal to the Meuse.

Summerall reasoned, correctly as it turned out, that the Germans dared not attempt to hold the roads for fear of his guns; put his advance divisions of infantry into columns of twos and sent them straight down these roads in a night march—a brilliant stroke of tactics. It worked; von Gallwitz' tenuous line was pierced at a dozen points, and now there was nothing for him to do but scramble back to the river as best he might.

In the pursuit the 2nd and 89th struck the river, which slanted across the corps front and beyond from right to left. Behind the two leading divisions the 1st and 42nd were practically pinched out. On Summerall's left, neither the I Corps nor the French beyond them had caught up with his furious advance; there were German elements there, of indeterminate strength, and an army boundary, assigned at a time when no such whirlwind victory had been contemplated, proved not to constitute a defensible flank.

This was the justification in the general state of affairs for the famous "race to Sedan" in which Summerall sent his 1st Division, on another night march, slanting across the rear areas of the 89th and 2nd, the front of the 42nd and the American I Corps, across the army boundary, toward that town of historic memories. The orders he had received from the high command were at least permissive of something, if not quite that. There has been a persistent rumor that the general had received oral assurance from someone representing high command that it would be all right.

But it was very far from all right; an overenthusiastic vanguard placed the commander of the 42nd under arrest, and when the 1st reached the hills south of Sedan, they found the French coming up on the other side in a thoroughly disagreeable mood, with the announcement they had orders to fire on those heights and were going to do so.

The 1st was pulled back under peremptory orders, but the incident closed Summerall's fighting career with something of a shadow; one of those shadows through which history finds it difficult to perceive the true stature of a man until a distance has been reached which allows the figure to stand above the mists. But even from this distance it seems not unreasonable to say that the figure of Charles P. Summerall will one day stand very high as that of the man who restored the structure of battle—who brought artillery and infantry back into that true relation to each other from which they had escaped during the static and useless fighting of 1916.

"Artillery exists only to protect and support infantry," he said, and on the field he demonstrated that by keeping this relation to the fore, even the machine-gun deadlock could be broken—not by the use of special arms which essentially avoid the issue, but by the proper employment and proportioning of arms already in hand; not by trying to give foot an additional mechanical mobility, but by restoring to it that flexibility which it has always possessed and which is its great asset. Surprise is a wonderful thing when you can have it; but it is noteworthy that not one of Summerall's successful attacks, not even that of November 1, was a surprise. He got his results through liaison, co-operation, and combination of the fighting arms; and this is, in the long run, the secret of all great officers.

A. A. VANDEGRIFT

Vandegrift of Guadalcanal

I

ALL OPERATIONS IN WAR ARE THE RESULT OF ENCOUNTERS between two mutually exclusive plans; and nearly all are undertaken on inaccurate information as to the enemy's strength and dispositions. These two facts are in general but poorly realized; a failure in apprehension that has led to the writing of most military history as though combat were an exclusive performance by one of the high contending parties, against enemies who have the unalterability and impersonality of natural forces. The normal leader of troops absorbs this attitude with his instruction, and considerable combat experience is required before he can overcome the tendency to be startled and shocked when he discovers his estimate of the situation was wrong, that he is launched into a chain reaction of improvisations.

When he cannot make an adequate improvisation to meet a situation radically altered from his original concept, a commander is surprised, in the military meaning of that verb—an event with whose results everyone is familiar. It follows that one of the more important elements in making command decisions is the question of the commander's state of mind at the time they are made; how far he has been surprised by the appearance of circumstances calling for a decision. It is not often that we have such accurate details as to the interplay of the four main nonphysical factors in a campaign—the state of mind and the state of information of both sides—as in the case of the fighting for Guadalcanal. Certainly there is no similar instance in a Japanese war, where most of the enemy commanders died without leaving any records.

What we know of that campaign is sufficient to establish General A. A. Vandegrift, of the Marines, as one of the ablest officers of our history, though he was advanced too rapidly ever to be a field leader in another operation. Many times astonished, he was never himself surprised, and constantly surprised the enemy. His operations were conducted under the unremitting observation of his opponents, but he managed to conceal from them all germane information both as to his strength and to his arrangements. When the campaign was over he had achieved a victory at a cost of something like a fifth of their casualties, though the total force they employed was nearly double his own. Guadalcanal was also a key campaign to the war, the point at which a decision was reached.

Of course he did not do it alone. By time the operation reached its climax, the 1st Marine Division (reinforced) was in so severe a state of mental and physical exhaustion that the need for withdrawal had become urgent. Army troops had already participated in numbers and would now complete the work. He was powerfully aided by the blows of the Navy and by the air arms of Navy and Army, which on one occasion nearly destroyed a Japanese division before it had placed a man ashore. But this is no more than to say that the campaign was fought under the modern conditions of war, in which the old sharp distinctions among arms and services tend progressively to disappear. The major responsibility, except in logistics, rested with General Vandegrift.

It is pertinent to look into the background of that flexibility of mind which emerges from any study of the campaign as its chief characteristic. It was no doubt latently present all the time and could not have been any more than developed; but it certainly was not in the least hampered by the early career of the man who got less of his learning from books and more in the field than almost any other high commander in World War II. There was a back door to an officer's commission in the Marine Corps in the early 1900's, and Vandegrift took it, being commissioned as second lieutenant after only half of a projected four-year course at the University of Virginia. One of the reasons appears to have been that after injuring a knee playing football, college had not very many attractions for him. Of course the early commissioning left him well behind officers of similar seniority in educational background, so the gap had to be made up; but at least the process was accomplished in the *gemütlich* open-air atmosphere of the Marine Officers' School at Fort Royal, the barracks at Portsmouth, New Hampshire, and the Wakefield rifle range.

His earliest field assignment was with the 1st Provisional Brigade in Cuba, then enjoying the revolutionary spasms of 1912. On his second day with the command he was under fire; and a month later he was detached and sent to join the expeditionary battalion in Nicaragua. There was some fighting there —the official records show him as "participating in the assault on Coyotepe"—but the event of decisive importance was nonmilitary. A one-horse train pulled into the town of Leon and from the tender of the locomotive descended a second lieutenant—melting with heat, swollen-lipped with thirst, covered with soot and coal dust, but smiling as he saluted his commanding officer. The lieutenant was Vandegrift; and fortune arranged it that the commanding officer should be Smedley Butler, who promptly tagged the young man "Sunny Jim."

The U.S. Marine Corps is probably about as free from the

COMMANDANT OF the CORPS!

"old school tie" influence as any military service can be, but a certain amount of it is natural and inevitable. Everyone in a military service or out of it likes to work with others whose training and experience have given them a point of view and method of performance similar to his own. A. A. Vandegrift had been a bit of an outsider among the Naval Academy and Virginia Military Institute graduates of the Marines, but from the hour when he stepped off the train at Leon that was done with. He was a protégé of the dynamic Butler, who regarded the young man as one of his best officers and saw to it that no appointment he could fulfill was withheld from him. Butler was a field soldier of almost violent activity himself, and the natural result was that Vandegrift was projected into a series of active employments far from home—duty against the Cacos of northern Haiti, first with his own corps and then as a loan officer with the Haitian gendarmerie. (He may have learned something about jungle warfare during this time, but the result is not discernible; jungle warfare was limited to the Caribbean in those days.) Duty under Butler in China, as his operations and training officer. Duty with the mail guards. Aide to the mayor of Philadelphia at the time Butler was cleaning up the police situation in that harassed city. A return to China; finally secretary and assistant to the Commandant of the Corps, then Major General Holcomb.

This is the background, one which, even for a Marine officer, runs heavily to foreign service and to active, if administrative, posts. In such a career there are few details that emerge above the level of gossip (that he is an epicurean eater and likes gardens, for example); but when a detail does show up there is usually in it a flash of the quick and ruthless action so characteristic of his old chief. It is 1927, for instance, and the Marine planes on the China coast are working out problems with naval vessels. Some Japanese observation planes came around. Protest was made to the Jap commandant, who replied that he was very sorry, it had been inadvertent, would not be repeated, etc., etc., etc. It was repeated the next day and by planes obviously photographing. As operations officer, Vandegrift sent up fighters to chase them away, with orders to shoot if they did not clear out. The Japanese commander protested in tones almost of anguish; he had lost face badly over this business and wanted an apology tied up in a pink ribbon to save his career. Vandegrift neither apologized nor refused; he simply sent no answer at all.

II

By the middle of 1941 it was pretty clear we were going to get into the war or be shoved in, and the war then meant a European leg of the tripod Axis, in control of every means of access to a continent. The apparent requirement was for beach-head operations on a massive scale. The U.S. Marines have gone through more variations of function than any other military service, but early in the 1920's they had decided that their purpose in the modern world had become that of conducting amphibious operations. It is hard to realize now that a good deal of the most pontifical opinion then held that landings on a hostile and defended beach were impossible. There was Gallipoli to back this and Marine experiments along such lines were regarded with some skepticism. The 1st Marine Division, organized that fall at New River, N. C., and trained for amphibious work, was thus both an experiment and a show piece.

It had to prove amphibious operations could be conducted and at the same time learn how to conduct them, a process including the invention of some of the equipment. General Holcomb sent Brigadier General Vandegrift down to New River as assistant commander of the division.

The date of Vandegrift's arrival was November 27, 1941; ten days later it became clear where the Marines would be conducting amphibious operations, and the matter of training for them became urgent. So did Vandegrift's responsibilities. The position of assistant division commander in the Marines is peculiar and rather difficult. Paper work is eliminated from his duties specifically so that he will be a means of liaison between the division commander and troops in the field; but at the same time the Marines have so few divisions that he is in some sense a crown prince, an heir apparent, and there are some fairly intricate personal relationships involved. In the case of the 1st Marine Division the problem was made more intricate still by the fact that Major General Torrey, the Division Commander, was not proving equal to his job. He was respectable and had a long record of service, but none of it under fire; a garrison general who cared more for a salute than a salvo of artillery, for parades than a platoon.

Vandegrift's approach to the situation was to get out into the boondocks himself on exercises and to make most of his suggestions downward rather than up. Under the freezing rains of the winter Carolinas the men learned that chances were excellent of seeing Sunny Jim's head poking from behind a bush and that he presently would be telling the platoon sergeant that the men were too closely bunched or the BAR team not properly under cover. In the meantime the Torrey matter came to a head; that general was relieved, and on March 23, 1942, Vandegrift was made a major general and commander of the division.

It has been related that this was over his own protest (one thinks of General Thomas in a similar situation), on the ground that he wished to give no appearance of having conducted an intrigue. He was overruled, of course. The training continued till June, 1942, on the 14th of which month he arrived in Wellington, New Zealand, with his staff, to prepare for a period of forward-area training looking toward action.

At the time he sailed, the assignment was vague and it was not contemplated that any attack action at all would involve Marines before some date early in 1943. But while the general was on the water the Battle of Midway had been fought and the whole strategic situation had been radically changed. The Japanese were for the moment deprived of their power of the offensive, but they would recover it unless an offensive were taken against them at least strong enough to prevent their building up fresh reserves. The fact that, if they placed the growing Gaudalcanal airfield in operation, New Caledonia and the New Hebrides—essential way stations on "the lifeline to Australia"—would come under direct attack, made the Solomon Islands the obvious objective. Less than two weeks after Vandegrift's arrival in New Zealand, he was summoned to Admiral Ghormley's headquarters and was informed that he would command the troops of the expedition.

The status of the division at that time was not one to encourage high hopes for success. General Vandegrift had never seen it assembled in one place and its best-trained infantry regiment, the 7th, had been sent to Samoa for sentry duty some time since. Only one of the other infantry regiments had come with him; the third was just sailing from San Francisco at the date of the Ghormley conference. Both these had been so heavily raided for cadres that they amounted to green formations little beyond the basic-training stage. On the voyage out the transports had been so crowded that there was not even opportunity for calisthenics. Many of the officers the general did not know, and the effect of all this was accentuated by the fact that instead of his 7th Regiment they gave him one from the 2nd Marine Division; a regiment still at San Diego which could hardly arrive much before the date when the division sailed to its objective. A Raider battalion and one of parachutists, similarly distant and unknown, were added.

The intelligence was sparse and the over-all plan that had

come from Washington touched the edge of fantasy. It called for a landing by August 1, with the capture of Munda in the Central Solomons by September and of Bougainville by November. There were no maps, no photographs of Guadalcanal-Tulagi, and only one chart, made from an old survey and liberally sprinkled with the initials that signified "position doubtful." The four higher commanders involved in the expedition could not be brought together before July 28, when the reinforced division was undergoing a brief and fairly unsatisfactory period of rehearsal training at Koro.

By this time a map of sorts had been made up from a single set of photos taken over Guadalcanal by a B-17 under fighter attack and General Vandegrift's staff had drawn an operations plan upon which Admiral Turner, who commanded amphibious forces, instructed his own staff. It was a backward arrangement, since Turner's command in a sense included Vandegrift's—actually would include it until the latter was ashore. There was no time to do things in any other way, since Admiral Turner was still en route from the United States when it became time to load the transports in New Zealand, something that had to be done with a definite method of operation in view.

At the Koro conference it developed that the two other commanders involved—Admiral Fletcher of the covering force and the Australian Admiral Crutchley of the naval screening force—had concepts of the proposed operation completely different from those of the Marine and amphibious force leaders. Fletcher thought of his part in the operation as a hit-and-run raid, in which he would see the Marines to the beaches, and then leave within twenty-four hours. It would have to be that, he explained; the Japs had available sea forces far superior to our own and could bring through Rabaul land-based bombers in such strength that with his slender complement of carriers he dared not stand against them. The Australian, who headed a strong cruiser squadron, was not much more helpful. He could give a couple of days but many of his ships belonged to the MacArthur command, were on loan, and must early be returned. Of course, Admiral Turner said that when the fleet left, his transports and cargo carriers would have to go too; he could not leave them unprotected in the waters off Guadalcanal.

Every commander encounters difficulties in setting up an operation, but up to this point those of General Vandegrift had been only intensifications of the normal type, solvable through command decisions. But for this question of supporting ships there was no solution he could apply. He had already heavily shaded the amount of supplies that Marine operating procedure would require him to carry on an expedition and the best estimates were that it would take nearly a week to unload the cargo vessels—not an outrageous figure for the full equipment of a reinforced division, since at least the first twenty-four hours would count for little, as he expected to be opposed at the beaches. Even after all the supplies were ashore, what would his men do for air cover during the period necessary to complete the Guadalcanal field and to bring in American planes?

A certain amount of heat seems to have developed during the discussion, which ended in the rather lame compromise of Admiral Fletcher agreeing to keep his carriers in the area till D plus 4 and Crutchley to keep his cruisers there "as long as necessary."

III

The landings showed that the maps were woefully inaccurate, which had been expected, and the intelligence estimates of Japanese strength were wildly wrong, which had not. It had been predicted there would be 1,500 Japs on the two islands north of the Guadalcanal channel, Tulagi and Gavutu.

To the former the raider battalion and one from the 5th Regiment had been assigned, to the latter the parachutists. On both the number of Japs exceeded estimates, and on both the Marines encountered the new form of war, outside their own or any other experience, that was to run like a refrain through

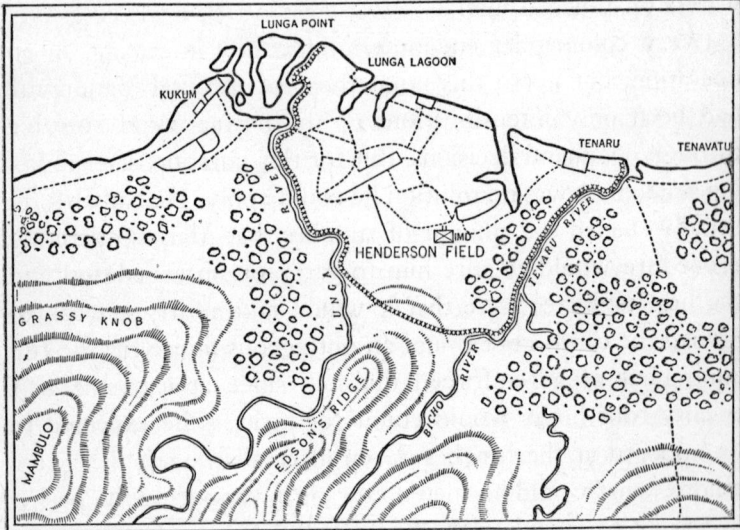

Guadalcanal drawn from an early map—the kind the Marines had when they landed

the whole of the Pacific conflict. The enemy were deeply dug into rock caves with connecting tunnels, from the mouths of which they maintained interlocking fields of fire. They used them with great cleverness, often letting a skirmish line through without firing, then attacking the support formation and striking the first one from the rear. The preliminary bombardment had by no means destroyed these positions, nor did the supporting fire. There was no way of dealing with them but demolition charges placed by hand. When operations halted for the night and the Marines dug in with both islands still far from conquered, all the Japs came boiling out of their holes for infiltration counterattacks of suicidal savagery. Casualties were heavy and it was the evening of the second day before Tulagi and Gavutu were secured; and then only after General Vandegrift, now on Guadalcanal, had put in two battalion combat teams from the reserve afloat.

On Guadalcanal, where 5,000 Japs had been expected behind beach defenses, the Marines went in standing up. Two battalions of the 5th Regiment were in assault. One of them, under Lieutenant Colonel Maxwell, was sent across the river Ilu at its mouth to work westward along the shore. The full 1st Regiment swung inland to cross higher up and move through an area of *konai* grass toward the airfield which the general proposed to encircle. Night of the first day brought both forces up to the next river, the Tenaru.* In the morning they crossed, pushing on past the mouth of the river Lunga and taking the airfield with a couple of prisoners, from whom it was learned that there were not over 600 Jap troops on the island and these had run away to the west, leaving their breakfasts in the kettles.

The supply situation was now the only one that caused concern. The original beaches were piled high with goods which not only offered an admirable target for air attack but had twice caused a suspension of unloadings, since the only available stevedoring force was suffering from exhaustion. Two air raids had still further delayed matters. General Vandegrift went to the top brass conference aboard Admiral Turner's flagship that night with the intention of trying to persuade Fletcher to stay beyond the allotted four days until the beach situation was cleaned up.

---

* The early maps were inaccurate and this river was not really the Tenaru. After the Army troops reached the island their maps corrected it to the Ilu; but it was not that either, the correct name was Alligator Creek. In view of the fact that the later battle was known as that of the Tenaru it seems more logical to preserve the original Marine designation.

He found that, so far from being persuaded to remain longer in the area, the events of the two days had brought Fletcher back to his position at the Koro conference. He was determined to withdraw his carriers the next morning, August 9, while something over half of the supplies were still in the holds of the cargo vessels. Forty heavy bombers had come down from Rabaul during the afternoon and he regarded it as only a stroke of luck that they had not found his ships. He could not afford to risk the attack of the more numerous planes that would come next time; must not lose his carriers.

Parenthetically, it is to be noted here that the fundamental decision was that our forces had undertaken an offensive while conditions still imposed defensive thinking. Fletcher was revising Washington's strategy, criticizing his orders as impossible of execution.

What mattered immediately was that Turner said he must take out the cargo carriers, the only ships of the type available in the whole Pacific. Any other decisions reached at the conference did not matter, for while it was still going on, the Japs ran down through the islands with their fast torpedo carriers and wiped out Crutchley's screening force in the deadliest defeat American forces suffered during the war, the Battle of Savo Island.

There was now no question; the ships must leave and did leave the following morning, supplies still aboard. General Vandegrift would have been fully justified in re-embarking and it is an interesting field of speculation as to what would have happened had he done so. Instead he issued strict orders for the conservation of ammunition and put his troops on a schedule of two meals a day, about half of which allotment consisted of captured Japanese rice with weevils in it. He was under constant air attack, day and night, with no defense but his antiaircraft guns. Worse; it was not more than twenty-four hours before he discovered that he was under an effective sea blockade. A submarine surfaced in the channel in daylight and shot up one of the small boats by means of which communications were being maintained between Guadalcanal and Tulagi. There was no means by which the 6,500 men on the latter island could be called to the aid of the 11,000 on Guadalcanal.

IV

With the Japanese in complete control of air and sea, the obvious immediate danger was that of being attacked from the water, and to this the general addressed himself first. He had a battery of naval 5-inch. They were established at Lunga Point and along the shore from a boundary line west of this point to the Tenaru River, machine-gun positions were set up with 50-calibers and mortars in support. The Tenaru itself is highly defensible; not very deep, but running most of its course between banks eight or nine feet high, passable only by a sand bar at the mouth. General Vandegrift made this his eastern flank, carrying the line south for some 2,000 yards along the stream till it turned westward across some of the ridges that are the outriders of Guadalcanal's central mountains. Just south of the airfield itself the single regiment of artillery was established and near it the general's headquarters. From the ridge covering these positions the perimeter generally followed the left bank of the Lunga down to the shore again, the western limit being just beyond the stream delta.

Inland there was a line of outposts in thick jungle and there was no wire except some raided from the coconut plantations by the shore, which provided a single strand for the most vulnerable spots. The position had a weakness on the western front, where a tall eminence, covered with *konai* grass and variously called Grassy Knoll or Mt. Austen, dominated everything. On preliminary information from planters and the few photographs, it had been planned to bring this feature within the defensive area, but when the Americans actually reached the place it was found to be so extensive that an entire corps would hardly have been more than adequate for the purpose. General Vandegrift attempted to control the height by extensive patrolling and did so to the extent that the Japanese were never able to use it for artillery or to assemble attack forces, but all through the campaign they kept observers up there and nothing that happened in the American lines went unremarked—an element in the tactical situation which must be always kept in mind.

These, then, were the physical arrangements with which the 1st Marine Division prepared to stand a siege. To the general's mind they were less important than getting his morale problem under control. It was obvious there would be a morale problem as soon as the news of the loss of the cruisers spread through the ranks and was confirmed by the obvious shortages of food and equipment. Moreover, these were Marines; they had been trained in a process of thought as well as physically to be beach-head assault troops who, as soon as they had won access to a land mass, would be relieved by Army men passing through their lines. When they found themselves doing garrison duty in a siege situation a reaction was to be expected.

Sunny Jim discounted this in advance and in more than one way. He insisted upon correct if informal uniforms and clean shaves, though the Guadalcanal situation was about as little inducive to cleanliness as anything the Marines had encountered this side of Haiti. The general never swore in public and always referred to the enemy at full length as "the Japanese," after the respectful formal manner of Stonewall Jackson, a character he greatly admired. This much, of course, is the old stiff-upper-lip, Englishmen-in-the-tropics; Vandegrift went beyond it to place an emphasis on aggressiveness, on fighting spirit, that even seemed excessive to those beneath him.

The word "retreat" was not even mentioned in his presence and the staff officer who did use it in some quite innocent connection was practically sent to Coventry for three days. "There will be no retreats," he used to say, and waving his hand at the maze of jungle-covered hummock which rose to the south: "One of those ridges is as good to fight on as another. We must make the Japanese see they cannot drive us out of anything we wish to hold." Not long after the landing he sent home the commander of the battalion that had led the advance along the shore. That officer had pushed his advance so slowly that the 1st Regiment, marching over ridges farther inland, had more than kept pace with him.

The insistence of aggressiveness led indirectly to the first setback on Guadalcanal, the Goettge Patrol, somewhat ill reported at the time, and consequently magnified to an importance it did not possess. Colonel Goettge was divisional intelligence officer. On August 12 a Japanese prisoner was brought in who said that a small group from the island garrison had collected at a native village beyond the Matanikau and might surrender if approached. A patrol had seen a white flag at the place. Goettge wanted to go pick them up. The general did not like the idea, but could find nothing precisely wrong on which to place a finger, and the proposed move was in perfect keeping with his own aggressive doctrine, so he consented.

After dark Goettge set out in one of the landing craft with a patrol of twenty-eight men and the prisoner, a rope around his middle. As the boat reached the shore where the Japs were, they opened a blaze of fire from every side that killed Goettge and all his men but three. The "white flag" turned out to have been the normal enemy battalion ensign.

A week later three companies of the 5th Regiment cleaned up the situation at the Matanikau village by a triple encirclement—down the river from the hills, across the bar, and from the water. By that date the Japanese reaction to the loss of their island was at hand and the correctness of General Vandegrift's insistence upon the importance of morale in this campaign was about to be demonstrated. The capture of Guadalcanal-Tulagi had caught the Japs badly off balance in a strategic sense and their high command at Rabaul had no troops immediately at hand with which to win back the lost position. The Army command at Rabaul had been assigned over 50,000 troops, but they were scattered all the way from Borneo to Manchuria, the nearest being a special storm-group known as the Ichiki Detachment, about 1,500 strong, then on Guam. They arrived at Truk on August 15. In the meanwhile the Battle of Savo Island had taken place and the incident of the Goettge Patrol, which the Japanese commander on Guadalcanal had reported as a strong attack beaten off with heavy losses. At the same time Japanese submarines reported that there was considerable American small-boat activity in the channels and the Americans appeared to be withdrawing to Tulagi for another Bataan defense.

Now Japanese intelligence had estimated the American forces on Guadalcanal with fair accuracy at 10,000 men, had noted the withdrawal of our ships and the fact that the airfield was not being used by our planes. (The strip was too short for them but the Japs did not know this.) Before the war it had been almost an article of faith with them that the British and Dutch were the hard fighters of the Allied team, the Americans panicked easily, especially under bombing, were effete, and could not stand close-range combat. In Java and Malaya the Japs had easily beaten the "tough" enemies and the accumulation of evidence from Guadalcanal now pointed to the idea that American psychology had been correctly understood. The high command ordered the Ichiki Detachment to the island at once to retake the airfield and wipe out 10,000 Marines—with 1,500 men and nothing heavier than a 70-mm battalion gun! It would be incredible if it were not true.

The first group, 900 strong, arrived on the night of August 18 aboard destroyers and were set ashore to the east of the field. One of our patrols ambushed theirs in the jungle next morning—they were marching along with slung rifles and no security detachments, apparently to show their contempt for Americans. From uniforms and documents on the bodies General Vandegrift learned that he was dealing with the expected counterattack force and that it would come along the coastal trail. He refused his lines a little on the upper reaches of the Tenaru, cut fields of fire for his machine guns, and moved up the 1st Battalion, 1st up to support the 2nd Battalion of the same regiment, which was holding the river line.

That day the first American planes reached the field and that night at three in the morning Ichiki attacked without waiting for the rest of his troops. His men charged across the bar at the river mouth with the fanaticism the Japanese everywhere displayed, but attained only the outer rim of our positions where they knocked out a couple of machine guns. They had no effective fire support and could not reinforce the footholds gained. By daybreak there was a fire fight. General Vandegrift sent the support battalion across upstream with five tanks, came down on the enemy flank and rear and wiped out the Ichikis to the last man. On the colonel's body there was found a diary in which he had entered his intentions of spending that day, August 21, "enjoying the fruits of victory." Marine casualties were under 120.

August 21 was a key date for other reasons than Ichiki. Up to this point General Vandegrift had been limited to dealing with questions of morale and mere endurance, since his outpost line took so many men he had almost no reserve and his patrols were limited to platoon strength. With the coming of American planes the blockade of the channels was raised and he could redistribute his forces on a more rational system. He brought over from Tulagi the battalion of the 5th Regiment that landed there, as well as the raiders and parachutists. The intensified patrols thus permitted speedily reported that a new enemy concentration was being built up east of the airfield by means of destroyers running in by night. With the arrival of our planes, in fact, the Japanese communications had become as insecure as the American. Both parties were limited to reinforcement by stealth or to fighting a major battle in order to run through a large convoy.

The new landings represented a reasoned effort to deal with American artillery power which the Japanese recognized as their chief difficulty. The land forces involved belonged to the Kawaguchi Reinforced Brigade, nearly as large as the Division. Their commander subscribed fully to the normal Japanese doctrine that the soldiers of his race were so superior in close combat that they could overcome even considerable numerical odds. He perceived his problem as that of moving his troops through the approach zone where American fire power would be encountered. This he proposed to do by landing the bulk of his brigade east of the airfield, with their light battalion guns and machine cannon, whence they should take jungle trails across the ridges to the rear of the American positions for an attack down the Lunga on a four-battalion front. Orders were issued against moving by day or crossing open grassfields where traces might be left; the approach was to be secret and the attack a surprise. One reinforced battalion combat team was to be landed in a single convoy west of the airfield at the last minute and to attack from Grassy Knoll simultaneously with the main movement. A combined carrier-borne and land-based air attack would eliminate the American planes at the field and provide the necessary preliminary bombardment. On the night of the attack heavy naval forces would enter the channels, bombard and conduct a feint at a counterlanding, which should so distract the American forces that a break-through could be achieved.

It will be observed that this plan was based on good observational intelligence of General Vandegrift's positions, which were strongest along the shore. It provided for neither supports nor reserves, but this was not a defect in Japanese eyes. The object of the plan was to eliminate the force in reserve; to place every Japanese soldier in immediate contact with the enemy.

However, it possessed other and real defects which General Vandegrift's aggressive defense and the support of American naval forces were most exactly calculated to develop. One of them was that the Japanese general counted on a control of the sea sufficient to let him land all his troops from one big convoy. He never obtained it; when the Japanese fleet swept down to lead the convoy in on August 24, they were intercepted by the U.S. Navy, lost a carrier, had two more badly beaten up, and were forced to turn back with their mission unaccomplished. Kawaguchi's brigade had to be sent in piecemeal by night aboard destroyers. As the artillery and logistic items represented the chief obstacles to movement across the ridges, these had to go in first. This was the concentration east of the airfield that Vandegrift's patrols had remarked. The arrival of the Tulagi detachments having given him reserves enough to work with, he promptly sent Colonel Merritt A. Edson with the raiders and parachutists on a strong water-borne night raid to the area on September 8, with a couple of destroyers running in to furnish covering fire.

The raiders hit the jack pot. The vanguard of Kawaguchi's infantry had already moved out along the trails, the remainder had not yet landed, and there was hardly a company to guard the accumulated medical supplies, ammunition, stores, and about half the artillery of the brigade. Edson's men eliminated the guards and destroyed everything; sent out patrols that traced the direction of the enemy movement and returned.

Their attack had two effects. It destroyed Kawaguchi's surprise, which apparently caused him no perturbation (it is remarkable with what singular fatuity Japanese commanders throughout the war clung to plans from which some essential element had been withdrawn); and by depriving him of half his artillery support, made him alter his stream of attack from a simultaneous movement by four battalions abreast to one by four battalions in succession, each supported in turn by what guns he had left.

On the American side General Vandegrift was now warned that he would be attacked from the south. He strengthened his east flank position along the upper Tenaru and carried along the rear of the perimeter to a high nameless ridge, where Edson's raiders were established in a line that was really a chain of foxholes, its flank resting on the Lunga.

Doctrine prescribed a defense in depth, but there was no depth in which to put up a defense; the airfield and artillery positions lay not more than a thousand yards behind Edson's ridge, and any attempt to push the line farther south into the mountains would have resulted in taking in so very much territory that there could be no line at all. General Vandegrift had to hold out a division reserve in view of the fact that the flank facing Grassy Knoll was open, and this had exhausted his resources in troops. What he did do was send forward patrols to reconnoiter the trails into the back country from Edson's position and register the artillery; and this act was to be decisive.

The first attack came at nine on the evening of September 12, against the center of Edson's line. Infiltrating Japs cut all the American communications wire, isolated one of Edson's companies after an all-night fight, forcing him back to a line of low hummocks at the northern part of the ridge. An officer of Vandegrift's staff who looked at the position toward noon found Edson's men utterly exhausted and mumbling; a counterattack had just failed. On his report the general ordered in a battalion from beyond the Lunga as reinforcement, but it never got there, as there was a heavy air raid lasting most of the afternoon and the men could not cross the airfield. For Kawaguchi this had been the move to his jump-off positions and he had achieved it with slight loss—so slight that he radioed a dispatch in terms which led Tokyo to announce the field was already taken. On the night of the 13th he proposed to attack by the left on the Lunga, each battalion in turn wheeling right as it crossed the airfield to roll up the American line to the Tenaru under a combined front and flank attack. He began the move, very early, at 6:30 P.M., wishing to be in possession of the field by time the Japanese cruiser squadrons arrived in the channels, an event scheduled for midnight.

No description of the fury of that battle can do it justice. The Japs used calcium flares, smoke grenades; they infiltrated wherever they could and once again cut all Edson's wires. Several times platoons were isolated, two Medals of Honor were won that night, and by ten o'clock the colonel had no more than 300 men in line. But the withdrawal of the previous night had provided the American artillery with still more accurate registry on all the approach trails and the few open areas into which Kawaguchi had brought forward his own guns. That artillery opened as soon as the attack began, and its effect was crushing. The outnumbered enemy guns were put out of action early, and the battalions waiting to follow the first into the attack were caught in their assembly area. A few Japanese did infiltrate—one was killed at the door of General Vandegrift's tent—but they could nowhere work up a concentration sufficient to drive home. By morning Kawaguchi had lost 2,000 men (the American casualties were under 200) and by afternoon his defeated remnants were streaming through the jungles toward the western end of the island, where not many arrived, since the raid of the Raiders had destroyed their food and medical stores.

V

On September 18, after a strange submarine and anti-submarine naval action which cost our forces a carrier, the first big convoy came in, bearing not only long-needed supplies but also the other regiment of Vandegrift's division, the 7th Marines, on which the general had finally persuaded the high command to accept his view that they could defend Samoa better on the shores of Guadalcanal than by doing garrison duty in the former island. The arrival of these fresh troops brought a re-examination of the whole theory of the defense. Japanese control of the approach routes was little abated, but the airfield was now so improved and had so many planes that enemy movement by day down the Slot of the Solomons was impossible. This meant they must continue coming in small groups by night and this in turn that the threat of a counterlanding was practically eliminated. They would have to work up a concentration and conduct an overland campaign.

There were now Marines enough to set up a defense in depth against such a campaign, and with our naval strength up to the point where convoys were a regular instead of an exceptional event, General Vandegrift had been assured of the support of the Army America Division. But the more he thought about defense in depth in that country the less he liked the idea. Edson's defense had been somewhat along these lines and the Japanese had thoroughly infiltrated. Their doctrine was infiltration and the jungle covers were admirably adapted to such a method. The obvious answer was a solid, continuous line of defense like that with which Ichiki's attack along the Tenaru had unavoidably been met. Now a line like this, when it encloses an area as large as the Guadalcanal perimeter, has a name; it is a cordon, the type of defense whose unsoundness Napoleon Bonaparte spent most of his career in demonstrating. All books of tactics since his day have raised a unanimous voice against it. The objection is that an artillery concentration blows a hole in the cordon, an infantry column rushes through the gap and takes everything from the rear.

General Vandegrift's experience was such as to have given him a lively sense of real as against ideal conditions and he did not think the normal objections to a cordon applied here. The Japanese artillery had been both weak and badly handled and it seemed likely that they would have continual difficulty in moving guns along the jungle trails. The defensive area was so small that from their central position his own guns could cover the approaches to every part of it.

The general had already learned that as a race the Japanese clung to preconceived ideas and plans with a determination so strong as to be almost inexplicable. That is, their mental make-up was such that having determined we would defend in depth, a cordon would be for them an incomprehensible surprise. In spite of their good observation of the interior of the perimeter, they were not likely to detect that back under the jungle, a line defense was being built. Vandegrift boldly threw away the book and established a cordon—wired in all around, with foxhole positions and visual contact and splinter-proof emplacements for automatic weapons. The 5th Regiment held the western flank of this position from the shore to the Lunga, the fresh and strong 7th carried it from this point past Edson's ridge to the upper Tenaru, and the 1st held the latter stream, while all the special formations were organized near the shore as a mobile infantry reserve.

In the meanwhile the arrival of the new regiment made it

possible to send patrols of battalion strength to the westward, where a good many Japs were floating around. They were mostly from the Kawaguchi command or the battalion of this brigade that was to but never did attack from the Grassy

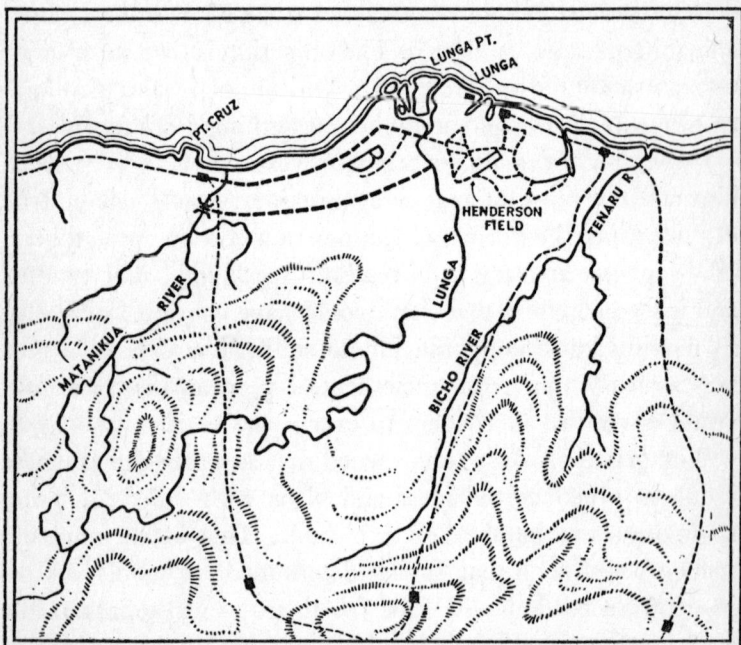

The 5th Regiment's Advance on Matanikau

Knoll region in co-ordination with the main assault. On September 22 one of these patrols found enough evidence of Japanese just west of the Matanikau to urge its commander to plan an attack on them there. It was to be a triple encirclement, one battalion crossing the sand bar at the river's mouth, another crossing the upper reaches of the stream by bridge, and a third making an amphibious landing behind the enemy positions. The general agreed. The attack turned into a complete failure with heavy casualties when the Japanese were found to be in strength and Marine communications failed as a result of a bombing raid which blew out the central switchboard at a crucial moment.

At this point it occurred to Vandegrift to ask himself why the enemy were so interested in the Matanikau. The answer he deduced was that across its bar and along the shore lay the one route by which they could move heavy equipment from the western end of the island toward the airfield. Once they got through there, there was no very defensible line till the western mouth of the Lunga was reached. They must not be allowed to work that close in, since from that area the precious airfield would be within easy range of light artillery served by the good observation posts on Grassy Knoll. There were insufficient troops to bring the Matanikau into the perimeter (it would have been necessary to engulf Grassy Knoll), but it was quite necessary to establish a forward battle position on the banks of the stream. The Japanese would evidently oppose such a step; Vandegrift decided to establish this position on the heels of an offensive action that would temporarily drive them from the region.

The whole of the 5th Regiment was to be brought forward to the right bank of the Matanikau. On the stream's upper reaches a special scout-sniper battalion that had recently been formed was to capture the bridge, cross and right wheel down the left bank, while two battalions of the 7th followed, each in turn extending westward beyond the scout-snipers and wheeling toward the shore. As soon as the way was cleared the 5th would cross the bar and attack straight ahead, driving the enemy toward the western capes and away from the heads of the trails leading inland. A plan of naval gunfire, artillery, and close air support was carefully worked out.

The advance opened on October 12 and provided another illustration of how thoroughly the events of war are the result of clashes between mutually exclusive plans. As the 5th advanced it encountered a force estimated above a company strong busily engaged in setting up a bridgehead on the right bank of the stream. It was the vanguard of General Maruyama's 2nd, Sendai Division, a force over 20,000 strong, one of the very best in the Jap army, which was being brought into Guadalcanal for almost exactly the operation Vandegrift had foreseen. They had a regiment at the Matanikau. One battalion each was to hold the right bank at bridge and bar until the arrival of the remainder of the division. Then tanks would lead an attack from the two bridgeheads along the coast, with artillery following. The guns would put the American airfield out of business and keep it out, then shell the southern rim of our perimeter while the remainder of the division's infantry, plus some scattered formations, attacked on both banks of the Lunga. The Imperial Navy would make a great sweep down from Truk to keep American ships from interfering, to provide bombing and naval gunfire support, feint a counterlanding, and fill the field with Japanese planes as soon as it was taken.

The date for Maruyama's attack and the fleet sweep was toward the end of October; it would take that long to get all the troops in there. But the Japanese general wanted his bridgeheads early and ordered the regiment already ashore to be in position by the night of October 6. They did not quite make it, some American planes catching them on the march and forcing them to take cover, so the night of the 6th found the bridge still in no-man's land, while the three companies that had crossed the bar were only in foxholes when the 5th Regiment struck them in the afternoon. It was quite a hot fight, the Japanese holding on with the skill and courage of a well-trained organization of proud tradition, but the Marines had tanks and the accurate support of an artillery complement nearly equal in strength to that of a full corps, while the Japs could call on only their battalion guns. The result was never

in doubt; by twilight the Americans had penned the fragments of the bridgehead force into a small pocket against the
stream and themselves held the eastern end of the sand bar.
Farther north the scout-snipers had won their bridge.

Next day it rained torrentially, which slowed up everything, but the flankers did get into position, while the 5th
cleaned out its pocket and made a move toward the sand bar
so menacing the Japanese attention was concentrated in that
direction. When the attack toward the sea got into motion it
penned a group of Japs against the water near Point Cruz and
wiped them out. In the meanwhile word had come through
from the South Pacific Command that there was every indica-
tion a major enemy move would soon take place. As the possibility must always be faced that they would succeed in
brushing aside our navy for long enough to set powerful
forces ashore, General Vandegrift felt constrained to call off
the remainder of the operation to keep his reserves in hand.

He was not very satisfied with a two-regiment operation
that had produced by count only 253 enemy bodies, but this
was another case of not being able to see into the minds on
the other side. Maruyama was lugubrious over having lost
nearly 600 men and his Matanikau positions. Two nights later
there was a naval battle in which he lost a couple of transports
with most of his heavy artillery ammunition and all his medical supplies but he persisted in carrying through the plan
without alteration. The date set for his Matanikau attack was
now October 21, with the main thrust down the Lunga one
night later and the fleet coming in on the 24th, as it was calculated there would be a slight lag in American naval reaction
to the loss of the airfield.

In the event hardly any of this timing worked out. Maruyama was late getting his troops ashore (another product of
the naval battle) and had badly underestimated the difficulty
of moving men and equipment along the jungle trails, so that

he was only crossing the Lunga on the 21st, with his men on one-third rations and in a sad state of exhaustion. The Matanikau attack did indeed jump off that night, a double move by the upstream bridge combined with a tank-webbed assault across the bar. But the lack of heavy artillery ammunition had prevented scheduled counterbattery shoots, and the moment the movement at the bar began it ran into an American gunnery concentration so fierce and so accurate that the infantry could not reach its assault positions. The failure was complete; officers on our side took it for a reconnaissance in force and not an attack at all.

Lieutenant General Hyakutate, the area commander, was on the island. He went up to the front the following morning and ordered the assault renewed at twilight. The heavy guns were to expend their slender store of ammunition without stint and the general summoned down all the planes available at Rabaul for powerful preliminary bombardment. Both guns and planes failed badly; the bombers were so harried by fighters as to be completely inaccurate and General Vandegrift had received only the day before the 155s of XXIV Corps Artillery, which was so effective in counterbattery that two of the Jap big guns were knocked out by direct hits and the rest had to move repeatedly, to the detriment of their performance.

The infantry attack had no better luck, though the Japanese had prepared concealed lanes through the jungle growth to let the tanks reach the bar by a short cut. The sight of tanks on the previous evening had caused General Vandegrift to move his single company of tank-destroyers up into support. As soon as the enemy appeared in the open on the bar these vehicles rushed forward to open fire from a range of not over 500 yards. In 20 minutes every tank was burned out; in 20 more, American artillery and mortar fire had broken the supporting infantry and not even snipers were shooting from the Japanese bank. The flank attack never got started.

One would have expected that the report of this action and his other difficulties might have caused General Maruyama to re-examine his positions and prospects. Not at all; with that inflexibility which Japanese officers call tenacity, he went ahead on the original line—or almost the original line, for the difficulties of the jungle had forced him, like Kawaguchi, to make his attack with units in succession instead of simultaneously. The first attack was on the night of the 24th, two battalions in assault and one in support against the east flank of the position, south of Edson's ridge.

When scouting had failed to detect the approach of the Japanese to this part of the line, which was held by the 7th Regiment, the General had withdrawn a battalion for the support of the Matanikau positions, unaware that the attack there had been so thoroughly crushed. The Japanese assault on the ridges accordingly fell on a 2,500-yard front, held by a single battalion. The enemy used mortars freely and tried to work through the wire in small groups, a method which much simplified defensive problems, but by midnight all the American local reserves were in, and with the fury of the onslaught showing no signs of decrease, the colonel on the spot asked for reinforcements.

General Vandegrift sent him a battalion of the 164th Army Regiment, which had reached the island on October 13 and had been held in divisional reserve. The men had little training in jungle warfare, but the exigencies of the case required them to be used in units as small as a squad as emergencies developed now here, now there, along the line—precisely the conditions under which their fresh energy and good basic training counted for most and their lack of experience for least. The Japs did break through at one spot to a depth of 100 yards;

there the advance piled up. When morning came the 164th surrounded this pocket, placed cross fires on it, and with the artillery laying interdiction fire on the supporting trails, wiped it out before noon. The rest of the day was spent in picking the little groups of Army men out of the line and settling their regiment into part of the position as an organization.

On the Japanese side there seems to have been a mood of self-congratulation during the day. Their losses had been severe, but their commander believed he had secured a firm lodgment inside the American battle positions, as indeed he would have had he been dealing with the defense in depth he thought he was facing instead of the Vandegrift cordon. One of his battalions, with the colonel of the assault regiment, was out of communication, but he had expected that during the day, when Japanese doctrine called for taking cover and remaining quiet. Also in accordance with doctrine, he prepared to exploit the advantage he imagined he had secured. The full regiment that was to have attacked west of the Lunga was brought across the stream to enlarge the previous night's gains and various formations totaling about two and a half battalions were placed on this regiment's right to expand the breakthrough and to eat up the American lines along the Tenaru.

This complete misapprehension of the character and solidity of the American position produced its logical result when the attack was launched about midnight. The lines of Japanese approach were thoroughly known; the artillery concentrated on them, smashing up the support formations before they could reach the front. The assault elements found themselves everywhere running into a wired line supported by machine guns and mortars. The attack was an abject failure; so was an attempt to renew it the next night, when the mortars of the 164th caught a Jap weapons company in tight column on the trail and wiped it out.

VI

That decided the campaign for Guadalcanal, or at least that part of it which concerns General Vandegrift and the U.S. Marines. The night that saw the last futile Japanese attack was also covering the retreat of their fleet from the hard battle of Santa Cruz, with its carrier decks void of planes. The enemy high command then reached a somewhat peculiar decision that the reason for their ill success had been piecemeal reinforcement and slow build-up. When they attempted to run a whole division in at once in November the result was the three days of violent naval fighting known as the Battle of Gaudalcanal, in which, almost incidentally, the new division was practically wiped out before it got anybody ashore.

This brought the total of Japanese casualties for the campaign to nearly 40,000 troops, a figure so far beyond our estimates at the time that it took postwar examination of Japanese records to make it believable. 32,000 of these casualties took place on the island itself as against an American total for the whole campaign, Army and Marines together, of 8,000; all theirs were dead while three-quarters of ours were wounded. This set of figures would support the very highest opinion of Vandegrift's generalship even if he had not retained the island which was the object of the campaign. To be sure, a large portion of the Japanese casualties (which, by the way, outnumbered the maximum total of American troops on the island) took place because the Japanese medical service broke down. Again, their losses were much heavier than they should have been because they repeatedly attacked before their method of reinforcement had built up sufficient forces to drive an attack home. Or they lost because they could never obtain control of the air; or because they never had adequate artillery.

To say these things is merely to state that in war there is always some reason why the loser loses. If they had put heavy forces in at once after the Battle of Savo Island and the withdrawal of Fletcher's carriers, these two events would have been the reasons why we lost. Underlying all these mechanical reasons is the process of reasoning which led to defeat on one hand and victory on the other. It was Vandegrift's special merit that he was able to throw overboard all preconceptions and to deal with the situation in its own terms. It was the Japanese failure that again and again they undertook operations on an "ideal" instead of a real basis—as when they put in 1,500 Ichikis against 10,000 Marines, and when the Sendai Division made an attack admirably calculated to break through a defense in depth against a continuous line which had no depth whatever.

By looking at the situation through his own eyes instead of through the textbooks, General A. A. Vandegrift achieved something more than the preservation of the Gaudalcanal airfield. He invented a new system of war—the system of seizing a beachhead on which an airfield could be constructed, setting up a cordon perimeter defense around it, and then proceeding to the next step. The process was repeated in endless variations throughout the southwest Pacific—at Bougainville, Cape Gloucester, Hollandia, Aitape, Geelvink Bay, Mindoro. The Japanese never did succeed in fathoming it, and never did succeed in breaking through one of those perimeters, even when, as at Bougainville, they could dispose of sensibly superior forces.

Admittedly it is not a system that could be applied anywhere and against all enemies. It required strong naval support and a large island with a coastal plain backed by jungle-covered mountains. The smaller islands—Tarawa, Morotai, the Admiralties, Kwajalein—had to be conquered entire. In other words, the Vandegrift system demanded the special conditions of the southwest Pacific and of having remarkably unalterable opponents. But at this point one might as well say that the victory of Saratoga required the special conditions of having riflemen who could shoot the left eye out of a squirrel and opponents drilled in the formal tactics of Europe. All war is made up of special conditions, and the ablest officers are those who recognize in what way the conditions they face differ from a norm that never really exists.

OMAR BRADLEY

Tactician of the West

I

EVERY WAR IS FOLLOWED BY A PERIOD OF DEBATE IN which history makes up its mind as to the merits of the officers concerned. The question is not one that can be resolved in any absolute sense—war is not a game of chess, the forces and responsibilities are always unequal—but it provides large areas of fascinating ratiocination from which occasionally something of critical value emerges. In this respect the case of the second World War is aberrant. There is not, nor is there likely to be, much disagreement as to the abilities of the commanders most prominently concerned; but the essential command decisions were so often arrived at in committee that there is a good deal of doubt as to who should be credited with what achievements. There was no question that the first high-command appointment of the war gave us an administrator and co-ordinator of genius in General Eisenhower. In fact the last M-day nomination to turn out so well was that of George Washington. Nobody doubts that in Omar Bradley we rather unexpectedly turned up one of the ablest field commanders in American history. The debatable points are along the boundaries of their mutual authority and in the region where both are rivals in reputation of Sir Bernard Montgomery.

It is a rivalry which neither of the American officers would recognize as against each other. Their personal relations were strikingly like the intimacy of Grant and Sherman. Though in most respects the men were so very different, there are some remarkable parallels between the career of the general whom the Count of Paris called "the true destroyer of the Rebellion" and the officer who broke those German armies that had laid half a world under contribution. Both Sherman and Bradley had roots deep in the Missouri countryside. Both were "sleepers" in the sense that no one ever heard of them until they came to the high command, literally out of nowhere. Both were distinguished by a perfect willingness to take the calculated risk, yet calculated the risk so extremely closely that subsequent criticism often denied that it was there to be taken. Both won to an extraordinary degree the affection of the rear-rank private. General Omar Bradley was never observed arguing strategy with his soldiers while poking a knife into a tomato can in pursuit of fragments of stew, but with allowances for differences in conditions, "Here comes Brad" and a hand-wave instead of a salute, with the name of "the G.I. General," come to pretty much the same thing. Also on at least one occasion Bradley was observed refusing the help of his aide in order to smooth out the ground for his own bed with an entrenching tool.

There is something symbolic about that last gesture—Bradley down on the ground where he will get dirt behind his ears in the manner traditional to infantrymen. When he was appointed to command the II Corps in Africa, the press could find very little to say about him except that he was "an infantry specialist" which, if it is a little like an attempt to identify a particular boxer by calling him a punching specialist, does set Bradley off to some degree from every other general of the war. He is the only one, Allied or Axis, to whom the phrase could reasonably be applied. One of the perplexities confronting the German High Command in dealing with a Bradley offensive was the realization that it would be based on the use of none of those spectacular mechanical devices against which it is possible in some degree to provide, but on the movements of combat infantry, which are subject to every variation that the temperament and training of the commander will allow.

The Germans of World War II gave a good deal of attention to temperament and training among the officers most likely to oppose them, and there is some reason to believe that Omar Bradley was rather deliberately kept in background positions where they would not work up a file on him as a potential opponent. Not that the man who heads the Infantry School at Fort Benning is exactly obscure; but any reasonable person looking over a sketch of Bradley's career down to the time he stood forth across the dust and rock of Tunisia in command of an army corps must certainly have concluded that he was far sunk in school-teacher appointments, unlikely ever to lead an army or even a division in the field.

His service with troops was limited to three years in training camps on the heels of his graduation from West Point and to the training command of two successive divisions (28th and 82nd) during the early months of 1942. He came to the 82nd after a year as head of the Infantry School, and to that from four years as an instructor at West Point, a year at the War College, and four other years as an instructor at Benning. The career is all like that; he had not even been overseas in World War I and anything he had done to indicate fitness for high command was concealed within the minds of the General Staff, therefore inaccessible to the enemy. If the latter had any psychological spies around watching him, they would have reported that he was an amiable, easy-going man, whom corporals found no trouble conversing with; that he never missed a baseball game he could possibly get to, and was so passionately devoted to hunting that at Benning he used to go out to a swamp and shoot the heads off half a dozen water moccasins before breakfast; that unlike most Army officers who get the edges rubbed off their speech by moving around, he had kept a strong twang from his native Missouri and a somewhat farmerish turn of phrase; and that his chief intellectual characteristic was common sense—for which the German language has no phrase. Not a dangerous opponent, if an opponent at all.

The general's procedures in his various training and staff tasks were so distressingly normal that there was little to report about them except the statistics of performance. At Benning he made few changes and those of no particular significance (one of them was the use of a somewhat wider front in infantry attack than had been considered feasible), and the divisions he commanded were well and thoroughly trained, but not to the point where they were outstanding in the A.U.S. He did give birth to the ambitious plan for expanding the officer candidate school, the plan that was later put into effect with 40,000 officers as a result. But this also was a school-teaching performance.

The emerging quality of his mind lies somewhat deeper. During the Benning period he disagreed with the feeling, common in our service in the summer of 1941, that the Germans had discovered all the secrets of modern war and that in building our new army we could not do better than imitate them. As of that summer and fall there certainly seemed less reason to contradict such an opinion than to accept it. Poland, Norway, the Low Countries, France, Yugoslavia, and Greece had gone down like ninepins; the Nazi armies were sweeping irresistibly across the plains of Russia. Bradley did not think they had achieved a perfection that we should imitate, but rather that the German successes were a warning to seek out more carefully and to emphasize the strong features of our own military organization. He held that there was nothing sacrosanct about German tactics or organization, but that they had achieved their results by getting the most out of the materials they had; and as of that date his opinion was heretical.

There is also the incident (it can be called no more) of the 28th Division, with a flash of that forthright and decisive action within the bounds of the common pattern which was to characterize Bradley as a field commander. The National Guard was a long way from readiness for war when called into Federal service in 1940. The responsibility probably rested at least as much on the regular army as on the Guard itself, but the empirical fact was a fact still to a considerable extent in 1942, with the guns already booming among the Pacific islands, when it was already evident that if Western Europe were to be recovered from German domination the Army of the United States would have to do most of the work. Many of the National Guard divisions had been "purged" by triangularization, the retirement of overage officers and the inclusion of selective-service men, but the process of preparing them to fight the ruthlessly efficient Germans had not been carried very far in some formations. One of these was the 28th.

When General Bradley arrived at the division's training area at Camp Livingston, Louisiana, he passed the word that he was not to be received with ceremonies on his first tour of inspection. In one battalion's area his arrival was signalized by the appearance of the bugler, who blew a complicated call no one had ever heard before, whereupon the entire battalion broke from cover and trotted across a field in an "attack maneuver" no one had ever seen before. The division was not all that bad, of course—it hardly could be—but it was by no

GLENDALE COLLEGE LIBRARY

means in good shape and General Bradley, investigating the cause, became convinced that the reason lay in the advanced state of friendliness among officers and enlisted.

Now he himself was a notably friendly man. He has been described by one of the newspaper panegyrists as the only General who ever said "excuse me" to a corporal. A great believer in the idea that orders are better executed in a spirit of co-operation than in response to bellowings. But he had not missed the point that friendly co-operation can be permitted in any military organization only when it rests on a solid basis of mutual confidence; when the men know their officers will give the right kind of orders and the officers know men will do the right things in response to orders. There is a great deal in war that cannot be put into any order; there are a great many points at which the leader must depend upon his men to think and act for themselves. This becomes increasingly true as the power of modern weapons turns the battle-field into an open, fire-swept area where no one man can give close support to another.

There was nothing basically wrong with the 28th, the General decided. The degree of fraternization his personnel had achieved was the legitimate product of efficiency, but it was efficiency in the performance of the peacetime duties of the National Guard. The division as a whole had not yet learned how much it had to learn, or that it must retreat into a past where everything was still to learn. The friendly atmosphere could only be re-established on the basis of a new achievement, or to put it otherwise, the bonds of severity had been relaxed and the men who relaxed them now found it impossible to tighten up against subordinates who had become their friends.

General Bradley tore the division apart till hardly one stone of it rested upon another. A few officers were relieved; nearly everyone who could be was sent away to a school of some kind; every sergeant in the division was transferred to some other company, where he would no longer be among men he had learned to call by their first names. It was one of the most thorough purges any National Guard division received, and it was a success precisely because it was not a purge at all in the normal sense, heads did not roll and there was no fuss or scandal. In an astonishingly short time the 28th became the division which fought off the attacks of no less than nine German divisions among the Ardennes without breaking.

There is a tale from this period which helps to illustrate how Bradley got himself called the G.I. general. He went out incognito with the men on a 25-mile night hike, walking along the moving lines to observe reactions. "God damn the guy that organized this hike," remarked someone out of the dark. "Yep," said Bradley, "they ought to hang him."

II

In February, 1943, the situation in Tunisia was that the Germans had broken through the Sidi-Bou-Zid and Kasserine Gap, badly defeating the U.S. II Corps. The loss of forward airfields that resulted was particularly hard to take as the Allied forces had only recently worked up to something like an effective command of the skies. While the enemy had not been able to push their drive deep enough to disrupt communications between Americans and the British as they hoped, the setback had cost time, casualties, and above all, damage to morale at that crucial moment when the change-over from defense to offense was in progress. General Fredendall was relieved from command of the II Corps; and although Eisenhower had the flamboyant Patton to replace him, all our commands in large units were still on an experimental basis, it was still uncertain how well any given officer would come out in a shooting war. There was a felt want for a general who could be a replacement for Patton in case that experiment did not work out, another officer who could be groomed for the command of the largest units in our expanding operations.

Just who made the decision that came to rest on Bradley is so uncertain that it was probably one of those committee arrangements. Eisenhower knew him as a classmate of that famous West Point group from 1915 which produced more than 30 generals, and had seen him since that time at Benning. It was under Marshall that Bradley had been an instructor at the Infantry School and the Chief of Staff reportedly marked him for a future high command at the time. Either way the unknown school-teacherish general began to move around the roads of Tunisia in a jeep during the early days of March. Patton broke through at El Guettar, Montgomery flanked the Mareth Line, and genuine command of the air was gained. The enemy, with von Arnim now replacing Rommel, were backed up against the final series of hill masses defending the northeast corner of Tunisia, and a campaign to breach them was the next operation.

The Allied aero-naval operations had by this time cut the Axis troops off from any hope of reinforcement and from all but the most fitful source of supply, so there was not much doubt that the task of cleaning them out of Africa could be accomplished in the long run. The difficulties lay in that final qualifying phrase—the question of time, which always works against the party on the offensive. The German objective was not on the ground but on the calendar. If they could hold the Tunisian bastion through the summer, not only could a Russian campaign be undertaken to retrieve the disaster of Stalingrad, but also any attack on the fortress of Western Europe would be delayed by a full year, with the opportunity thus accorded for building new fortifications, training new reserves, bringing nearer to perfection new technical devices.

There was an excellent chance that the Germans could

achieve this. Although reinforcement had been cut off, they did not lack for men or weapons or food to make a summer's fighting along the lines reached in mid-April. On the southern front the British Eighth Army was faced by a series of ridges extending without a break to the tip of Cape Bon peninsula, too rough for the employment of armor and affording admirable emplacements for artillery and the observation posts that supported it. The place could be taken by the application of sufficient weight, but that would be essentially a siege operation, with the implications of delay involved in that type of attack.

North of this front and around the angle were the two main corridors through the hills into the coastal plain—the valleys of the Miliane and Medjerda rivers. Here General Alexander, in tactical command, planned to make his main effort with two British corps and one French, his ten divisions including three of armor which were highly suitable for valley country. The difficulty was that the Nazi commander knew that the main attack must come through there and would be prepared to meet it, especially by means of those fire-covered mine fields whose employment the Germans understood so well. North of the two valleys another set of rugged hill masses rises and does not cease till it reaches the sea.

The decision to use the American II Corps against these northern hill masses was no doubt partly political. There was a good deal of feeling on the American home front that the decision to fight Germany before Japan was a mistake, and an effective American part in the Tunis campaign would go far toward eliminating that idea. There was also the sound military point that if Cape Bon offered an area where the Axis troops might hold out for a long time, there was another hardly less good in the rough northern tip of Tunisia, terminating in the great fortress of Bizerte, to which all approaches were canalized between mountain and water. The mountain front west of this complex might be difficult ground for fighting; but unless the Germans were badly defeated among the hills there, a break-through along the Medjerda might easily leave them capable of an impacted defense around Bizerte.

This was the situation and these the problems when Bradley took over II Corps on April 17, 1943, while Patton was sent to prepare for the invasion of Sicily. The new chief had three infantry divisions, 1st, 9th, 34th, with the 1st Armored; all now being moved north from the central sector, right across the communication lines of the First British Army, amid an atmosphere of considerable secrecy. That move was later considered one of the major logistic achievements of the war, and if the Germans did hear about it they didn't believe it. Attempting a move like that under an unknown general would confirm for them Der Führer's remark that the Americans were military idiots.

When the move had been completed on April 22, Bradley had in line a small French formation, the Corps Franc d'Afrique, next to the coast and operating tactically under General Eddy's 9th Division, which was next southward. Before the latter formation lay the Sedjenane Valley, which, since the run of the ridges is southwest to northeast, looks on anything but a very large-scale map like a direct highway to Bizerte. The appearance is deceptive; the ridges from both sides constantly throw off interlocking spurs, the whole valley is covered with heavy man-high scrub that imposes a barrier on visibility and makes easy those infiltration counterattacks on a small scale which do so much to disjoint an offensive. Beneath this vegetation the valley was heavily mined and booby-trapped.

To the right of the 9th Division's zone rose a hill, Djebel El Hara, overlooking a watercourse called the Oued Djumine which runs through a rather wider and flatter valley than that of the Sedjenane to Mateur, the key road center of northern Tunisia. This valley looked like a good route for an armored thrust, but British intelligence on the area indicated that it was even more heavily mined than the Sedjenane and it was dominated through nearly half its length from the south by a commanding bare ridge, Hill 609. Not only did this hill

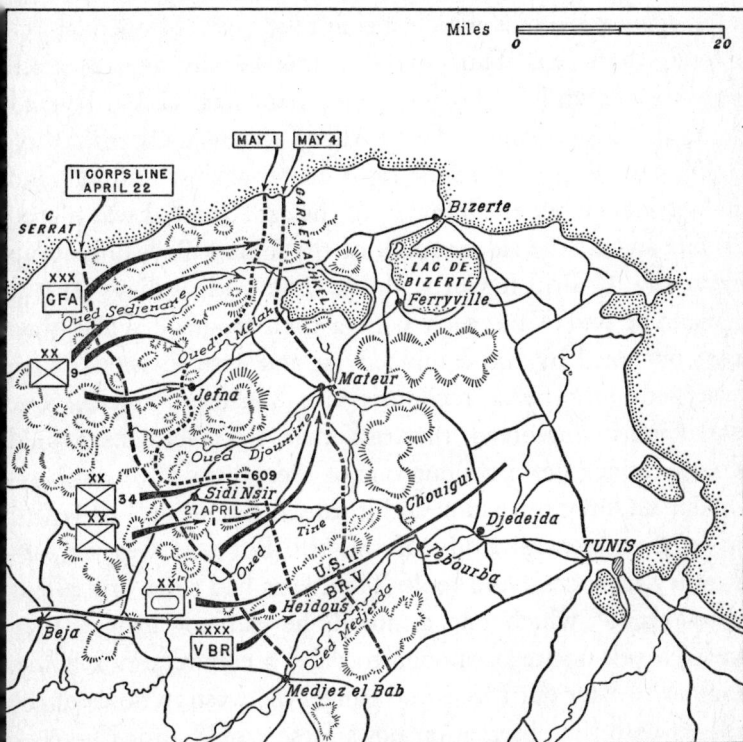

Bradley's Attack

afford observation positions; it was filled with 88s practically bore-sighted to take in flank any advance along the valley. With hardly a break Hill 609 leads into another complex which dominates the widest valley of all, that of the Tine, but this valley narrows and after some ten miles turns sharply north toward Mateur under the shadow of another hill mass overlooking it from the east. It became known to our troops as "Mousetrap Valley."

Bradley's plan of attack was as unorthodox as those of that other famous mountain fighter, Marshal Masséna. The overall scheme was that of ignoring the inviting valleys and their roads except as supply routes; using his infantry in direct attack against the hills which, being taken, would uncover the ground between. Thus the 9th was heavily concentrated toward its own left, the 34th (Major General C. W. Ryder) and 1st (Major General Terry Allen) were equally massed on a still narrower front at the right center against Hill 609 and its outriders while the infantry of the 1st Armored was placed in line against the ridges south of the Tine valley, linking up with the V British Corps there. The wide valleys of the Djoumine and Tine, each with a total frontage wider than that occupied by the combined 1st and 34th divisions, were watched only by a reconnaissance squadron apiece. The arrangement involved the risk that the Germans would counterattack heavily along one of the valleys into the flanks of our infantry formation and it caused a good deal of worry at least to General Eddy of the 9th. But that was the risk Bradley calculated and took. The Nazis had three and a half divisions, of which one armored; he did not believe they could work up steam enough to drive a counterattack home, especially after our forces had gained the western noses of the ridges with the observation posts these would afford.

The attack began at 0300 on 23 April, under a moon, and the fighting was extremely hard. The Germans were well dug in on reverse slopes with only observation posts and small groups of machine-gunners forward. Their artillery and mortars could sweep the western faces of the hills with high-trajectory fire which struck fragments as damaging as steel splinters from the bare rock. If preliminary air bombardment had shaken them they showed few signs of it. In the first days of the attack the 1st Division by its right and the 9th by its left worked forward along the ridges under heavy casualties. By 28 April the 1st was at least in partial possession of a series of long vertical crests running nearly east and west to the south of Hill 609 and could put fire not only on the approaches to that eminence but also onto the rear slopes of some of the supporting hills from which the Germans were using artillery and mortars. Two attacks on 609 itself had been repulsed but Bradley had front-line evidence that the Germans had moved most of their antitank guns to the Medjerda Valley, where the British were using abundant armor. He sent in ten tanks, which got across the supply line to the key crest. On 30 April the 34th assaulted the tall, flat-topped, cliff-sided hill simultaneously from southeast and northwest and it was taken in the face of constant local counterattacks, in some of which bayonets were actually used.

The right wing of the 9th meanwhile had come up against a pair of tall conical hills known as Green and Bald hills, with a narrow valley holding the town of Jefna between. The British had tried this position earlier and had come a cropper in an attempt at direct assault. Now on the extreme southern front of the corps zone of action the 1st Armored had been making good progress against resistance which, though it could not be described as light, had a less formidable character than that faced by the 34th—partly because the Germans were so much concerned in holding the Medjerda corridor farther southward against the British drive, partly because the terrain consisted less of ridges lying over against each other than of a series of almost round hills, which failed to offer the same opportunities for mutual support. In taking these hills the 1st Armored had put a good deal of fire on the trails in their rear to interdict supply. On the testimony of prisoners this had been very effective; they could get enough of neither biscuits nor bullets. By evening of 26 April they were beginning to abandon positions as soon as fire came down on their rear.

It seemed to General Bradley that this psychological habit, this willingness to concede the game when outmaneuvered, might be exploited against Green and Bald hills. He pushed the two left combat teams of the 9th still farther forward among the low hills north of Green and Bald, brought nearly all the divisional artillery into the area with some from corps, and put them all to work on the roads supporting the double Jefna position. It worked; on 2 May patrols brought in some prisoners who said they had been ordered to withdraw to Mateur and on 3 May Green and Bald were taken without a battle.

III

As of that date the II Corps line was long zigzag, farthest forward on the front of the 9th Division and that of the 34th, farthest retarded at the entrance to the Djoumine and Tine valleys. Farther south the Germans were holding solidly against the British who had tried to force the valleys and then the ridges facing them by direct attacks with armor. One Nazi counterattack had even gone as far as a British divisional headquarter. But von Arnim's position was now in fact fatally shaken. The hard fighting in the Medjerda corridor was absorbing every man he could find and he dared not draw troops from the southern front, where Montgomery was maintaining the kind of intensive artillery fire accompanied by patrol actions which always preceded one of his attacks. The Germans were reduced to the device of trying to plug gaps as they developed.

But the situation on their right wing opposite Bradley was no longer one in which such palliatives would be of service. On the extreme north the hill defenses had been broken through, the country to Bizerte was neither very rough nor very well organized, and there had not been time to do much mining. The route up the Djoumine was American whenever our forces chose to take it. Any attempt to hold it from the hill mass to the east would result in the troops left there being cut off, for the mousetrap of the Tine valley had been sprung and the way was open for Bradley's tanks to go rushing right to Mateur.

Under these circumstances German orders were issued for the evacuation of all North Tunisia, with a retreat through the central plain to the Cape Bon peninsula. The forces in the area were to hold as long as they could along the line Chouigi–Mateur–Lake of Bizerte. On 3 May the movement of stores out from behind this line was begun. The pivot of the defensive system was the Chouigi Hills, a rough roadless district running some ten miles from Chouigi town to Mateur, thence to Ferryville, with the three towns controlling all routes to the east and south. Geographically this complex was quite as difficult as the whole fortressed terrain already crossed, but Bradley instantly recognized that the defense did not possess the same validity. The Germans had not had time to fit the area with the elaborate mine fields and fortifications with interlocking fields of fire they employed earlier; and they could no longer count on the same quantity of fire support.

A great deal, then and later, was heard about the effectiveness of the German 88. There is no doubt that it was a dangerous weapon, but it is necessary to look on this artillery question from both sides. The German side of it is that although they did not give American infantry a particularly high rating, they found themselves in constant trouble as the result of the activities of our 155 medium artillery. In their system of war guns of similar caliber had been largely supplanted by dive-bombers because of the superior tactical mobility of the latter. Our forces had a good deal to take from the Stukas earlier, but by 4 May this was no longer true. The dive-bombers appeared only fleetingly and our control of the air was virtually complete. The enemy had thus lost all capability of making an effective counterattack and was committed

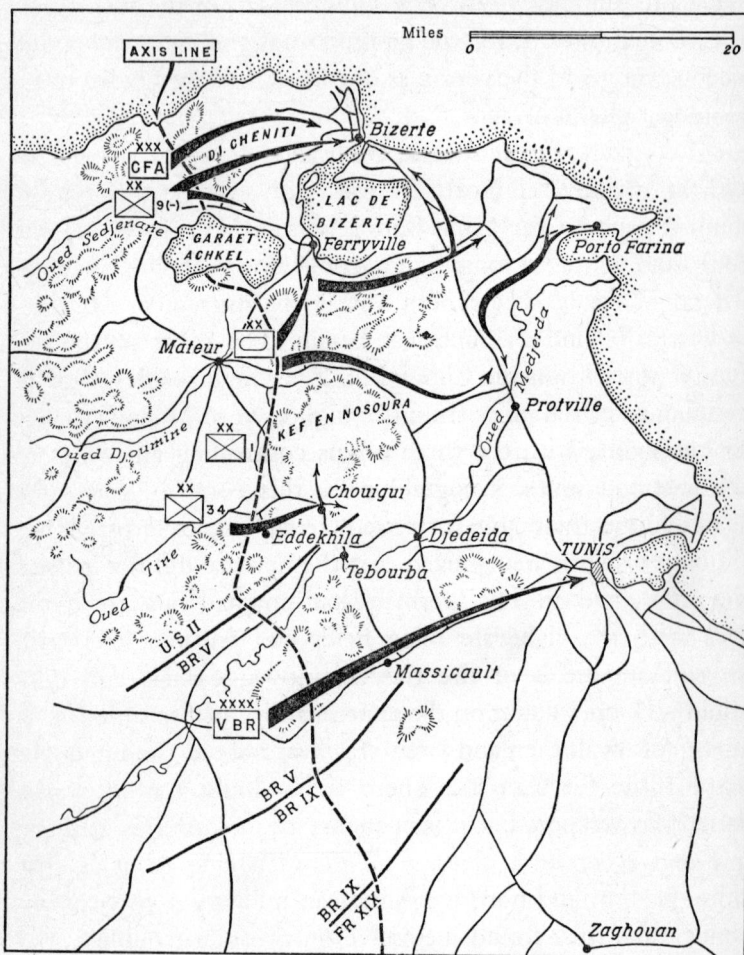

The Attack Breaks Through

to using his reserves in piecemeal operations. His defense had become passive; Bradley was permitted to embark on a period of completely uninhibited maneuver and he did so in a manner reminiscent of Summerall's movement along the roads in column during the final drive to the Meuse.

Parenthetically, it is worth noting that there was another and major calculated risk here. The whole thing rested on a basis of deduction; there were a few broken low-grade ciphers used at the front, air reports of German movements, prisoner interrogations, and above all, Bradley's personal reconnaissance, conducted daily in a battered jeep, usually in company with a division commander—reconnaissance in which he climbed into artillery observation posts, looked into everything, and asked his subordinates for their ideas before issuing orders. The sum of evidences from these sources had become very strong, but the fact that Bradley was perfectly right should not be allowed to obscure the risk. Previous Allied commanders in Africa had more than once assumed that the Axis troops were on their last legs and had been made to pay heavily for underestimating the recuperative powers of those wily warriors.

If there had been any recuperative power left in the Afrika Korps, that command could certainly have done a great deal with the disposition Bradley now adopted. He flung the 1st Armored down the Tine Valley, right across the front of both the 1st and 34th and heedless of any counterattack that might be made into its flank. The 81st Reconnaissance Battalion was in Mateur at 1100 on 3 May. By evening it had been followed in by medium tanks.

The 1st Infantry Division, from its more southerly but more forwardly position on the right flank, followed the armor, crossed the main route from Mateur to Chouigi, and came up against the hills there in a holding attack. The 34th, using the same road net over which both the other divisions had passed, went straight eastward against Chouigi town. "I never saw that one in the book," said the General, whose solutions to map problems at Benning always had a touch of the fantastically unorthodox, "but it seemed like a good idea so I did it." Then, a little nervous over the outcome of this rule-or-ruin piece of tactics, he went out in a field and had a couple of his aides toss rocks for him to shoot at.

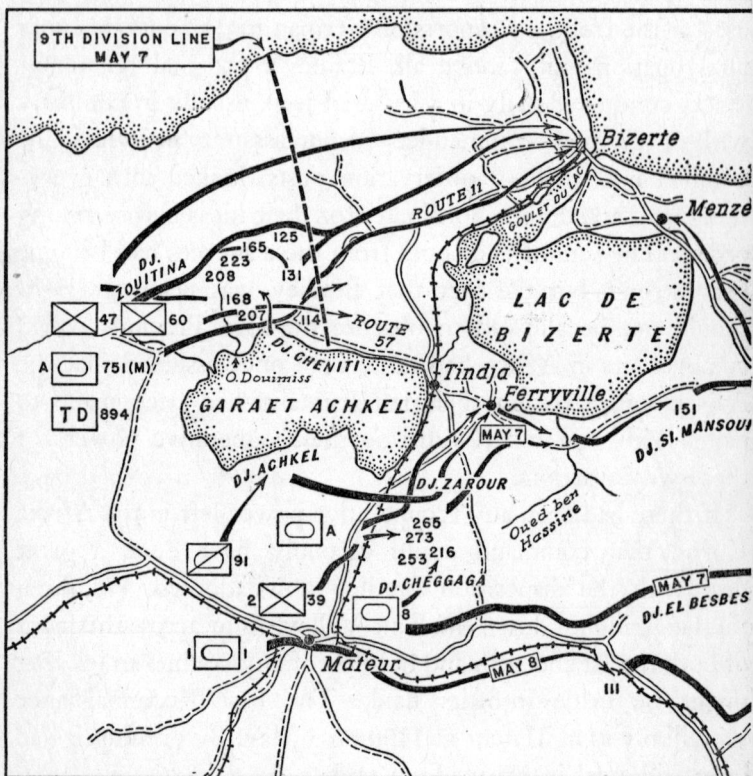

Mop-up in

He might have spared his apprehensions. The German commander, as Bradley hoped he might, regarded Mateur as the key to the whole situation and brought in infantry, artillery, tanks, planes, everything he could assemble, to retake the place or at least to pen the audacious Americans within it. It was a siege. In a three-day battle of the most violent character, the Nazis did succeed in preventing the 1st Armored from debouching from Mateur, either east toward Ferryville or southeast to the break of the hills. But their local victory was worse than Pyrrhic; while the battle swayed back

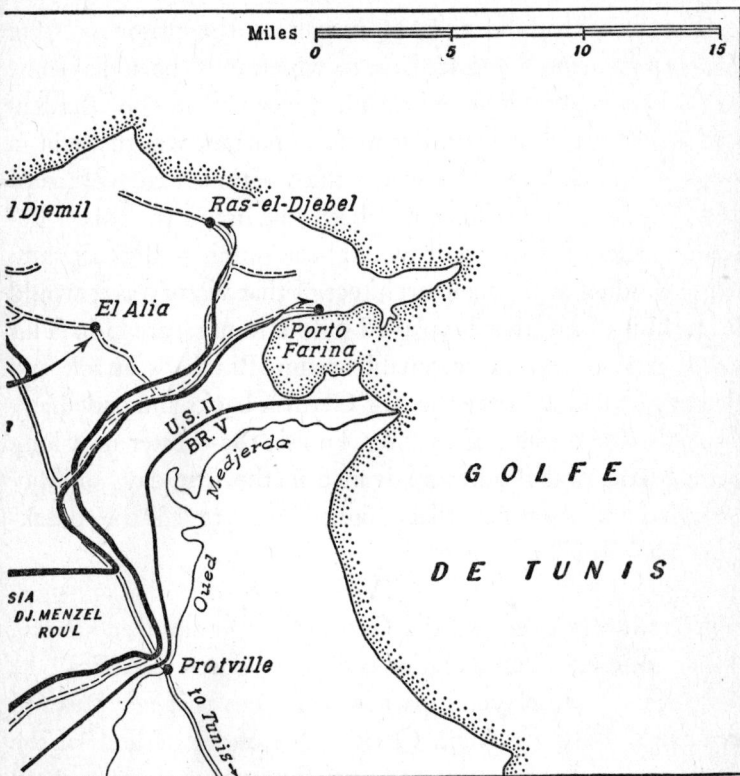

Tunisia

and forth at Mateur, the 34th, operating on a broad front, had worked through the Chouigi hills, outflanked the town of that name, and now came rushing toward Teborba and the last escape route from northern Tunisia with nothing to stop them. The bulk of the German forces were held pinned in the north by the 1st Armored and the steady pressure of the

9th. That same day, 7 May, the British broke through into the Tunis plain, and though there was still some fighting on the approaches to Ferryville and Bizerte, all that really remained of the campaign was an extended mop-up ending in a mass surrender.

The price had been 4,434 casualties, the prisoners were 35,934 Germans, 5,861 Italians, to which must be added some 3,000 enemy dead, not quite eight times the number Bradley had lost in the same way. Far more important was the gain in time; in a little over two weeks the positions that were sup-posed to hold all summer had been taken and the forces defending them destroyed. It would be as unfair to the British to name Bradley as the main architect of that victory as it would be to him to say that he played only a minor part in it. This much is not beyond reasonable claim—Bradley's attack and Bradley's victory broke the stiff German backs and ended any hope they cherished of making Tunisia the theater of a long siege battle, and Bradley's advance in the first days of May engulfed the reserves that might have stayed the breakthrough to the Tunis plain.

IV

After it was over and the General had announced simply, "This concludes the operations of the II Corps in Africa," he disappeared. He played a part in Sicily but that was Patton's campaign; Italy was Mark Clark's. One of the oddities of the American army that appeared out of nowhere between 1940 and 1944 is that no one in it had any experience in high commands so that the officers who had corps and armies reached their rank after the very briefest experience in subordinate roles. Bradley's performance in Tunisia and later in Sicily rendered it inevitable that he should be one of the very upper-bracket commanders for the invasion of the European Continent. The decision to make him commander of the American armies was really another committee operation, though it rested technically in the hands of Eisenhower alone. Probably it owed a good deal to Bradley's easy-going ability at getting along with people, especially that able but extremely difficult character, Sir Bernard Law Montgomery.

Ralph Ingersoll has reported that "unpleasant things were said" by the two men over the question of army boundaries during the Sicilian campaign. His evidence is not thoroughly satisfactory, and assuredly if such things were said they were rapidly forgotten after Bradley reached England in September of 1943 and began to work on plans for the invasion. The American leader's position was peculiar and rather delicate at the time—commander not only of the first U.S. Army, which was a going concern, but also of a group of U.S. armies, which placed him theoretically over Patton, to whom he was junior on the list, and made him the equal of Montgomery, who as commander of ground forces for France, ranked over him. In practice this tangle, which apparently left Bradley so far below where he belonged, was important only in seatings at formal dinners. The heads worked smoothly together and the arrangement was largely one of Bradley's own making. When Eisenhower asked him whether he would like command of the Twelfth Army Group he replied, yes, he would, but only when Third Army was set up as an operating organization; a single commander could do better at extricating the forces from the inevitable beach-head tangle than could two.

In the planning, the new army commander demonstrated a considerable capacity for minding his own business. He was a tactical officer and he remained one, concerning himself exclusively with the terrain of the Cotentin Peninsula and how he would accomplish the serial objective outlined in the preliminary plan. That plan was roughly for the British forces on the left of the beach-head area to clear the ground south and southwest of Caen, where forward airfields could be most readily established, work into the Vire-Falaise area and anchor this flank against an expected German counterattack. It had to be anticipated that this counterattack would draw in the enemy Fifteenth Army from the Pas-de-Calais—though every effort would be made to keep that force amused by the threat of a second landing. Bradley's was the more active part; he was to cut across Cotentin, then with one arm (V Corps) to prolong the British flank while with the other (VII Corps) he gripped Cherbourg. V Corps was supposed to gain the St. Lô road center by D plus 9, and with the aid of VII Corps, the entrances to Brittany by D plus 20; Patton and his Third Army then to pass through the lines for the reduction of Brittany and the capture of the ports there.

The first command decision Bradley was called upon to make after the right-flank beach-head had been established with difficulty and bloody fighting, the left-flank beach, with comparative ease and little loss, was with relation to the capture of Cherbourg. It has been stated that within three days from the landing beach supply was working so well and the artificial harbors were so far along that General Montgomery no longer considered the possession of a port important. Very possibly; but the point is that relations between the British commander and the American were by this time so thoroughly established that the former treated his position at the head of both forces as purely nominal. "What do you want to do?" he asked Bradley at a historic conference on the day the two American beach-heads were linked up. "Let me know and I'll write the orders that way." From that point on he never interfered with Bradley's operations, especially as he had his own hands full with that sudden flood of German armor belonging to Panzer Group West, which was preventing the planned expansion beyond Caen and even holding him short of the vital road nexus.

What Bradley wanted to do was to flank out Cherbourg by cutting across the neck of the supporting peninsula, in spite of the fact that intercommunication among the beach-heads was not yet solid. Such a move had been foreseen only as a possibility. The actual situation as of 12 June was a good deal different than had been expected, but Bradley perceived that most of the alterations from plan were actually in favor of the American armies, in spite of some lagging behind schedule.

Rundstedt and Rommel had been deceived beyond all reasonable expectation; were holding their Fifteenth Army intact in the Pas-de-Calais and throwing the bulk of the strength they had against the British, under the impression that theirs was the main effort in what Germany still interpreted as a diversionary landing. The Allied aerial offensive had also outrun hopes. Not a Seine bridge was standing west of Paris and the enemy were clearly having great difficulty in moving reinforcement and supply. That is, for the moment their major units were substantially fixed in position, with the opportunity this offered of throwing large forces onto small. This condition of paralysis and confusion in the German ranks could not be expected to last forever. When the Nazis woke up they would either reinforce Cherbourg or abandon it, concentrating their forces in one direction or the other. Therefore, despite the fact that it would leave him temporarily with a flank in air, Bradley shot his 9th Division through and cut the peninsula on 18 June.

It was just in time. The Germans at the Cherbourg of the peninsula had formed a battle group something than two infantry divisions strong, under orders to down the west coast road and join the formations there in an attack to extend the wedge-shaped salie toward Carentan, to which Rommel attached great impor nce. This battle group was now cut off and under violent ack by the three divisions of Collins' VII Corps (4th, 9 , and 79th). Collins succeeded in breaking the enemy bad when Hitler intervened with one of his characteristic inspirations to order a defense made in the open country round Montebourg.

Apparently he failed to realize the speed with which Bradley could drive infantry through *bocage* country where tanks could move only slowly and with difficulty, or the boldness with which the American general would turn the 9th in on the flank of the Germans in the north without securing the American left and rear by anything but the psychological factor. The Montebourg position broke; on the heels of the break VII Corps poured right through the Cherbourg outer defenses, never giving them a chance to organize; by 25 June there was fighting in the streets and on the next day the place was ours except for mop-up operations against a few fanatic detachments.

V

The great Channel storm had delayed matters and the Allied armies were already a long way behind the schedule that called for the capture of the St. Lô road center by D plus 9. Despite pressure from Eisenhower, Bradley now proceeded still further to delay the attack on that vital place. He had a fairly close count on the enemy by this time and rather better than a general idea of what they would do. It ruck him that here was an exception to the Clausewitzian l of time favoring the defender. The Germans had, within th ariations caused by loss and reinforcement, some 16 infant divisions and eight armored by the early days of July, but m t of them had been so battered that the real strength was not bove three-quarters of this figure. All but two of the armored visions were facing Montgomery in the Caen area, trying to revent him from enlarging the bridgehead the British force had gained east of the Orne River. The enemy were peculiarl sensitive about this region, desperately anxious to keep Allied orces out of the Seine Valley. The reason is clear enough from the fact that their Fifteenth Army, 19 divisions strong, remained on sentry-go in the Pas-de-Calais, quite evidently waiting for Patton and the Third Army to land along that shore, quite evidently determined not to let the two landings link up.

This picture of German intentions was reinforced by information pouring in in a flood from the Maquis, that all the rest of France had been sucked dry of troops in order to help Rommel. Southwest France contained only limited-service units, there were but eight divisions along the Mediterranean shore, the six Brittany divisions had been milked of a good third of their force, and the latest troops to arrive in line had come all the way from Holland. The difficulties of the German reinforcement program were patly illustrated by the adventures of this formation. The Seine bridges were out and the railroads all across France were under constant attack both from the air and by sabotage. The division had to move through Belgium and the Rhineland to the east end of the Seine-Loire corridor, then make its way to the front on foot and on commandeered bicycles, while the equipment followed in horse-drawn transport with the Maquis not infrequently stealing the horses by night. It was far easier for the Allies to reinforce across the Channel and the reinforcements were in fact coming rapidly.

General Eisenhower seems to have been somewhat concerned lest the Germans detect the fact that Patton's troops had already begun to flow into France and put in their Fifteenth Army before the break-out from the Cotentin Peninsula was achieved. With these troops the enemy could work up a mass of maneuver that would make any break-out extremely hazardous. Bradley thought they would not move; at least not within the time necessary for our forces to build up the break-out so strongly that it could hardly fail. The main reason was that the enemy commander was Field Marshal Erwin Rommel. Bradley later rated him as the ablest opponent with whom he had to deal (making a footnote that with Nazi leaders one could never be sure whether they were acting on their own ideas or merely another inspiration from Hitler), but he had one weakness. He repeated his tactics, and of all his repetitions, none was so marked as the habit of throwing a reinforcing unit into action the very moment he received it.

Several times during that June when there was such fierce fighting all along the line, there had been attempts to build up reserves on the German side—as we know now, on orders from Rommel's superior, Rundstedt. Each time, partly because of the vigor of the Allied pressure, but more because of Rommel's incurable mental habit, the reserve had dissipated before it was formed. As Bradley now saw his problem it was that of cracking a very thick and tough shell; there would be nothing behind.

He wished not only to accumulate force enough to be sure he got through that shell; he was also faced with the necessity of creating a tactical position in which there would be maneuvering room for him to thin the enemy's lines by over-extension. This was not achieved till the Battle of St. Lô came to an end after mid-July. There seems to have been some hope around SHAEF that the series of attacks beginning on July 3 would itself be the break-out. Bradley has mentioned that his original thought was to swing down the west coast of the peninsula, with the VIII Corps on his right opening the attack, each other corps in line taking up the action in succession on order, engulfing the German left flank and all making a vast pivot on V Corps, which was in line next to the British. Unfortunately VII Corps, next east of VIII, had to work up a narrow peninsula of dry ground between marshes, and the Germans had fortified this peninsula in great depth. VII Corps could obtain no room for maneuver and was held in siege fighting; the Germans concentrated toward VIII Corps and stopped that too.

XIX Corps, between VII and V, did however, make its advance and on 18 July won St. Lô in a battle of unparalleled fierceness. This was the event that had been foreseen in the new general plan, a plan which was in effect one of those committee decisions—Eisenhower modified by Bradley and Montgomery. On 18 July Montgomery with his armor was to launch an attack from the area of Caen into the rolling Seine basin which is so suitable for tank warfare. As soon as it had engaged the German attention, Bradley would attack from just west of St. Lô, swinging his spearhead to cut off the German forces opposing VIII Corps against the coast, then pouring everything he could through the gap toward Brittany. The tactical part of the decision was Bradley's and Bradley's alone. It was his masterpiece; designed to make use of precisely the factors on which the Nazis counted most heavily for a successful defense.

The most important of these factors was the character of the *bocage* country, a region of narrow depressed roads running between hedgerows enclosing small fields, the hedgerows themselves so old, tall, and thick they cannot be seen through. In such terrain every hedgerow line is a fortress where men and guns may lie concealed yet have admirable fields of fire. Tanks must expose their bellies to short-range fire in tilting up to crash the hedgerows. It is strictly infantry country, and this quite as much as the demand for armor around Caen had led Rommel to entrust the defense almost exclusively to infantry. There were less than two Panzer divisions on the American front. The German conceived that even should the American infantry get through his lines, it could not move fast enough to exploit any gain.

Bradley's particular merit in this case was the realization that military speeds are relative. If his infantry broke through the *bocage*, the Germans would experience far more difficulty in moving armor to the rescue than our forces would in passing armor through the gap into open country behind. Bradley therefore made it an infantry attack; his armor was to pay no attention to anything till it worked through the gap created by the infantry; and the infantry was to attack in such numbers that the enemy would be overwhelmed. That domination of the air played so large a part in all this perhaps owes more to Eisenhower than to Bradley—or to the air forces supported by Eisenhower, another committee decision.

The "carpet bombing" in which many of the heavies of the strategic air force joined the tactical air force to lay 7,000 tons of bombs behind the German lines in preparation for Montgomery's attack of 18 July was something new. Small fragmentation bombs were used to prevent extensive cratering. The air-force people appear to have believed that the carpet would so lie over the enemy as to leave them nothing but squashed bedbugs and, indeed, some claims of the sort were made at the time. In Montgomery's attack the actual German casualties from bombings were light; the Nazis were too well dug in. But they did suffer a loss which no one on our side had quite anticipated and which was to prove a key factor. Their communications in the bombed area went out, two German divisions were badly mauled, and the advance proceeded seven miles before encountering serious resistance.

The attack as a whole was a comparative failure because if Rommel tended to repeat his tactics, so did Montgomery, and the "Fox of the Desert," though fatally wounded on 25 July, was granted time to place his antitank guns deep enough behind his lines to escape the rain of fire from the air. When Montgomery's tanks reached this zone the British leader's losses became extremely heavy, he was stopped, and on 19 July rain and overcast came down so tight that the similar aerial carpet which was to have preceded the American attack could not be laid.

In the event it turned out to be a blessing in disguise that Bradley's attack was thus postponed until the 25th. For one thing it allowed the American general to get reports on the actual effects of the bombing attack and to digest them. Accuracy was a question. When the fall of St. Lô forced the Germans to abandon the highroad from that place to Périers, Bradley halted his men along the line of that road to provide the planes with a marker they could not miss.

Another benefit from the halt in the British attack was that the Nazis became convinced the main Allied effort was being made by the left, that Bradley had fought himself out in the desperate combat for St. Lô, that the Pas-de-Calais invasion was still on and Montgomery was attempting to clear a way for it. When 1,588 bombers laid a carpet five miles long and one mile wide behind the St. Lô-Periers road on the morning of 25 July, it came as a complete surprise to the enemy. Nothing in the operation went entirely according to plan and it is only fair to remark that the bombing was a good deal of a surprise to Bradley as well. He had expected the bombers to fly laterally along the road line, laying their eggs on one side so as to give close support without hitting our lines. For some reason known only to air-force officers, they decided they had to fly across instead of along the road, dropped a good many bombs on our side and killed, among others, General Lesley McNair.

The reverse of this incident was that the air support was far closer and the follow-up far quicker than in the Caen area; and the attack was made not by tanks in fairly open country but by infantry among *bocage*, where the Germans could not tell what was coming until they were in the very article of close combat. The effect of this quasi-invisibility

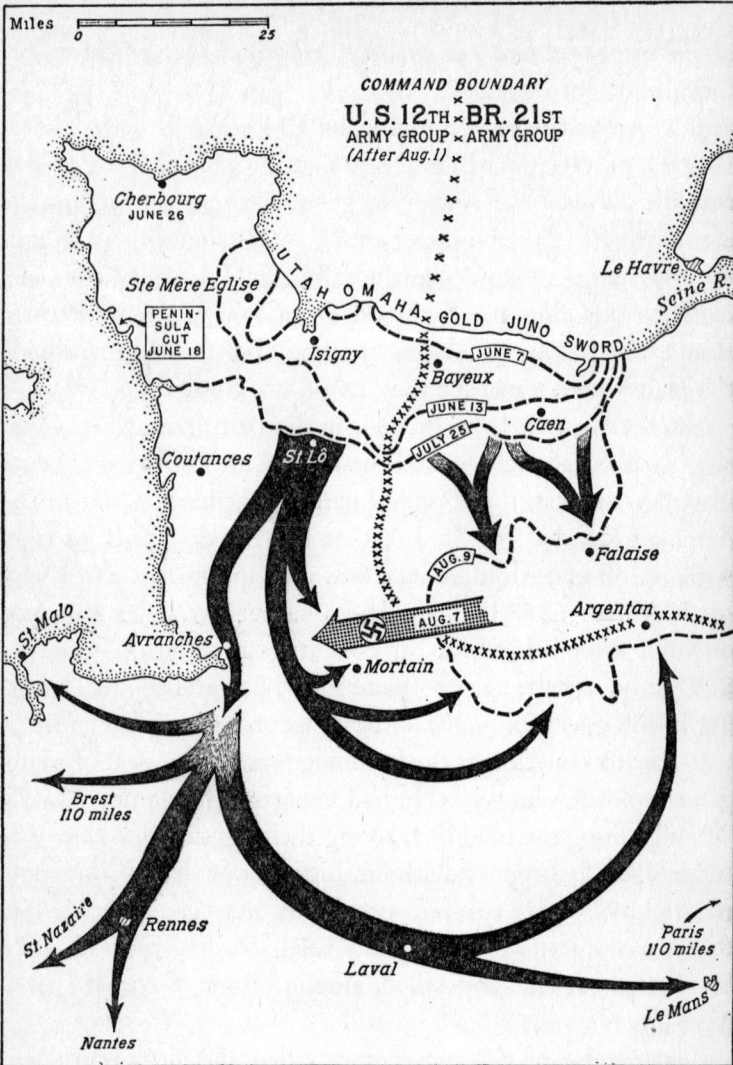

St. Lô

of the attackers was powerfully aided by the fact that as at Caen, and as Bradley had hoped here, the German communications broke down. Their upper commanders could obtain only the most inaccurate and fragmentary picture of what was going on at the front. Nothing in that picture told them that instead of the book maneuver of breaking down a flank and turning in for an encirclement, Bradley was throwing the weight of his force into a movement essentially eccentric, turning their outer flank back against the sea.

Their forces north of Coutances made vigorous local counterattacks, but generally in a northerly direction until the evening of the 26th. By this time Bradley's point had penetrated five miles through all organized defense, the 2nd and 3rd Armored Divisions were in open country and the 4th and 6th Armored were attacking Coutances from the east. The latter two belonged to VIII Corps, the other two armored divisions to VII Corps, which was making the thrust through, while XIX Corps was attacking due south from St. Lô to turn back the new flank of the broken German line.

It would seem to have been that night when the failure of communications south of St. Lô, the direction and force of the Coutances attack, told the Germans they had been penetrated. There were fragments of no less than six infantry and two SS Panzer divisions in the now narrowing pocket, all in the most frantic confusion and with many small groups beyond the reach of orders. The Germans reacted with a typically Nazi piece of tactics—orders to get the SS Panzers out and let the infantry go to pot. They had no time to practice the usual night marches; by day the American armor got into their transport and American planes were over everything, down to artillery observation cubs, from the windows of which observers fired tommy-guns. By evening of 28 July over 18,000 prisoners had been taken and the western flank of the German line had ceased to exist. By night of the last day of July our troops were at the road junction of Avranches and the way lay open to Brittany and the south.

VI

That night also saw the formalization of what had been an actuality for several days—Bradley's promotion to be an Army Group commander, with General C. H. Hodges taking over the First Army and Patton in charge of the Third. It was the day of command decisions on both sides, for inspiration again descended upon Hitler, who ordered that instead of the normal procedure of pivoting back on the strongly held position before Caen for a stand along the line of the Seine, his Seventh Army in Normandy should shift its Panzers westward, close the gap to the coast, and cut off whatever American formations had passed through. To hold the line the Seventh would be reinforced from Fifteenth Army in Pas-de-Calais. The earliest of its divisions began crossing Seine that same night.

The plan seems a mad one now, but that is in the light of subsequent events, on which decisions can never be made. Actually Der Führer had good reason to believe that if the line through Avranches could be cut or even seriously pinched down, Patton's Brittany offensive would wither like a huge blossom on a too slender stalk. The German had learned something from the affair at Montebourg and the quick loss of Cherbourg; his Brittany garrisons were under orders not to accept action in open country, but to hold hard in the inner lines of Brest, St. Malo, Nantes, and L'Orient, denying their use to Patton as avenues of supply.

In connection with the counterattack toward Avranches the over-all German plan was thus a blow at the enemy's lines of communication and by that token one of the most effective forms of action. But there is this difference between Hitler's unorthodoxy and Bradley's; that the German's was a sand-table solution which ignored actual conditions at the front, while the American varied from the book precisely because conditions at the front did not correspond to those on the map. To reach the area where the counterattack would have meaning, the Panzers had to move through *bocage* country under American control of the air. That is, their advance to the jump-off positions could be no more rapid than that of the infantry and artillery which would meet them there. A surprise in dimension was also waiting for them; at no time did the Germans correctly estimate the number of troops Bradley had available. Finally, the infantry forces in their counterdrive had been badly hurt and their organization was in none too good shape.

The result was that the Germans could not complete their build-up for what became the Battle of Mortain till 7 August, at which date they attacked with four and a half armored divisions. By that time Bradley had in line three infantry divisions (4th, 9th, and 30th) under his best corps commander, Collins, supported by one armored division and part of a second. These defenders far outnumbered the Nazis in artillery, the key factor in a combat of infantry against armor in such country. Equally important was the fact that the delay in moving up forced the Nazis to hurry on their attack under the most unfavorable possible weather conditions of clear skies and bright air. Swarms of Allied planes came down, especially the rocket-firing Typhoons that are so deadly to tanks. Armor against infantry in the *bocage*, their attack gained three miles the first day to where they could look across the level ground toward Avranches, but gained it at such a cost that the drive turned into confused hill fighting on the second day. That first night, after a day of some worry, during which Bradley had halted at the Mortain corner a corps destined for the support of Patton, he relaxed and let the columns go through within sound of the guns, sixty miles of trucks, moving bumper to bumper.

Hitler's orders; the attacks went on throughout 9 and 10 August. By that date Patton's armored elements had cleared all of Brittany but the ports. The risen French forces had taken over most of the duty of sealing the Germans in there, while the armor had begun to flow eastward whenever it could get the fuel.

Already when the St. Lô break-through was achieved, when it became evident the Germans were going to counterattack through the *bocage* to close the Avranches gap, the American general had begun to adumbrate the most gigantic of all his projects, the real reason why he had shot Patton out on an apparent eccentric after the penetration. It was the encirclement of all the German forces south of the Seine—forces now being constantly added to as Fifteenth Army sent over more infantry to release Panzers for the Mortain push—an encirclement on a scale that makes Ludendorff at the Masurian Lakes look pinch-penny. To do this it was essential to close the gap Fontainebleau-Orléans, between the southmost swing of the Seine and the northmost loop of the Loire, as an avenue of escape from the west or of reinforcement from the east. The bridgeless rivers would then hold the enemy pocketed; Bradley would lean his right on the Seine and come down on the rear of the forces facing the British at Caen and the Americans at Mortain. Partly this was a committee project, no doubt; Eisenhower seems to have urged an effort to pocket the enemy, since we had mobility and he had none. But it was Bradley the tactician who found the means and set up the project on so gigantic a scale.

The news on the morning of 9 August was that the new XV Corps had taken Le Mans and was already in the German rear; the XX Corps had struck the Loire and had begun to turn northwest on the outside of XV Corps' already gigantic left wheel. Next morning early there was a conference in a hayfield with maps spread out on the fresh, sweet-smelling haycocks. Montgomery and Bradley talked over their plan. For the British forces, which now included Canadian and Polish, it meant only turning the axis of their present effort slightly southward to make Falaise the objective point instead of the Seine valley; Montgomery thought it could be done. There was a little friendly argument over army-group boundaries; it seems Montgomery wanted his own area to come down as far as Alençon, but a compromise was reached on Argentan. Bradley remarked amiably that he would bet he could have Falaise before the British could reach Argentan and the generals dispersed to their tasks.

It seems to have been all of two days later before Hitler, or whatever cats-paw was at the front for him, realized the significance of what was going on between the rivers. Again this was partly a matter of communications, for the activities of the French, the omnipresent American planes, and the isolation of small German units were causing combat intelligence to reach Nazi headquarters in the oddest and most disjointed forms, which could not be pieced together to make a rational picture. On that 12 August the battered American infantry divisions of Mortain found the Germans were no longer attacking. Alençon had fallen the day before, XV Corps was already halfway to Argentan. The Germans had perceived their danger and were withdrawing armor from all over the front to hold open the jaws of the trap till at least their Panzers could escape; the infantry, as at Coutances, being left to make the best of a bad business, a fact which did not improve their morale.

In fact, after five days of hard fighting, when the greater part of seven Panzer divisions had managed to get out of the gap, German morale collapsed all along the line from the lowest to the highest. There was a wave of mass surrenders and another of men in vehicles trying to get away across open fields with Allied airplanes diving on them. The moral collapse was not merely because of the preference accorded the Panzers and the pounding of the American guns, but also because the counterattacks by which German high command had promised to relieve the pocket had been broken off in less than twenty-four hours.

Bradley, now so opulently provided with reserves that he could do everything at once, had released Patton toward the Seine with two full corps. One of his wings seized Orléans and struck the northern river east of Paris on the 20th. Next morning another corps was on the Seine west of Paris in two places, paused only long enough to set up a bridgehead on the north bank, and began to come down toward the river mouth at railroad speed, threatening the Germans on the south flank with another and still deeper encirclement. They were forced to abandon everything and get away as best they could, claiming as they did so that their Seventh Army had escaped.

This is true in a sense, since enough representatives of most formations could be found to permit a statement that the divisions themselves were there. Actually seven infantry divisions and two of armor were down to nothing more than a headquarters guard, all cohesion and power of maneuver had been lost and the Seventh Army would never again fight as a unit. Even its commander, General Hans Eberbach, was captured at his breakfast on 31 August.

VII

In the tremendous pursuit that carried to the frontiers of Germany Bradley's own part was not especially significant. The only engagement in it was the accidental battle at Mons, when the 1st Infantry Division captured or killed twice its own strength in Germans during forty-eight hours, because General Hodges had had the good sense to put this unit in trucks and send it forward to seize the road centers in the rear of his armored advance. The Allied armies had spread across so broad a front and were now moving so rapidly that any coordination below General Eisenhower's headquarters had become an impossibility, and that headquarters assumed operational field command on 1 September. It was Eisenhower who

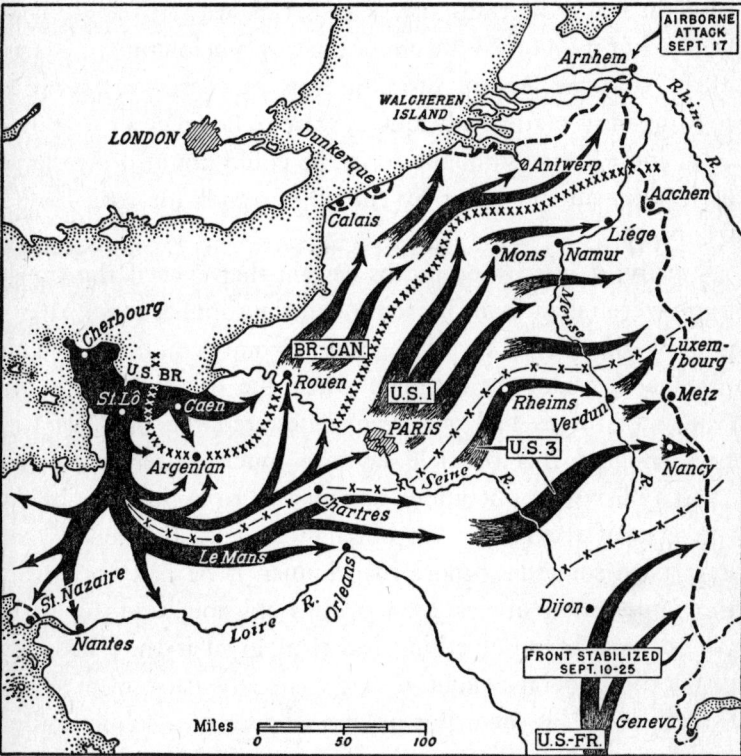

Advance to the Siegfried Line

made the often criticized decision to assign Montgomery's drive in the north priority on the all too slender resources of supply. Aside from the political-military need of clearing the rocket-bomb coast, the reasons for this decision were quite adequate. Montgomery had before him the bulk of the German field army and fundamental objective was that army, not any stretch of territory. Both Hodges with our First Army and Patton with the Third were, in the fading days of August, already so far beyond railhead and so deep in the area where all lines of communication had been systematically devastated by our bombers, that a large part of their supply was being brought up in air transport. The device was amazingly successful but it involved the use of the C-47s belonging to Brereton's Airborne Army. Brereton was quite reasonably protesting that if tactical advantages were to be taken of his powerful and extremely mobile force, he could not afford to have his equipment worn out by running errands for road-bound troops.

Finally, it was by no means certain that even if the transports were taken from Brereton and the supplies from Montgomery, Bradley's Twelfth Army Group would be able to reach a decision. At the date when the question arose the American forces had not even penetrated the old Maginot Line. Behind this obstacle lay the much better organized Westwall, where operations tantamount to siege were called for, even if the forts were but lightly held. Bradley would have been something more than human if he had not urged the importance of his own army's mission, and his staff would have been something less than loyal if they had not given the general's point of view an advocacy even more forceful than his own. But he was enough of a soldier and a friend to the supreme commander not to feel called upon for protest when the decision went the other way.

The incident is strikingly similar to the discussions in which Sherman objected to Grant's plan for crossing the Mississippi below Vicksburg—except in its military outcome, for where the Civil War leader's attack went right through, one wing of Eisenhower's offensive ground to a halt before Metz and the other failed at Arnhem. Metz finally was taken by an inching attack, Aachen fell to another, and the situation reached those December days in which Bradley came to the conclusion that the only way our superior mobility could be exploited was by a slow, difficult attack across the river Roer from the west and southward.

It was essentially the same situation the Allied forces had faced in trying to make the Cotentin break-out, though both area and armies were now so much larger. The essential strategic factor was to move the Allied forces up to the Rhine on so broad a front that a crossing at more than one spot would be possible and the German concentration opposite an indicated point of attack impossible.

The time factor was also compelling at this point. General Eisenhower has related how Bradley urged upon him that the Volksgrenadier formations manning the greater part of the Westwall would become perfectly valid troops for their purpose and place if let alone, whereas if attacked immediately, and in the face of the still urgent supply difficulties and those provided by winter weather, it would be possible to break them with relative ease. This was the basic thought behind the heavy, slow-moving November attacks which brought the Ninth Army on the left of Bradley's forces and the First Army at their center up to the line of the Roer, while Patton's Third Army on the right more or less marked time. Now arose the question of the dams. The Germans had brought their Sixth Panzer Army into the flat lands between the Roer and Cologne, and an attempt to pass the river while they could at any moment flood our lines of communication and attack our troops on the east bank with mobile forces would be very perilous. An attempt to destroy the dams from the air failed. Thus in spite of the winter weather, in spite of a probable shortage of artillery ammunition, Bradley directed an attack to reduce the area of the dams; an infantry operation by hand work, like the Battle of St. Lô.

While this positional and limited offensive was in progress, Rundstedt launched his Ardennes counterattack. The facts surrounding that operation immediately became the subject of violent controversy and they have remained so; it is perhaps important to place them in order. The opposing force was the reinforced Sixth Panzer Army. Our front-line intelligence correctly identified six enemy infantry divisions in it along the narrow Ardennes front, far more than were necessary for security against the thinly stretched forces of our Ninth Army opposite. Ninth Army therefore believed an enemy attack imminent.

Bradley's staff—and this is clearly Bradley's responsibility —rejected the idea. For one thing it had been an absolute rule in the German army since the days of Frederick the Great not to undertake winter offensives. For another, many of the Sixth Panzer's formations were new units insufficiently trained for offensive warfare. The Germans had no control of the air and no prospect of gaining it. Although the Nazi armies contained armored formations, there were hardly enough to launch a major offensive, and the supply dumps were inadequate for any large move. Finally, the defense around the Schmidt Dams showed every sign of cracking and the Nazis knew as well as we that the loss of the dams would involve that of the Roer Valley and the destruction of the Westwall down to the Eifel Range.

This was all true except the part about the German armor shortage, Intelligence having failed to identify two armored divisions recently arrived. But from the Rundstedt-Hitler point of view, most of it added up to reasons for conducting an attack at that time and place. The front at Schmidt was weakening?—The attack would have to be made before it broke and whether the men were adequately trained or not. The Allies controlled the air?—Obtain surprise by attacking in weather when planes could not fly and the advantage they

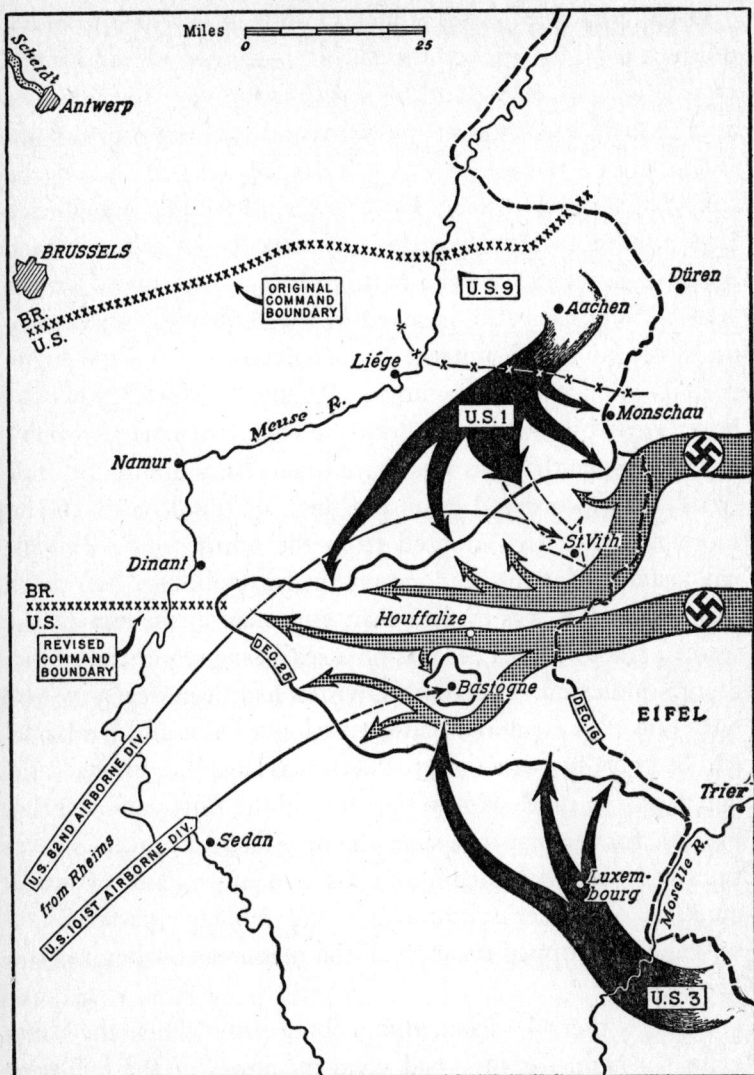

The Ardennes—Offense and Counteroffense

gave would be canceled. The tradition was against winter offensives?—The greater the surprise. If there were insufficient supplies, more could be seized from the Allied dumps, as Napoleon had supplied himself from the magazines of his enemies.

While Bradley was at Eisenhower's headquarters on the afternoon of 16 December for a conference on replacements, which had become a very burning subject, the word ran in that the Germans had attacked in the Ardennes, principally on the front of the untried 106th Division on its first night in line. They were using tanks and shouting that they would be in Paris by Christmas. Both American commanders perceived at once that this was more than a local affair; the 10th Armored was ordered in on the flank of the drive from the south and the 7th Armored from the north, while Bradley left instantly for his headquarters in Luxembourg. Before he reached them it was evident that, important as the attack had seemed from SHAEF, it was on a scale far greater than early reports indicated. The 106th Division had been nearly wiped out. The 10th Armored had been caught front and flank and had been badly beaten up; the 28th was hard hit. There was a gap nearly 15 miles wide in the line and the Luftwaffe was out in force for the first time since the invasion of France. 24 divisions had been identified in the push; an entire Panzer brigade appeared in American uniforms and sabotage paratroopers were being dropped through all the rear areas far beyond the Meuse.

In Paris there was something like a panic when the news came through, for they had vivid memories of the last time the German Army went into the Ardennes. At Twelfth Army Group headquarters "We were far less worried than they were back there," said Bradley later, a little astonished to learn how much excitement there had been over Rundstedt's attack. Himself, he had considered the possibility for some time; it was part of the calculated risk he took in concentrating toward the left for the Roer offensive. "The Ardennes is still the safest place in which to thin the line. But, you point out, the enemy has the capability of striking there? All right, let him come there if he wants to. We've got to destroy his army some place."

With these ideas in mind Bradley had already introduced one major miscalculation into the German plan before its execution began. They had expected to find supply dumps, especially of gasoline. There was not one for 60 miles behind the screen of troops at the Ardennes edge, the place had been set apart as an untenanted reservation in which a battle could be fought. A second error was immediately introduced by Bradley's tactical arrangement. The Ardennes is a territory poor in roads, most of those that exist running north and south; and it is so rough that armor and its supply must needs travel by road. A glance at the map shows that no serious advance to the west could be made without possession of the routes that run through Bastogne and St. Vith.

The 7th Armored had been ordered in on St. Vith, close behind the front, as soon as the guns began to shoot; the 101st Airborne was ordered up from area reserve to Bastogne. At St. Vith nothing was gained but a delay of some hours; but at Bastogne, where the 101st Airborne was surrounded before it even had all its men in position, the whole German plan went to wreck. The town was held; the attack that should have been a river changed to a ribbon, the men who should have been in Antwerp on 20 December were still trying to batter down the 101st on Christmas day. The Germans had not enough armor up front, not enough supply, they were counterattacked, and the offensive that was to have won the war for them came to a wild wailing halt as the skies cleared, the Allied air force came out, and Patton pinched off the southern roads across the salient with the 80th Infantry and 4th Armored divisions.

The stand of "Nuts" McAuliffe and his men in the battered town for six days was an act of collective valor to compare with that at Chickamauga, and the march of Patton's men has few parallels, but emotional admiration should not be allowed to obscure the fact that Bradley foresaw and planned for something like that. If McAuliffe had not held at Bastogne further reserves would have stopped the enemy at Rochefort or Namur; if the 80th Division and 4th Armored had not relieved the besieged town there were others behind them. The Krauts never had a chance, and the fact that they never had a chance is due more to the planning of Omar Bradley than to any other one man.

VIII

By mid-January the Ardennes salient had been effectively collapsed and the First Army, which with the Ninth had been assigned to Montgomery's tactical command for the emergency, was back under Bradley's orders. It was possible to assess results and to make plans in the light of a new situation. That situation was such as fully to have justified the Germans in their tradition against winter campaigns. Their bottom-of-the-pot reserves had been spent and the expenditure had produced absolutely nothing, not even an appreciable gain of time. The enemy were now substantially without mobile forces and if they could be forced from the barriers of river and mountain into anything approaching field warfare the result was reasonably certain. The most obvious area in which to exercise this compulsion was on the left flank of the enormous front, where Montgomery's command looked across the Rhine into the extensive North German plain. The stream is one of the great rivers of earth, but Napoleon has remarked that of all natural barriers a river is the least defensible, particularly when attacked by an opponent who can conceal his precise point of impact. Eisenhower planned to make the main Allied effort on Montgomery's wing.

Bradley's part was to be a covering offensive, designed to clear the mountainous country along the left bank of the stream and looking forward to the seizure of bridgeheads in the Mainz-Frankfurt region, where there was a wide gap in the hill systems on the opposite bank and an avenue of approach to all central Germany. The attack to penetrate this gap had been the plan urged by Bradley during the previous fall, when supply difficulties brought Twelfth Army Group to a halt.

It is worth noting that, compared to the northern attack, this was to be a poor man's offensive. There were not enough troops to launch major efforts in both sectors. A good part of the Siegfried Line before Bradley remained unscratched. It was extremely likely that the Germans would have all the bridges down when the Rhine was reached, the airborne troops would have to be used in the north, there was no way of getting heavy bridging equipment up to the stream at an early date, part of the First Army's strength would have to be employed in covering the flank of the Ninth, which imposed a limiting condition on any attack of its own.

Indeed, the prospects of Twelfth Army Group's accomplishing anything looked so poor that the British sought to have Montgomery made commander of all ground forces north of Luxembourg, under the impression that everything from that point south must stand on the defensive. It would be about the time of this request that Montgomery issued a highly injudicious press statement minimizing the American part in stopping Rundstedt. Omar Bradley had always so hated publicity that up to this point he never gave press conferences and had permitted interviews only under pressure from Eisenhower. But the matter had now become one in which justice to his troops and hence the morale of his armies was involved—and beyond that, the question of breaking the hearts of the Germans and forcing them to fight against a certainty of ultimate defeat. He summoned the press to his headquarters and gave a counterstatement. Meanwhile his staff was working like mad on the plan that was to turn the covering attack into the the true deathblow, leaving the British forces once more in the position of having engaged the enemy's attention while Bradley cut them to pieces from an unexpected quarter.

A certain amount of disagreement is inevitable when the armies of two nations are fighting together side by side. That is why Napoleon preferred to make war against alliances. The important thing to note here is the pattern that repeats throughout Bradley's operations, the fact that by various routes, in campaigns whose military styles were completely different, it fell out always that he delivered the decisive shock. An event so often repeated ceases to be fortuitous; one is forced to seek another explanation than coincidence.

One such explanation is that Bradley had by now thoroughly taken the measure of the German strategic mind, which was most frequently and essentially Hitler's. They would give up nothing until forced. This entailed the difficulty that it was necessary to assemble strong attacking elements against the most insignificant objective, but it had the advantage that the enemy would always withdraw too late from positions no longer really tenable. Once their mobile reserves had been wasted in the Ardennes attack, the Rhineland positions, heavily defended by the Westwall though they were, were in effect a return to the Eighteenth-century cordon system. A single rupture in the typical cordon produces not only an entry for the attack but also the loss of most of the troops composing the cordon.

This much on the level of wide strategic thinking. In tactics Bradley's uniform successes may be traced precisely to the fact that all his operations were in different styles and this in turn to his failure to forget that he had been head of the Infantry School. When new weapons come into warfare there is an inevitable tendency to treat them as irresistible—as they usually are till the means of defense has been worked out— and to seek means of assigning to them the stellar role on every battlefield, rather than inquiring whether they are peculiarly suited to the situation. The Arnhem operation is a good example. Doubtless paratroops were the most rapid means, in a physical sense, of obtaining bridgeheads across rivers. Unfortunately this could be seen from the German side of the stream as clearly as from the Allied. Bradley's special merit was in the realization that infantry is the most flexible of all arms and that the province of the fancy special weapons is to add to the infantry's power, not to replace it. The very fact that his offensive was to be a poor man's war was an advantage in his eyes.

The more spectacular operation in the north, which opened on 19 February to clear the way to those parts of the Rhine not yet held by the Allies, attracted so much attention that the movement of Patton's Third Army was worth no more than a line or two in the communiqués and an ill-understood line at that. Actually Bradley was destroying an army group in that Rhineland country which commanders throughout history have found too confused for regular campaigning. The area is split midway by the winding valley of the Moselle, north of which parallel ridges rise sharply to the crests of the Eifel Range. South across the valley a similar series of north-south ridges runs up to the backbone of the Hunsrück Mountains. The city of Trier is the western anchor of the Moselle valley. Just west of it the Saar River falls into the Moselle from the south and the Prüm-Sauer system from the

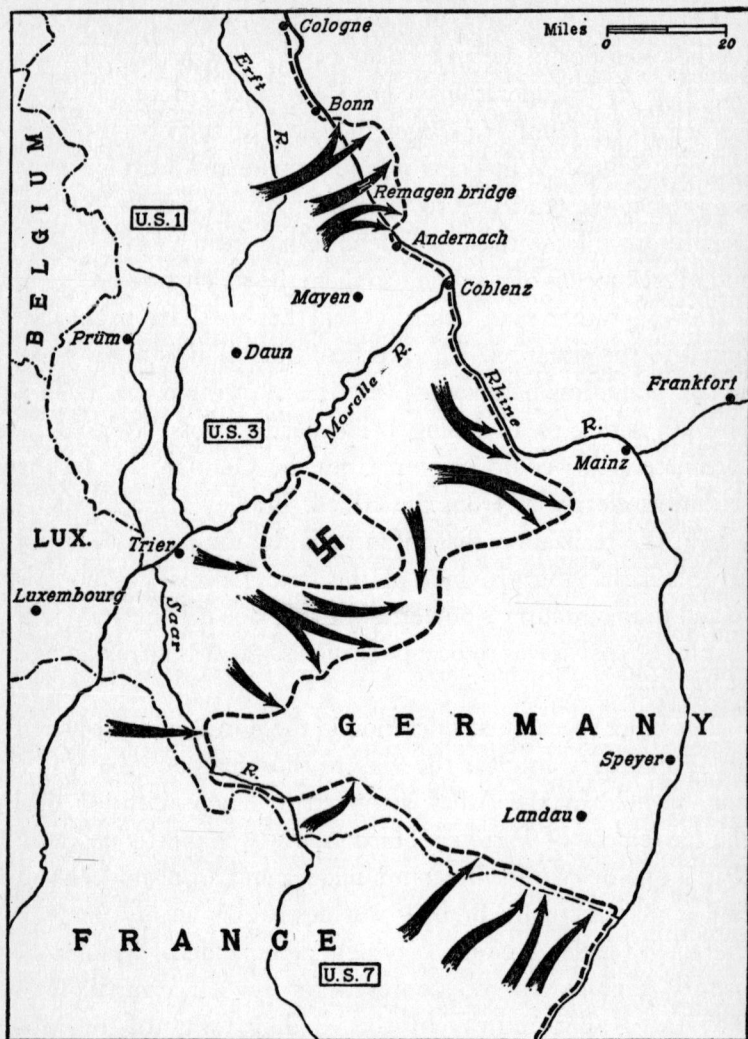

Remagen to the Frankfort Gap

north, almost at the same place; west of this the Moselle itself comes up from the south to bend sharply rightward, forming a triangle of high broken ground between it and the Saar. At the opening of his attack the Allied line was approximately Prüm town—Sauer-Moselle.

On 19 February, when the big bang went off in the north, an offensive of objectives so strictly limited that it was described as an "aggressive defense" began in this area, both north and south of Trier. There was fighting between the Prüm and Sauer that day; during the night Patton pushed an entire infantry division across the Moselle, took the Germans by surprise and began to clear out the triangle up to the Saar. This was accomplished by the 22nd and Patton's men won several bridgeheads across the upper Saar, which were extended and linked up during the next several days in the face of vigorous counterattacks. The offense through Prüm town and across the river of that name similarly gained some two miles. Bradley now had salients both north and south of Trier, which Patton pinched together on 1 and 2 March, using one armored division on each front. There was fighting in the town on the latter day and the enemy gave it up, but put on an infantry counterattack into the flank of Patton's head of column on the south bank the following morning.

The Germans had now worked out both the method and direction of our attack. It was aimed on the valley of the Moselle and would consist essentially of infantry advances against the outer knuckles of the ridges, followed by short armored penetrations along the valleys between these ridges toward the Moselle. Such an offensive could best be contained by holding the ridge knuckles in force to narrow down the front of the American attack, then counterattacking into the flanks of the narrow American stream as it lengthened. The counterattacks could be made especially from the Hunsrück direction, where the forests offered such good cover from our aviation. This is what the Germans concentrated to do, and they were allowed time to make this concentration by the inching nature of an infantry offensive. The only trouble was that their analysis was completely wrong, they had been taken in by the most gigantic of Bradley's surprises.

On 5 March the 4th Armored Division attacked in force on a very narrow front in the Prüm area; broke through at once and went racing northeast and away from the Moselle Valley across the parallel ridges toward the Rhine. They were right off the roads; tanks had to tow 6 x 6 trucks. But they were also right off the map; there was no resistance to speak of, the division made over 20 miles the first day and camped for the night among some crater lakes south of Daun. On 6 May the advance was as rapid, washing all the way up to Mayen; but this place is on a highway, the alarm had spread, and the division found it held in some strength. Doubtless a way could have been forced through, but battle was no part of the division's mission. It pulled back, swung around Mayen by the south through country again roadless, and next day dipped its standards in the Rhine north of Coblenz. Through the gap it had made the 11th Armored came pouring along to the Rhine, which it reached at Andernach on 9 March, followed by all the infantry of VIII Corps.

The left flank of the German forces had thus been turned in an operation which Bradley himself later described as the most orderly and military ever accomplished under his command.

IX

He might have added that it was the most effective. The 11th Armored, swinging leftward downstream, encountered the vanguards of Hodges' First Army coming up—an almost fabulous example of that timing which Bradley so often made the center of his tactics. It involved the co-ordination of the movements of two armies, each embracing more men than the United States had under arms on Pearl Harbor day, and one of these armies bound to conform to the movements of the force on its own left which was not under Bradley's command. First Army did not really begin its offensive until the last days of February. There is a partly canalized river called the Erft with a ridge before it which turns into the Rhine east of the Roer, forming a fortified bastion behind which lies the communications center of Cologne. A stiff counterattack could conceivably be launched from this area into the right flank and rear of Ninth Army as it slanted northeast toward the Rhine. The attack of the First, in the view of everyone but Twelfth Army Group people, was to clear this flank up to the Erft. He has never said so but there is little doubt that under the doctrine of exploiting an opportunity, Bradley meant from the beginning to let First Army go as far as it could.

The opportunity certainly presented itself. When VII Corps on the First Army's left pushed up to the Erft and captured its ridge on 1 and 2 March, the Germans attempted to bolster their position by inserting three armored divisions. The weather cleared, the armor was caught in motion by Allied aviation and badly broken, on the heels of which the First gained a wide and deep bridgehead across the Erft toward Cologne by 3 March. By the 5th, VII Corps was in the outskirts of the city. Now it seems the German High Command determined on evacuating all the left bank of the great river as far up as the Eifel Range, leaving only some of the Volkssturm to hold the ruins of Cologne to the last. Their more valid troops would keep Bonn, the Eifel itself, and the pass where the river plunges through the hills, just as farther south at this same date they had decided on a main defensive effort around Trier. It was a plan for holding everything by holding the essential avenues of ingress.

As on Patton's front, it was spoiled on that of the First Army by the weight of the American attack being thrown in an unexpected direction. First Army used only VII Corps against Cologne city. Hodges had two more corps. One of these, III Corps, was given a direction southeast, behind a long ridge that juts north from the Eifel to enclose the narrow Rhine plain. III Corps made its advance on a narrow front with the 9th Armored Division leading. On the map it was as perilous a maneuver as the similar jag of the 4th Armored across the roots of the Eifel, since a quite minor effort on the part of the enemy could have cut the narrow ribbon of men in two.

But Bradley took a risk calculated on the speed of an armored division and his judgment that the Germans would make no more major counterattacks which might reduce the forces they needed to carry out their defend-all policy. The primary purpose of the drive was to link up with Patton's left wing near Andernach, giving the forces on the left bank of the Rhine alternative lines of support and supply; but the result ran beyond anyone's wildest hopes and introduced a completely new element into the situation. On 7 March the 9th Armored captured Remagen bridge.

It led into the region where the Westerwald Hills pinch all communications close into the river valley, apparently to no great future, but all up the chain of command there was little doubt about what to do. Every general in it approved the acts of his subordinates in rushing troops across the bridge and added something more from the resources under his command. By time the matter reached Eisenhower the orders were to get not less than five divisions across as fast as they could move. Corps and army artillery was flooding in from all the country north of the Eifel to enfilade the lines with which the hastily gathered German forces were trying to keep the bridgehead from expanding north and south. By 11 March the holding on the east bank was 11 miles long and three miles deep; Hodges had gained all the crests the Germans could use for observation posts.

By 11 March also the Nazis were in deep trouble in the zone of Patton's Third Army. The arrival at the Rhine of the 11th Armored with the 89th and 90th Infantry Divisions close behind relieved the 4th Armored of all apprehensions with regard to fighting battles. The last division turned back, cleared Mayen, gained the supporting road system, and swept out the whole left bank down to the junction of Moselle and Rhine. German forces north of the Moselle dissolved into fugitives and German forces south of that river were under orders to get across it as soon as possible.

There were three main difficulties about carrying out these orders. One was that another of Patton's corps, spearheaded by the 10th Armored was already south of the Moselle and digging into the retreat. It moved so freely by day under the excellent American air cover that it outpaced the retreaters. The second difficulty was that General Devers' Sixth Army Group in Lorraine and along the south face of the Rhineland had attacked and was so closely clutching the German forces there that they dared not go on the move for fear of more armored spearheads being launched into their retreat. The third and most serious German trouble was that between the demands of the Remagen bridgehead (which had already absorbed some of the forces guarding the lower Rhine against Montgomery) and those of the Lorraine front, there were no reserves to hold the Moselle-Rhine junction. Or it may merely have seemed to them the least important of the many itching spots they had to scratch. But it was in this area they lost their battle.

For Bradley pressed Patton on to make his main thrust southward across the mouth of the Moselle instead of pouring Third Army's troops into the Remagen bridgehead as the

Germans expected him to do. On 15 March the 11th and 4th Armored crossed the Moselle and worked six miles south. In the next three days four infantry divisions followed them. All the weight was now on that flank, close up to the Rhine. Coblenz was taken; the advance pushed on to seize Mainz on 22 March, while many of the Nazi troops were still out in the Siegfried Line, far to the west. By 25 March only the Speyer-Landau exit remained open, so far as any exit from the Rhineland can be said to have existed under the constant rain of projectiles from American aviation. Organized resistance west of the Rhine was in fact at an end. Bradley's achievement (which he must share with Devers, who contributed the indispensable function of making an attack with forces which the Germans thought only capable of static action) was overlaid at the time by the fact that public attention was focused on the great crossing of the Lower Rhine by three armies abreast.

That operation was carried out with spectacular success, but at the date it took place, it was already something of a work of supererogation. At the time there was a great deal of talk, in Germany and out of it, of a Nazi retreat to the "national redoubt" in Swabia and the Alps for a prolonged stand of incalculable results. The preparations made by the Germans would indicate that such a program was on their agenda, but the performance had become impossible. The troops which should have been the flank and rear guards for such a retreat had been destroyed in the Rhineland campaign. As General Eisenhower himself has noted, only Tunisia produced so complete an elimination of all the enemy's forces engaged. Equally important was the fact that at the date of Montgomery's big crossing, Third Army already had three solid bridgeheads across the Rhine in the Frankfurt gap area, and Hodges with the First at Remagen was in line with three full corps.

Napoleon said once that he never planned what to do in the event of victory, since victory plans for itself. This is doubtless sound doctrine, but it requires a certain amount of revision in the light of modern technology, since the Napoleonic pursuit is hardly possible unless adequate supplies of gasoline are up. Actually nothing is more remarkable in the whole Rhineland campaign than the fact that as far back as the date when Patton's men were working around Trier, Bradley clearly foresaw that if the thrust of the 4th Armored broke through, the Germans would be in no condition to oppose crossings along the middle river. He brought up bridging equipment into his forward area and the infantry divisions had not passed Coblenz before convoys of engineers were rumbling through the streets. The three bridgeheads were seized in a series of *coups de main*, it would be wrong to say without preparation, but by the application of the minimum amount of force necessary to take the objectives. At the date of Montgomery's crossing, Bradley's forces had already taken 19,000 prisoners on the east bank of the river.

X

The operation which followed has been, and is likely to be, regarded as something in the nature of knocking out a fighter who cannot get his hands up. It is true that German mobility was even less than it had been, but it is important also to recognize that the Russians were already closing on Berlin in those days at the end of March and if worst came to worst the Nazi leaders far preferred surrendering to the western Allies. We do not know what hopes of secret weapons or wearing out Allied patience by endless guerrilla operation they cherished, or what expectations they had of destructive counter-attack at the moment when the rushing columns should have outrun their supplies. The point is that the Germans still regarded their case as by no means hopeless, gathered their best

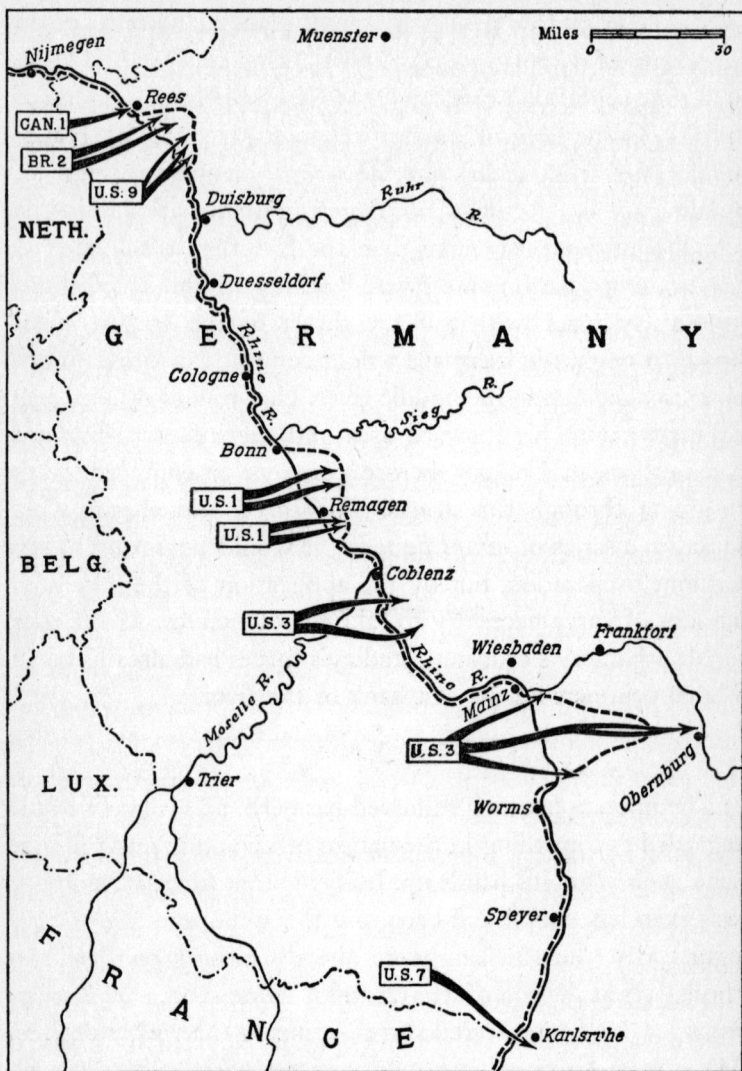

The Rhine Crossings

armies in the Ruhr area with supply lines running east and southeast, and prepared to sell at a price higher than the Allies could afford to pay. Their chances of making a stout stand and a fighting retreat looked so good that General Eisenhower planned to drop the whole First Airborne Army in the Kassel area to cut off the enemy's main line of retreat and communication.

It proved unnecessary. Bradley had planned too well; the old plan of the Frankfurt gap which he had hatched the previous fall, when Siegfried Line, Rhineland, and Rhine still lay between him and that gap. There was one important modification now. On its north the Mainz-Frankfurt corridor is flanked by the Taunus Range, which Bradley had expected to use as his left-flank cover. Remagen Bridge brought the First Army north of the Taunus and made this flank guard unnecessary, permitted Patton's army to advance without concern over its left, and allowed one more deception, the final one. Hodges was facing the Germans on the south flank of the Ruhr along the river Sieg, deep and rapid, running between high hills, a true military obstacle. The enemy were dug in on the north bank with emplaced artillery, observation posts, detachments detailed for local counterattacks, and all the paraphernalia of German defense that had made the campaigns of St. Lô and Aachen so slow and exhausting. They clearly expected Hodges would have to attack them in that position.

The deception was that Bradley ignored the river line. There was never anything but a pretense of attack northward across it. While a mere screen of troops held the hills on the south bank—fully as defensible as those north of the stream—Hodges moved straight eastward, with the 3rd Armored Division of VII Corps leading, then turned north. Far south Patton's Third Army burst through the Frankfurt gap in a still more gigantic left wheel, covering the right of the First Army as the First covered the Third's left. The degree of co-ordination achieved between the two is something to remark and compares with that between the same two armies in the Eifel offensive.

In the meanwhile Ninth Army had attacked on the right wing of the Montgomery offensive north of the Roer. Its primary mission was to contain the German concentration in that industrial area, restrain them from cutting into the flank of Montgomery's British-Canadian offensive as it spread across the North German plain. But as Simpson's Ninth penetrated, each division in turn passing around the rear of the one preceding it to wheel right against the Ruhr, it found so great a proportion of the Nazi forces had been attracted to the siege front that there were more than enough troops to form a flank drive. The army was returned to Bradley's command for an operation downright offensive in character. He ordered Simpson to keep going; Simpson shot his XIX Corps right around the Ruhr and on 1 April his 2nd Armored Division met the 3rd Armored coming up from the south in the Kassel-Paderborn area.

There was much fighting to be done still and many men to die, but the essential step had now been taken, the last of the German armies had been encircled and 300,000 fighting men were cut off from every source of supply and communications in the largest operation of the kind in recorded history. When it was complete the war was over.

. . . The steps that led up to that result have been given in some detail in an effort to clarify what General Omar Bradley's particular contribution was. That contribution is and will remain extraordinarily difficult to assess. It was a committee war; many of the ideas came from his subordinates and some were imposed by the command above. His part was often to say, "Go ahead"—yet in uttering this simple phrase he so frequently added one touch more that he made the campaign entirely his own. In Tunisia, for example, the plan of using only a single reconnaissance squadron as a link between divisions was his. In the Eifel campaign the idea of feinting an infantry drive along the Moselle Valley, then jabbing an armored spearhead across the hills, may have been fairly due to Patton, a good deal cleverer tactician than his press clippings would imply. The plan of having the First Army operate by its right may have come originally from Hodges. But the plan of combining the two moves, giving both columns of advance double lines of communication, coordinating the paired attack, was all Bradley. The turn-around after the invasion of Brittany seems also to have been his idea in very large proportion. At that time supply was a burning question, with fall storms that might ruin the artificial harbors imminent. The orders were to take Brest, which no one realized the Germans would defend so skillfully or demolish so thoroughly. It was Bradley's merit to have recognized that, though the problem of supply might be important, that of the German Seventh Army was far more important. The former question could be solved when it arose; the latter had to be solved at once, because the conditions that made it possible to destroy the German army south of the Seine might disappear, never to recur.

It is in such instances, in the calmness that could recognize the Ardennes break-through less as a defeat than an opportunity, that the greatness of Bradley as a soldier lies. He could think big; relate every detail of a complex structure to a broad general plan. Almost alone among eminent commanders his career as a leader of troops shows no change of concepts, no development. He never had to develop; the ideas that led to the destruction of the German armies were there from the beginning.